ANGLISTIK UND ENGLISCHUNTERRICHT

Herausgegeben von
Gabriele Linke
Holger Rossow
Merle Tönnies

Band 73

PASCAL NICKLAS (Ed.)

Ian McEwan:
Art and Politics

Universitätsverlag
WINTER
Heidelberg

Bibliografische Information Der Deutschen Nationalbibliothek
Die Deutsche Nationalbibliothek verzeichnet diese Publikation
in der Deutschen Nationalbibliografie;
detaillierte bibliografische Daten sind im Internet
über *http://dnb.d-nb.de* abrufbar.

Herausgeber:
Prof. Dr. Gabriele Linke
Dr. Holger Rossow
Prof. Dr. Merle Tönnies

ISBN 978-3-8253-5654-5
ISSN 0344-8266

Dieses Werk einschließlich aller seiner Teile ist urheberrechtlich geschützt. Jede Verwertung außerhalb der engen Grenzen des Urheberrechtsgesetzes ist ohne Zustimmung des Verlages unzulässig und strafbar. Das gilt insbesondere für Vervielfältigungen, Übersetzungen, Mikroverfilmungen und die Einspeicherung und Verarbeitung in elektronischen Systemen.

© 2009 Universitätsverlag Winter GmbH Heidelberg
Imprimé en Allemagne · Printed in Germany
Druck : Memminger MedienCentrum, 87700 Memmingen

Gedruckt auf umweltfreundlichem, chlorfrei gebleichtem und alterungsbeständigem Papier

Den Verlag erreichen Sie im Internet unter:
www.winter-verlag-hd.de

Contents

Preface.. 7

Pascal Nicklas
The Ethical Question: Art and Politics in the Work of Ian McEwan.. 9

Peter Childs
Contemporary McEwan and Anosognosia.............................. 23

Anja Müller-Wood
The Murderer as Moralist or, The Ethical Early McEwan...... 39

Roland Weidle
The Ethics of Metanarration: Empathy in Ian McEwan's *The Comfort of Strangers*, *The Child in Time*, *Atonement* and *Saturday*... 57

Katherina Dodou
Dismembering a Romance of Englishness: Images of Childhood in Ian McEwan's *The Innocent*....................................... 73

Lynn Guyver
Post-Cold War Moral Geography. The Politics of McEwan's Poetics in *The Innocent*.. 87

Lars Heiler
Unleashing the Black Dogs: Cathartic Horror and Political Commitment in *The Innocent* and *Black Dogs*........................ 103

Elsa Cavalié
"She would rewrite the past so that the guilty became the innocent": Briony's House of Fiction.. 119

Caroline Lusin
'We Daydream Helplessly'. The Poetics of (Day)Dreams in Ian McEwan's Novels.. 137

Erik Martiny
"A Darker Longing": Shades of Nihilism in Contemporary Terrorist Fiction.. 159

Helga Schwalm
Figures of Authorship, Empathy, & The Ethics of Narrative (Mis-)Recognition in Ian McEwan's Later Fiction................. 173

Barbara Puschmann-Nalenz
Ethics in Ian McEwan's Twenty-First Century Novels. Individual and Society and the Problem of Free Will..................... 187

Contributors' Addresses... 213

Preface

The short stories and novels by Ian McEwan as well as the films based on his novels have become very popular in recent years and made McEwan one of the most important contemporary English authors. His readiness to react to cultural and political changes and concerns is one important reason for the great resonance his works provoke. So, it comes as no surprise that he is regularly on the agenda in the classroom in schools and at university.

This volume focuses on central topics in his writings: politics and art. These two aspects merge in the fundamental question of the ethics of writing. The contributors to this volume met for a few days in March 2009 at the Humboldt University in Berlin to discuss their readings of McEwan's texts. The lively debates did not only show how controversial McEwan can be and how sensitive some readers are to the increasing presence of Englishness in the novels, but they also showed the importance of the ethical question. Not all of the articles address this problem head-on but it seems to be underlying the entire discussion of the connection between politics and art. The articles in this book are ordered as much as possible according to the chronology of McEwan's work.

A number of institutions and individual people made this volume possible. There was easy cooperation and generous support from the Department for English and American Studies at Humboldt University as well as from the University itself. The British Council helped and most of all the Deutsche Forschungsgemeinschaft. Annemarie Taeger-Altenhofer – as so often – was there to unstintingly right wrongs. Katharina Christ and Brian Greenhill were great in organizing, proof-reading and editing. Thanks are due to the editors of the series anglistik & englischunterricht, particularly to Merle Tönnies whose ready enthusiasm and moral support were well-timed. The book is dedicated to Liam Maximilian and Jona Benjamin whose arrival is closely connected to the gestation of this book.

Pascal Nicklas
Berlin, 1 November 2009

Pascal Nicklas (Leipzig and Berlin)

The Ethical Question: Art and Politics in the Work of Ian McEwan

> *It is not the first duty of the novelist*
> *to provide blueprints for insurrection,*
> *or uplifting tales of successful resistance*
> *for the benefit of the opposition.*
> *The naming of what is there is what is important.*[1]
> Ian McEwan 1989

In Plato's Πολιτεία there is no place for the art of imitation. The philosopher's critique of Art is particularly directed against the questionable ethical standing of fiction: its influence on the minds of the recipients and the relation to truth do not pass his ruthless examination which is based on a fundamentalist conception of Good. It is particularly the borderline between reality and fiction and the readiness of the recipients to confuse their own existence with that of the characters which worries the philosopher. It seems inevitable to him that the imitation leaves its traces on the imitator. This – depending on the nature of the imitated – can be a dangerous thing. And in the first place it is the poet himself who (Πολιτεία 393 a/b) lets himself appear to be someone else speaking. This difference between the other (ἄλλος) and the self (αὐτός) is for Plato the central concern when it comes to the ethics of fiction.

At the heart of McEwan's poetology is the desire to look through the eyes of someone else. The confusion of the self and the other which Plato identified as the great potential – and moral danger – of the epic and imaginative writing in general opens up for Ian McEwan the ethical dimension of literature. This becoming someone else for a while is part of the activity of the writer but also one of the recurring themes in McEwan's short stories and novels. There are a number of essays and interviews in which McEwan talks about this act of imagination as a fundamental human capacity which informs moral behaviour just as well as creative writing. Most notably, and many of the articles in this volume refer to this statement McEwan made in *The Guardian*, McEwan talked about the consequences of lacking this faculty in the aftermath of the terrorist attack on the World Trade Centre on 11 September 2001. Here, the moral and the literary coalesce in the political. – It is this field of overlapping and interdependent aesthetic, politological and philosophical discourses in which the voices assembled in this volume are engaged. The aesthetic and the political are inextricably entangled with the ethical.

Ian McEwan is not a philosophical writer or someone with an ideological mission using literature to propagate his ideas.[2] Despite his strong scientific leanings[3] and his interest in experiments his novels are not schematically plotted but develop from individual scenes and explore fictional characters and situations. In his poetological remarks on the political novel, McEwan summarizes his view on the novel as a form:

> The very form of the novel, or the very nature of the possibilities it affords – imaginatively pluralistic, humanistic, intrigued by the fate of individuals, sceptical – suggests a clamorous democracy; anyone might become central to the story, every point of view must be heard. The freely conceived novel sits as uneasily with the Czechoslovakian state apparatus as it does with Islamic fundamentalism. If you want to argue with Caesar on Caesar's terms, then you had better write expository prose in which to propound in the clearest terms your vision of an alternative social order. (McEwan 1989: xviii)

The ideological and political constellations and figurations which become visible in the scenarios of his own novels are always very much contemporary even when the setting is historical. Peter Childs demonstrates in this volume the acute relevance of McEwan's fiction particularly in the context of the social and political bearings scientific debates have. The genome and theories of the mind and brain as well as Darwinian evolutionary models or ecological problems of climate change are the background to much of McEwan's fiction and his many articles. Childs draws a connection between these theories and McEwan's art of writing which hinges on the poetics of becoming someone else: "For me the moral core of the novel is inhabiting other minds"[4], McEwan says. This imagining of the reality of someone else is one of the sources of compassion and sympathy the latter of which is innate according to Darwin. Particularly in *Saturday*, Childs argues, McEwan works on a Darwinian matrix balancing the contradictions of the survival of the fittest and innate sympathy. It is Perowne who throws the term eponymous for Childs' article into the debate: anosognosia. It is the medical term for the missing awareness of one's own situation, i.e. patients who are not conscious of their own disabilities. McEwan translates – according to Childs – this medical condition into a diagnosis of contemporary society.

The not-knowing of one's own position is equally dangerous as not being able to imagine what it is like to be the victim or the object of our actions. This moral reasoning can be easily and continually detected in McEwan's work. It is not a recent development in his fiction. It rather seems that it is his particular way of writing something in the vein of *littérature engagée* though literature is always more than a vehicle of opinions or convictions for McEwan. It makes sense to some extent to compare his stance with that of Sartre. And it is helpful to remember that McEwan belongs to the European "Generation Joschka Fischer", that he is a contemporary of Daniel Cohn-Bendit. It not only McEwan's delight in a decent bottle of wine which he shares with these two activist politicians but it is the ecological concerns and the vicinity to the peace movement, the engagement in the disarmament movement in the seventies and eighties. The choice of the pair of spectacles in the photograph used by McEwan's publisher's for a long time served as a link to the John-Lennon-iconography[5] connected to the movements McEwan identified with at the time of his most obviously political output, before and after *The Child in Time* (1987). And it is probably because of this political heritage that McEwan seems to some of the contributors in this volume quite at odds with postmodernism. There is a belief in human universals, in some common traits of all humanity which goes against the grain of the dominant constructivist credo of our day. And it is in this vein of believing in some potential for compassion, some deeply rooted Rousseauist patterns of thinking that the imaginary identification with others becomes such an important ingredient of McEwan's poetics.

In her contribution to this volume on the "Poetics of (Day-)Dreams in Ian McEwan's Novels", Caroline Lusin shows how the motif of dreamplay and daydreams is one consistent and under-researched feature in McEwan's works. She can cite many instances where characters dream themselves into other people or beings. One of the most striking examples might be the stories in *The Daydreamer* where young Peter slips into the skin of the family cat. The cat in turn takes over his body and goes to school with it while he stays at home in the cat's world. After changing back, Peter feels a little estranged to his own body and needs some time to adapt to his physical self. This story about Peter metamorphosing into a cat may be understood as mirroring the experience of the reader after having finished a gripping novel. It may also be understood as a metaphor for the agency or *poiesis* of the writer who becomes someone else while he is writing. This identification of poetics with metamorphosis is older than Ovid's work who himself transformed the mythical heritage into his *carmen perpetuum.* The mythical basis of this literature of metamorphosis is fundamental to the experience of story-telling and the listening or reading of stories. It is not only the world that is transformed by literature but both the writer and reader: literature makes a difference.

This poetological grounding has got for McEwan clearly not only aesthetic implications but also political consequences. His politics as well as his poetics are not based on ideas of the collective but rather rest in the individual. His characters do not appear as puppets standing in for large ideas and ideologies but they experience their lives as though they were the first human being on earth – only in special moments or with hindsight do they realize that they belong to a group or a nation. The collective memory is at the bottom of their experience but they have to go through their experience by themselves.

Talking about the novel which is to come out in 2010, *Solar*, McEwan tells Daniel Zalewski from *The New Yorker* an anecdote about a reading he gave of his work in progress at a literary festival in Wales. In the comic excerpt McEwan presented, the main character, Michael Beard, gets onto a train with a bag of crisps in his pocket.

> He is incensed when his seat mate opens the package and starts eating. ("One of those guys in their mid-thirties with a shaved head and gym-thickened neck," McEwan told me. "Millions of them in Britain.") Beard notices that the man has a bottle of

> water and retaliates by grabbing it and taking a sip. Upon disembarking, McEwan said, "Beard puts his hand in his pocket and his package of crisps is in there, untouched."[6]

One member of the audience in Wales pointed out that Douglas Adams tells a similar episode in his *Hitchhiker's Guide to the Galaxy* (1978) and next day "the British press halfheartedly raised the question of plagiarism – a pale retread of a furor two years ago, when the *Mail on Sunday* revealed that sveral phrases in *Atonement* resembled medical descriptions in a nurse's wartime memoir" (ibd.). McEwan's reaction to the question of origins raised in Wales elucidates his ideas about the relationship of the individual to the collective:

> McEwan claimed to be unfazed by the Wales incident. The cips story, he said, was an urban legend dating to the nineteen-twenties. "The scene is partially about what happens if you have an experience, and then you're told it's an urban legend. Your life is suddenly rendered inauthentic. Now, one of Beard's friends can say, 'But I read that in a Douglas Adams novel!' So it's even better. (*Ibid.*)

Everyone – and particularly narcicistic characters like Beard who might remind one of the antagonists in *Amsterdam* (1998) (another comic novel deriving its drive from the incongruity of male self-images and social realities) – wants to live an authentic life and is, every so often, reminded of the secondariness of one's life and ideas.[7] These delusions of grandeur of the Ego are described in psychoanalytical terms as one of the sources of daydreams which, for Freud as well, form one of the anthropological sources of literature.[8] The Self as king and ruler of the universe whose wish-fulfillment collides with the reality principle dictated by social norms and the restrictions of human existence serves easily and frequently as a butt of ridicule. But it is a figuration bearing much truth about the author (Briony ordering her toy animals that they all face her while she is sitting at her desk writing her *Arabella*-play[9]) who serves as an Everyman in Freud's reading. Being an artist is no special illness, it is normality blown up out of proportion. The individual treasures its precarious individuality just like the artist whose anxiety of influence leads to artful strategems of camouflage. But just as the artist is flowing in the stream of tradition his characters are shown by McEwan in their larger social and political contexts. Robbie with his individual *histoire* of disgrace and prison is swallowed in the masses marching to Dunkirk.

Atonement (2001) easily appears as the most English of McEwan's novels. It firmly sets itself in the tradition of the English novel and is full of direct or indirect meta-fictional reflections on the art while the act of writing is tightly connected to the moral shortcomings and the desire for atonement of the intradiegetic author. In her article for this volume, Elsa Cavalié points out, however, that the Englishness as displayed metonymically by Tallis House is the product of invention; in Hobsbawn's terminology[10] it is an 'invented tradition'. The field of referentiality evoking Brideshead and Howards End reinforces the impression of the artificiality of Tallis House and serves as an "indictment of the myth of Englishness" (122). The political implications become most obvious when the idea of Englishness is confronted with the otherness Briony is experiencing and ineffectually trying to condone by her orderliness. Atonement in these terms becomes only possible by embracing otherness and avoiding nostalgia.

Englishness as one of the more prominent topics in *The Innocent* (1990) is seen as a political topic connected to McEwan's continued interest in childhood by Katherina Dodou: *Dismembering a Romance of Englishness. Images of Childhood in Ian McEwan's The Innocent.* At a time of national re-definition in terms of renewed political and international grandeur under Thatcher, the close connection of Englishness and childhood-imagery questions the innocence of the boyish schemes climaxing in the brutal dismemberment of Otto's corpse and the rape of Maria. Leonard is shown in all the ambiguity of individuality and belonging to a national community. He identifies strongly with the English nation and is shown as feeling his Britishness with childish naïveté. His being a member of a collective is hinted at in almost Orwellian detail when the narrator of *The Innocent* describes Leonard unpacking his suitcase in Berlin. The delusions of individuality are neatly set in contrast to the sad sartorial uniformity Leonard conforms to having three categories of gray suits:

> He luxuriated in the choice of bedroom, and unpacked with care. His own place. He had not thought it would give him so much pleasure. He hung his best, second-best and everyday gray suits

in a wardrobe built into the wall whose door slid at the touch of the hand. On the bureau he placed the teak-lined, silver-plated cigarette box engraved with his initials, a going-away present from his parents. By its side he stood his heavy indoor lighter, shaped like a neoclassical urn. Would he ever have guests?[11]

His wondering if he ever would have guests highlights the social show value of his commodities whose appreciation by Leonard depends on the impression they can make on others. Having his initials on the cigarette case stands in stark contrast to his insignificance signified by the gray suits. To demarkate ownership it would need his complete name and home address. Similarly the sadly ridiculous "indoor lighter" in the shape of a neoclassical urn does not evoke an aristocratic aura but quite the contrary. In a different context it could have been a mocking reference to Keats, here it looks like a trashy piece of prop. Leonard's misconception about himself gains greater political resonance when his "proprietorial swagger" (6) is described while he is walking through the residential part of Berlin where his new home is. McEwan leaves no doubt how inappropriate this show of self-confidence is. His claims to be one of the conquerors of Berlin are dismantled in both personal and historical terms. Leonard was only fourteen on V-E Day and it was the Russians anyway who liberated Berlin.

Lynn Guyver is concentrating in her contribution to this volume on *The Innocent* which is just like *Black Dogs* (1992) an overtly political novel and tackles the phase of the Cold War from a complementary perspective to that of the latter novel. Though both stories are set almost entirely or at least partly in Berlin, they are despite all their historical accuracy not historical novels. They are rather probing the human condition in a political context, inquiring into the question "of what constitutes human morality at public and private levels." (97) This fictional investigation works as much in terms of content as it does in terms of form. Guyver points out how McEwan undercuts the cultural drive for distinction and distinctiveness as Bourdieu puts it, particularly detabilizing concepts of Britishness by diffusing the binary patterns intrinsic to the form of the spy novel.

A similiar diagnosis is offered by Lars Heiler, who, however, concentrates on the meaning and effect of cartharsis through the experience of horror in McEwan's spy-novel and its unequal twin,

Black Dogs. Both the disection of Ottos's corpse and the encounter with the black dogs are moments of personal horror and political enormity. The private and the public merge at these moments and function like the *pharmakon* as dicussed by Derrida (comp. 114): both as a remedy and a poison. The consequences of these intense moments – which have a haunting effect on readers – are existential for the characters and change their lives. The intersection of the personal and the political is clearly visible.[12]

Looking at the development of Ian McEwan as a writer in the chronology of his works, a continuity of interest in ethical questions which lie at the heart of the relationship of art and politics becomes obvious. Particularly the early work, from the collections of short stories to *The Comfort of Strangers* is driven by a probing of the human in extreme situations demanding a moral stance from characters and readers alike which the characters more often than not cannot live up to. In her analysis of the early story *Butterflies* in the collection *First Love and Last Rites* (1975) Anja Müller-Wood draws attention to the mode of narration and its ethical implications. The unreliable narrator of the story – in whose mind of sick distortions the reader is drawn into – forces the reader to contemplate the conditions of the confessional mode the narrative is unfolded in. So, the story is more than a presentation of the shocking abuse and murder of a child. It is also the self-reflection of the responsibilities of the artist representing 'reality'. In this early short story, Müller-Wood shows the treachery and deception of confessional rhetorics which intentionally dissemble the truth to provide the basis for an unjustifiedly sympathetic reading. Suddenly, it is the girl's agency which led to her death and not the narrator's atrocious crime. In a way, this short story anticipates the *chef-d'œuvre*, when the reader is forced to contemplate the art and rhetorics of Briony in *Atonement*.

In order to clarify the textual strategies employed by McEwan to reflect on the narrative nature of his art, Roland Weidle distinguishes with Ansgar Nünning between 'metafiction' and 'metanarration': the former is the self-refentiality of the text on its fictional status while the latter concerns comments on the narrative nature of the narrated within the narration. This diffentiation helps to analyse the relationship between fiction and reality in the novels of McEwan. Weidle argues that McEwan has to be seen as a pre-postmodern (61) author as he employs metanarrational strategies charcteristic of postmodern writing but does not subscribe to the text-centred 'ontology' of postmodernism. According to Weidle, McEwan remains with his concepts of empathy and imagination in a realm of realities which still constitute a universalism very much at odds with contemporary concepts of the self.

Similarly critical is Helga Schwalm's analysis of McEwan's political ethics when it comes to the question of recognizing the other. Employing philosophical categories from the ethics of Axel Honneth's theories of intersubjectivity and ethics, Schwalm sees McEwan's view of empathy in a very problematic light. She argues that the novels *Amsterdam, Atonement*, and *Saturday* "display and explore various dimensions of authorial and figural patterns of empathy" (174). The effect, however, is a paradoxical movement between the poles of empathy as "a fundamental quality of intersubjectivity" (*ibid.*) and empathy as a transgression, appropriation by the author and "potential misrecognition" (*ibid.*). – Schwalm takes her cue from McEwan's response to 9/11 in *The Guardian* in 2001.

> If the hijackers had been able to imagine themselves into the thoughts and feelings of the passengers, they would have been unable to proceed. It is hard to be cruel once you permit yourself to enter the mind of your victim. Imagining what it is like to be someone other than yourself is at the core of our humanity. It is the essence of compassion, and it is the beginning of morality. (McEwan 2001)

This quotation is almost like a shibboleth for those who discuss McEwan's ethics and ideas concerning empathy. It easily connects with his comments on the imagination and the function of fiction. Therefore, it rests on the shoulders of a consistent corpus of narrative texts and essays which circle around this central topic of McEwan's moral poetics. But, I think, it is not sufficient to distil from it McEwan's comprehensive political position on the terrorists' acts he is responding to not very long after the event. And it is certainly no basis to develop a philosophical position from especially because McEwan does not actively participate in a self-consciously professional philosophical debate. His perspective is that of a writer of narratives. As that he has, obviously, missed the chance of imagining himself into the world of the terrorists. He identifies only with the obvious victims of the terrorist attack, he does not ask in this article how it feels like to be human collateral damage of

American and British troops. On the contrary, he argues on the basis of his Western essentialism, referring to human universals, that the terrorists would not have been able to act if they had been able to imagine "themselves into the thoughts and feelings of the passengers". This is a rather limited outlook on the world and falling much short of his usual insight into the human potential for violence and surprising acts of cruelty.[13]

It is exactly this world of terrorism, Erik Martiny explores in his paper which contextualizes *Saturday* (2005) with other – mainly English and American – novels dealing with terrorism. Martiny discovers in the great range of novels he reads a predominantly nihilistic outlook which can be distinguished into a number of types of nihilism. McEwan's novel is the only one where literature carries away victory over the dark forces: the recital of *Dover Beach* by Perowne's daughter Daisy in the face of imminent rape stretches the limits of verisimilitude almost beyond the breaking point. But it is the author's humanist convictions of the power of literature which are highlighted in this improbable scene which Martiny finds – despite all – "utterly convincing" (168).

Saturday certainly shows McEwan's art of writing at a very high level and it merges the private and the political in the prominent moment at the beginning of the novel where Perowne's nightwatch turns from the "pleasurable" (3) sensations to worried musings: "And now, what days are these? Baffled and fearful, he mostly thinks when he takes time from his weekly round to consider." (4) The pleasurable animal mode of the beginning, "the elation is passing, and he's beginning to shiver" (13). This marks the point where his reflections and memories make place for the imaginary. Perowne is imagining himself into a "nightmare" (15). This is where the topic of terror enters the novel and shows the character – whom some deem a gallingly happy and successful citizen – in its most unprotected, endangered and fearful mode which metonymically brings politics into the private seclusion of the bedroom.

Barbara Puschmann-Nalenz's contribution, which closes this volume, rounds up the problems of ethics and narrative in the latest three novels *Atonement*, *Saturday* and *On Chesil Beach* (2007). It is particularly the theoretical framework developed by critics like Wayne C. Booth, Martha Nussbaum, Richard Rorty and Colin McGinn which puts emphasis on the identificatory invitation of fiction and its potential to move the readers and thus instil patterns of ethical thinking. Puschmann-Nalenz inquires exactly into the narrative strategies which serve McEwan's moral poetics of identification and imagination and questions its implications. The article tries on one level to reconstruct the way the reader's response is achieved in these novels. On another level, the extratextual and metafictional ethical positions of the writer are examined and finally the question is raised if the fictional work establishes any sort of ethical normativity. All this seems to suggest a philosophical positioning of McEwan which stands in contrast to postmodern standards. It is rather some kind of essentialism we find, reflecting human nature in universal terms reminiscent of Platonic ideas.

Notes

1 Ian McEwan: *A Move Abroad:* or *Shall We Die?* and *The Ploughman's Lunch.* London: Picador, 1989, xv.
2 This is being very general in terms of McEwan works: there would, of course be some contention concerning specific novels. Kiernan Ryan, e.g., critizises *The Child in Time* for its being too obviously political: "Yet in wedding his narrative so openly to a feminist vision McEwan inevitably attracts the charge of sacrificing imagination to ideology, exploration to opinion, and thus breaking his own golden rule for the novel." (Ryan 1994: 51) He is sharing this view with D.J. Taylor (1989: 58-59).
3 Amigoni characterizes McEwan quite aptly as "an intellectual who has contributed to shaping the discussion of scientific public culture, and the contemporary novelist that scientific intellectuals like to lionize." (Amigoni 2008: 157).
4 Appleyard (2007: 2).
5 "In 1972, McEwan and two friends bought a used microbus and drove from Munich to the Khyber Pass. 'Ian was more of a hippie than I was,' Amis says. 'I was an opportunistic hippie – more velvet suits and flowered shirts. He was more ... '*Afghanistan*, yeah.' He had several caftans, you know. And beads, I think. A bit of that.' (McEwan denies ever owning a caftan, but a diary entry from 1976 is instructive: 'We eat *Psilocybe* mushrooms, canoe, swim naked in the electric-cold water, take saunas, play volleyball, drink wine and talk about Jimmy Carter, and Ezra Pound.')" Daniel Zalewski: "The Background Hum. Ian McEwan's Art of Unease", *The New Yorker*, 23 February 2009. http://www.newyorker.com/reporting/ 2009/02/23/090223 fa_fact_zalewski (last accessed on 5 November 2009).
6 Zalewski (2009).

7   Authenticity is a big topic when it comes to placing McEwan in a postmodern or pre-postmodern tradition. There seems to be some sense of 'reality' and 'truth' in McEwan's thinking which perhaps stems from his scientific leanings and has a strongly modernist rather than postmodern feel to it. For her elucidating comments on authenticity see Richter 2009.
8   Freud (1999).
9   "She was one of those children possessed by the desire to have the world just so. Whereas her big sister's room was a stew of unclosed books, unfolded clothes, unmade bed, unemptied ashtrays, Briony's was a shrine to her controlling demon: the model farm spread across a deep window ledge consisted of the usual animals, but all facing one way – towards her owner – as if to break into song, and even the farmyard hens were neatly coralled." (McEwan 2002 : 4-5) This scene is brilliantly adapted in the film where Briony is shown writing her play being looked at by her animals. In the text it is a bit unclear how the animals can be "facing towards their owner" as it is not said where Briony is.
10 Comp. endnote 6 in Elsa Cavalié's article.
11 McEwan, Ian: *The Innocent*. New York, Toronto etc: Bantam Books, 1991, p. 3-4.
12 Domic Head (Head 2007: 200) refers to Judith Seaboyer who had already in *The Comfort of Strangers* seen the connection between the literary realism of McEwan and the mirroring of the private sphere in the public domain. (Seaboyer 2005: 24). (Comp. also McEwan 1989 : xviii-xix).
13 In his discussion of *Black Dogs* Tim S. Gauthier argues, "A good portion of McEwan's fiction in fact works on the premise that a very thin line separates the majority of us from the dark individuals he presents. The acts of evil committed are 'presented as things anyone could find him/herself involved in under the right (or wrong) circumstances' (Malcolm [2002:] 17). In *Black Dogs*, he creates an elaborate system of connections and juxtapositions that serve to highlight the gap that separates innocent bystander from Nazi commandant. McEwan offers his text in reply to those individuals who forthrightly state that they would have never taken part in such activities [...] The occurence of the Holocaust jeopardizes any assertion of innocence and in fact immediately invokes the possibility of complicity and guilt." If this interpretation with all its generalizing implications holds true for the Holocaust it should also be applicable to 9/11. Therefore, I believe, the *Guardian*-article should not be overrated.

Bibliography

Amigoni, David: "'The luxury of storytelling': Science, Literature and Cultural Contents in Ian McEwan's Narrative Practice." in *Literature and Science*, ed. Sharon Ruston, Cambridge: D.S. Brewer, 2008, pp. 151-166.

Appleyard, Brian: "The Ghost in My Family" News Review Section, *The Sunday Times*, 25 March, 2007, 1-2.

Freud, Sigmund: "Der Dichter und das Phantasieren" in *Gesammelte Werke, chronologisch geordnet, siebenter Band, Werke aus den Jahren 1906-1909*. Frankfurt am Main: Fischer, 1999 (London: Imago Publishing Co., Ltd., 1941), pp. 213-223.

Gauthier, Tim S.: *Narrative Desire and Historical Reparations. A.S. Byatt, Ian McEwan, Salman Rushdie*. New York & London: Routledge, 2006.

Head, Dominic: *Ian McEwan*. Manchester and New York: Manchester UP, 2007.

McEwan, Ian: *A Move Abroad:* or *Shall We Die?* and *The Ploughman's Lunch*. London: Picador, 1989.

---: *Amsterdam*. London: Vintage, 2005.

---: *Atonement*. London: Vintage, 2002.

---: *Black Dogs*. London: Jonathan Cape, 1992.

---: *Enduring Love*. London: Vintage, 2004.

---: *First Love and Last Rites*. London: Picador, 1976.

---: *In Between the Sheets*. London: Picador, 1979.

---: *On Chesil Beach*. London: Jonathan Cape, 2007.

---: "Only love and then oblivion. Love was all they had to set against their murderers", *The Guardian*, 15 September 2001, http://www.guardian.co.uk/world/2001/sep/15/september11.politicsphilosophyandsociety2 (accessed 30 October 2009), n.pag.

---: *Saturday*. London: Vintage, 2006.

---: *The Cement Garden*. London: Picador, 1980.

---: *The Child in Time*. London: Picador, 1988.

---: *The Comfort of Strangers*. London: Picador, 1982.

---: *The Innocent*. New York, Toronto etc: Bantam Books, 1991.

Malcolm, David: *Understanding Ian McEwan*. University of South Carolina Press 2002.

Richter, Virginia: "Authenticity: Why We Still Need It Though It Does not Exist", in *Transcultural English Studies. Theories, Fictions, Realities*, ed. Frank Schulze-Engler and Sissy Helff, Amsterdam, New York, NY: Rodopi, 2009, pp. 59-74.

Ryan, Kiernan: *Ian McEwan*. Plymouth: Northcote House. 1994.

Taylor, D.J.: *A Vain Conceit: British Fiction in the 1980s*. London: Bloomsbury, 1989.

Schemberg, Claudia: *Achieving 'At-one-ment'. Storytelling and the Concept of the* Self *in Ian McEwan's "The Child in Time", "Black Dogs", "Enduring Love", and "Atonement"*. Frankfurt am Main etc.: Peter Lang, 2004.

Seaboyer, Judith: "Ian McEwan: Contemporary Realism and the Novel of Ideas", in *The Contemporary British Novel*, ed. James Acheson and Sarah C.E. Ross. Edinburgh: Edinburgh UP, 2005, pp. 23-34.

Slay, Jack: *Ian McEwan*. New York: Twayne Publishers, 1996.

Zalewski, Daniel: "The Background Hum. Ian McEwan's Art of Unease", *The New Yorker*, 23 February 2009. http://www.newyorker.com/reporting/2009/02/23/090223fa_fact_zalewski (last accessed on 30 November 2009).

Peter Childs (*University of Gloucestershire*)

Contemporary McEwan and Anosognosia

The expression 'Contemporary McEwan' might open up the possibility of several different kinds of context for McEwan's work as a writer. It can place him among current novelists; it can consider his writing about the contemporary; and it can examine McEwan's own recent output.

One launching point might be McEwan since the year 2000: this decade, this century, this stage of his career. This is the fiction since he won the Booker prize and since the world took on a different kind of seriousness in September 2001, the month *Atonement* was published. It is also a period in which McEwan has started on what appears to be a new phase of writing, inaugurated by *Atonement*, during which he has produced three novels praised for their prose as much as anything they have to say. These have been written in what has been called McEwan's "mature style" of writing,[1] notable for crafted, detailed, cursive sentences.

Contemporary McEwan is also McEwan on pressing global topical issues, especially in *Saturday*, and in the newspaper responses to 9/11, through to recent writing on climate change since he joined the Cape Farewell artists' expedition to the Arctic in March 2005 and wrote on solar technology for the Edge Foundation in New York. Importantly, this last activity illustrates a continued concern with ecological issues from at least the time of *A Move Abroad*, the portmanteau collection of *Or Shall We Die?* and *The Ploughman's Lunch,* which still arguably stands as the best introduction to the feelings that inform McEwan's writing, though its emphasis has been reinflected by more recent focus on terrorism and environmental change. Thus, back in September 1982 he wrote in the Introduction to *Or Shall we Die?* about how the "growing science of ecology places us firmly within the intricate systems of the natural world and warns us that we may yet destroy what sustains us."[2] In that Introduction he also writes that: "our science and our art describe the same reality";[3] With such sentiments McEwan posited a Newtonian and Einsteinian observer of the universe: the second he characterised in his phrase "And shall we live in womanly times". Of this observer in the Einsteinian universe, a prototype for the physicist Thelma in *The Child in Time*, McEwan says: "[she] believes herself to be part of the nature she studies, part of its constant flux; her own consciousness and the surrounding world pervade each other and are interdependent".[4] McEwan says he means by this "rethinking our world view so radically that we might confront an evolutionary transformation of consciousness?"[5]

"Love one another or die" remains McEwan's humanist message on Climate Change, restated in an article of 2008 entitled "The World's Last Chance":

> There is a rendezvous next year [2009] in Copenhagen which [...] is the global successor to Kyoto. [...] If it does not result in practical, radical measures, the fight to control our future could well be lost. Every nation on the planet will be represented. The general feeling is that the conference cannot be allowed to fail.[6]

This is McEwan on the most globally pressing contemporary question, yet it is one with which he has been occupied for 30 years, and the expression in his fiction of this interest in a parallel between natural change and human transformation is something to which I will return at the end of this essay.

McEwan's concern over humans' interaction with nature is mirrored by his interest in the reanimated question of 'human nature'. In terms of art, McEwan's work as a novelist has especially concentrated on the interlinkages between consciousness and emotion affected by the agency of imagination. Mirroring McEwan's comments in the Introduction to *Or Shall We Die?* on a hypothetical Einsteinian observer, June notes at the end of *Black Dogs*:

> Human nature, the human heart [...] has to develop and expand, or the sum of our misery will never diminish. My own small discovery has been that this change is possible, it is within our power. Without a revolution of the inner life, however slow, all our big designs are worthless. The work we have to do is with ourselves if we're ever going to be at peace with each other. I'm not saying it'll happen. There's a good chance it won't. I'm saying it's our only chance.[7]

Political change, our only and last chance, may result from a shift in perspective, which is dependent on the exercise of the observer's imagination.[8] Yet, while this sentiment is laudable it is also deeply unprogrammatic, in contrast to the collectivism and direct political action advocated by June's husband Bernard. The novel's narrator, their son-in-law Jeremy, wavers between June's and Bernard's positions in ways that highlight an equivocation in McEwan's own politics and anticipate the vacillations evident in *Saturday*.

More convincingly, the consciously altered perspective of the imagination straddles art and ethics for McEwan. He expresses this in his fiction but also directly in several interviews: for example, he says that

> For me the moral core of the novel is inhabiting other minds. That seems to be what novels do very well and also what morality is about: understanding that people are as real to themselves as you are to yourself. [...] I've taken a lot from cognitive psychology about the way children develop theories of other minds. It's part of the emerging into full consciousness.[9]

He adds in words that describe Briony Tallis, Henry Perowne, Edward Mayhew and others of his characters: "We are all on a scale between an icy pursuit of self-interest and being overwhelmed by an awareness of what other people think."[10] Empathy and imagination can be over-indulged and dangerous, as is plainly depicted in the actions of Jed Parry in *Enduring Love*, while their absence can also be detrimental to relationships, as is evident in the behaviour of Joe Rose, the narrator of the same novel, towards his partner Clarissa.

McEwan is notably contemporary among British novelists because of his abiding interest in drawing on and drawing parallels with current debates in popular science subjects. For example, when a 'rough draft' of the human genome was finished in 2000,[11] McEwan noted on its publication that the mapping of the gene was performed on not one individual but on a composite from 15. Once again intimating that "our science and our art describe the same reality", he concluded: "That which binds us, our common nature, is what literature has always, knowingly and helplessly, given voice to. And it is this *universality* which science [...] is set to explore."[12] Such language suggestively aligns McEwan with humanists sceptical of the more relativist contentions of postmodernism,[13] but he is far from a functionalist[14] and narratives such as *Saturday* insinuate the interaction of culture and biology at the most fundamental level; for example, when Baxter, in large part susceptible to emotional swings because of Huntington's disease[15], moves away from an aggressive intent in reaction to the emotional appeal of spoken poetry, where the aesthetic imagination moves him at least temporarily to alter behaviour. As Catherine Belsey argues, "If there is such a thing as human nature, [...]" it perhaps exists in the interaction between biology and the cultures that "evolved brains make possible".[16] This implies that the contents of imagination are culturally shaped but the capacity to imagine is biological, and appears to be universal. In one interview, McEwan conjectures that: "The imagination flows into unwanted places, and perhaps this is its evolutionary function: to foresee bad outcomes and try to avoid them. Fear may lie at the root of the imagination itself."[17]

The contents of the imagination are less easily aligned with genetics than circumstance but that the imagination is a human biological universal is both underlined and undermined by, for example, autism, where meta-representation is far less prevalent. Underlining the significance of perspective within what is now denoted as "theory of mind",[18] McEwan has said he most values fiction for its ability to portray "what it means to be someone else"[19] and in his fiction, the limits of imagination are repeatedly foregrounded as major drivers of character and plot. This is also the case in his libretto for Michael Berkeley's 2009 opera, *For You*. As often in his novels, the plot hinges on a terrible misunderstanding, and McEwan explains the appeal of such a device: "I like the cognitive moment of dissonance when people are so persuaded by something they want to believe that they see or hear differently [...] We're almost defined as a species by our willingness to misunderstand" (or "believing is seeing" as he puts it in *Enduring Love*).[20] Fabrication and delusion repeatedly stand alongside sympathetic identification in the imagination.

The same concern with theory of mind informs McEwan's portrayal of Briony Tallis in *Atonement*, Joe Rose in *Enduring Love*, and Peter Fortune in *The Daydreamer*, which is a compendium of childhood transformations through imaginative identification. Envisaging the perspective of others has long been the preserve of literature's concern with the imagination: "How do we let ourselves be moved by pity if not by transporting ourselves outside of ourselves and identifying with the sufferer; by leaving, as it were, our own being, to take on its being?"[21] So says Rousseau in *Emile*; and so also says McEwan in his pieces on 9/11 for *The Guardian*, on September 12th and 15th 2001. These assert something that the novel has frequently been used to argue: that, in contemplating the real, the exercise of the imagination enables us to 'extend our sympathies'. Here, as in many other cases, McEwan's position is informed by social and applied science as much as philosophy and the arts. Darwin argued in *The Descent of Man* (1871) that "sympathy and cooperation were innate to man".[22] Or as the psychoanalyst D.W. Winnicott concludes:

> A sign of health in the mind is the ability of one individual to enter imaginatively and accurately into the thoughts and feelings and hopes and fears of another person; also to allow the other person to do the same to us.[23]

This last point is one that is stressed too little but again impinges on any analysis of, for example, the relationship of Joe Rose and Clarissa Mellon in *Enduring Love*.

At the time of writing his 2005 novel, *Saturday*, set on the day of the February 15 2003 anti-Iraq-war march in London, McEwan was reading Darwin, referring to him extensively in his contemporary essay on "Literature, Science and Human Nature."[24] In the essay he also cites Saul Bellow's 1964 novel *Herzog*, which provides the epigraph to *Saturday*, from which I quote: "what it means to be a man [...] in a mass. Transformed by science. [...] you yourself are a child of this mass and a brother to all the rest".[25] In *Saturday*, Darwin and Darwinism play a complex and ambivalent role. On the one hand, Henry Perowne seems to understand human agency in strictly biological terms. He describes people as:

> hot little biological engines with bipedal skills suited to any terrain, endowed with innumerable branching neural networks sunk deep in the knob of bone casing, buried fibres, warm filaments with their invisible glow of consciousness. (13)

On the other hand, Perowne's poet daughter Daisy has set him to read a biography of Darwin as part of his humanist education. Nature is Darwinian, but Darwinism is a part of culture, which for Daisy is a potentially redemptive force. The night before the day of the novel, Perowne has been reading the Darwin biography in preparation for an unnamed volume of Conrad Daisy wants him to embark upon (6). Later in the novel, McEwan's narrator however calls Perowne the sharer of Baxter's secret (95), and I would suggest that Conrad's paradigmatic short story of that name – "The Secret Sharer" – is one key intertext for *Saturday*.[26]

The recognition, through imagination, of others as 'secret sharers', lies I think at the heart of *Saturday*'s concerns, and is tied to its literary and Darwinian message of innate sympathy and co-operation. Yet, there is a counter-message in the novel running against this grain, placing a limit on fellow-feeling and suggesting that individual human success relies on such a constraint on empathy; in Beckettian terms of the human theatre of the absurd, the inability to feel another's pain is both a necessity and a tragedy. At the start of Chapter Two, Perowne recalls a phrase he has read in the Darwin biography: "There is grandeur in this view of life." (55) This is the start of the last sentence of *On The Origin of Species*:

> There is grandeur in this view of life, with its several powers, having been originally breathed into a few forms or into one; and that, whilst this planet has gone cycling on according to the fixed law of gravity, from so simple a beginning endless forms most beautiful and most wonderful have been, and are being, evolved.[27]

Perowne has earlier noted that there was a change that Darwin made to this conclusion after the controversies generated by the first edition of his book, but he has not remarked what the revision entailed, which was to include in the second edition the phrase "by the Creator" in the passage's descriptive image of the breath of life. Twenty pages later in Saturday Perowne thinks to himself:

> if the present dispensation is wiped out now, the future will look back on us as gods, certainly in this city, lucky gods blessed by supermarket cornucopias, torrents of accessible information, warm clothes that weigh nothing, extended lifespans, wondrous machines. (77)

This is not an isolated reference and Perowne, with powers of life and death, is implicitly or explicitly likened to a God several times (e.g. 13, 23, 77-8, and 128), in contrast to Baxter who is on three occasions called simian or ape-like. (e.g. 88).

Perowne also reflects, before he meets Baxter, on

> [h]ow restful it must once have been, in another age, to be prosperous and believe that an all-knowing supernatural force had allotted people to their stations in life. And not see how the belief served your own prosperity – a form of anosognosia, a useful psychiatric term for a lack of awareness of one's own condition. (74)

Anosognosia is a medical term when a person who suffers disability due to brain injury seems unaware of or denies the existence of their disability, but McEwan describes it simply as "a lack of awareness of one's own condition", and this arguably presents a view of modern Western living presented in the novel, as well as being an observation on the limitations of the contemporary.[28]

Saturday thus repeatedly posits opposed Darwinian views of human life (88), crudely presented the self-focussed survival of the fittest (enacted in modern form on battlefields ranging from the Iraqi desert to the squash court) and Darwin's observation noted earlier that "sympathy and co-operation" are innate to humans. On Perowne's first meeting with his sharer Baxter, he thinks: "Among the game theorists and radical criminologists, the stock of Thomas Hobbes keeps on rising."[29] On this day of the anti-war march, it seems that the hawks have ascendancy over the doves, and in Hobbesian terms the worse aspects of human nature are accorded the status of psychological facts. However, McEwan subscribes to an alternative tradition of Rousseau, Hume, and Adam Smith in which even the most isolated Conradian self is a secret sharer; or as the novel's epigraph has it: "you yourself are a child of this mass and a brother to all the rest." As is evident in McEwan's fiction elsewhere, the self is inherently social, formed inter-relationally,[30] and where Hobbes and others see fellow-feeling as a by-product of self-concern, Smith sees it as a projection of self into other, countering arguments of a complex form of selfishness by querying how acts that are for the sole benefit of others can be deemed 'selfish'.[31]

While *Enduring Love* is the paradigmatic McEwan text here, the sense that all are connected to one another is echoed by Perowne's feeling just before the car accident with Baxter's vehicle when he walks by a road sweeper and their eyes meet: "For a vertiginous moment Henry feels himself bound to the other man, as though on a seesaw with him, pinned to an axis that could tip them into each other's life." (74) Is this sympathetic identification or the fear that McEwan says may be at the root of the imagination? We are all 'secret sharers' in Herzog's modern world but Perowne's rationalism is limiting in ways that make him happy and successful: "the growing complication of the modern condition" he complains halfway through the book, "the expanding circle of moral sympathy.... The trick, as always, the key to human success and domination, is to be selective in your sympathies." (127) At the conclusion of the book, 24 hours after the start, he has operated on Baxter and is about to go home, and considers himself once more to be extremely happy, such that "there must be something wrong with him." (258)[32]

Many critics have found little to like in the figure of Perowne, and we might surmise that his failings are akin to a form of anosognosia. He is forced to be Baxter's 'secret sharer' in Herzog's modern city mass, but Perowne remains out of step with many others, including the anti-war marchers whose route he avoids in his personal urban journey. As quoted above in the different context of his feelings about a 'God delusion', Perowne's beliefs serve his "own prosperity – a form of anosognosia"; and while it is up to the reader to consider the extent to which Perowne has extended his sympathies over the course of his Saturday, it is perhaps something analogous to a lack of awareness of his own condition that is "wrong with him".

When Daisy recites "Dover Beach" at the end of Saturday, Perowne imagines the poem concerns her lover, by whom she is pregnant. In terms of mood however, what registers with him from the poem is the following: "this evening the lovers hear only sadness and loss in the sound of the waves breaking and retreating from the shore." (221) Inevitably this anticipates McEwan's next book, especially as *On Chesil Beach* attempts to place itself at a turning of the tide in human sensibilities and beliefs, though this time about sex and communication rather than faith and god. Like the allusions to Philip Larkin's "Aubade" in *Saturday* and McEwan's libretto *For You*, *On Chesil Beach* also clearly returns to another famous Larkin poem, "Annus Mirabilis", most famous for its observation that sex started in 1963, the year after Chesil Beach is set. However, it is the second verse of Larkin's poem that better describes the socio-historical moment McEwan attempts to portray in *On Chesil Beach*:

> Up to then there'd only been
> A sort of bargaining,
> A wrangle for the ring,
> A shame that started at sixteen
> And spread to everything.

The selection of 1963 as a watershed is of course imprecise and only a general marker of change. McEwan himself notes the same point about Virgina Woolf's choice in her essay "Mr Bennett and Mrs Brown" of December 1910 as a moment when "human nature changed". Describing a possible inspirational incident for *On Chesil Beach*, McEwan goes on to note in his essay "Literature Science and Human Nature" that Woolf also wrote in her memoir "Old Bloomsbury" how in 1908 Lytton Strachey, on entering a room, asked Woolf's sister Vanessa whether the stain on her dress was semen.[33] "With that one word," Woolf notes, "all barriers of reserve and reticence went down".

This is in part a separation between age groups suddenly eroded, and in McEwan's novella the strangest detail is how Edward and Florence are caught at a tidal moment between generational sensibilities.[34] McEwan consequently uses geological and natural imagery throughout *On Chesil Beach* to suggest a gulf between generations and a turning point in social history. Florence's vagina is termed "a naturally formed cavity",[35] marriage is "a new pinnacle of existence" (6), the "matter" between them is a "mountain" (139) and a word is "a starburst" (149). The shingle and waves are repeatedly cited at the time of the couple's "failure" (83), and most prominent is imagery associated with the Fleet. This is "shingle between the sea and the lagoon" (5) representing a sliver of land between two epochs:

> thousands of years of pounding storms had sifted and graded the size of pebbles along the eighteen miles of beach, with the bigger stones at the eastern end. The legend was that local fishermen landing at night knew exactly where they were by the grade of shingle. (19)

McEwan suggests that temporal orientation is achieved by the behaviour of people situated at points along a stretch of time. Thus, of Edward and Florence the narrator says:

> And what stood in their way? Their personalities and pasts, their ignorance and fear, timidity, squeamishness, lack of entitlement or experience or easy manners, then the tail end of a religious prohibition, their Englishness and class, and history itself. (96)[36]

As we see here, the narrator sits above the characters and action repeatedly passing a comment from the twenty-first century about "the times": in terms of sexuality, history, and even cuisine. This implied narrator's attitude of an omniscient commentator from a distanced world is apparent from the book's first sentences: "They were young, educated, and both virgins on this, their wedding night, and they lived in a time when a conversation about sexual difficulties was plainly impossible. But it is never easy." (3) The final two sentences of the book, describing Florence striding away to the future along the beach, and Edward in "righteous silence", are a clear culmination of this opening, brought home by the narrative hierarchy of discourse, where the characters are fixed in time before a heavily analogised moment in social history.[37]

As though describing his own contemporary fiction, McEwan says that "At its best, literature is universal, illuminating human nature at precisely the point at which it is most parochial and specific."[38] While he concentrates on individuals, like many writers in the humanist tradition before him, he is interested in what anthropologist Donald E. Brown calls "Universal People", and on what "all people, all societies, all cultures and all languages have in common".[39] McEwan's focus in his recent writing is clearly on the observation of human behaviour: "The expressions of emotion are the products of evolution, Darwin argued, and therefore universal."[40] McEwan acknowledges that for a good part of the twentieth-century the notion of a universal human nature was reviled, but he follows E. O. Wilson in asserting that humans have a nature but that its "values are self-evident to us to the point of invisibility" and "human literature does not define human nature so much as exemplify it".[41]

Finally, in his article "Save the Boot Room, Save the Earth", an essay on his involvement in an expedition to the Arctic, McEwan says of human beings: "We are the beneficiaries and victims of our nature (social primates, evolved through time like wind-sculpted rock), merry and venal, cooperative and selfish."[42] In this longview, humans always suffer from anosognosia. McEwan arguably suggests in *On Chesil Beach* that we never extensively know our condition any more than Edward or Florence understand his anger[43] and her feelings of "dread" and "disgust" and "shame" about sex (7, 84): all Florence knows is that, possibly isolated from Edward by hinted-at childhood abuse which she cannot admit to herself,[44] she feels "Alone", like her new husband (86).[45] Yet, it is the back story of Edward's family that epitomises the contemporary McEwan condition: a conspiracy of silence and denial over his mother's brain-damaged condition, summarised as a "a form of make-believe". (68)[46]

For this reason, describing not anosognosia but fiction, McEwan has said in interview: "The reason I like novels is that they're good at dramatising the ways in which we fool ourselves."[47] If this is the case then it provides a powerful lens through which to read his later work. *Enduring Love, Amsterdam, Atonement,* and *On Chesil Beach* have all been read in this way, so it may well be that this is also a key to unlocking fresh readings of *Saturday*. This leaves a question concerning the way in which Perowne, in particular, might be fooling himself, and whether in a novel about consciousness such self-deception is linked to "a lack of awareness of one's own condition", which is also one way of looking at the fragility of the dominant contemporary Western *Weltanschauung* as well as the impulses behind myriad abuses and such violences as war.

Notes

1 For example, see Walter (2007).
2 Ian McEwan, Introduction to *Or Shall We Die?* in McEwan (1989: 16).
3 McEwan (1989: 14). McEwan also adds that 'Niels Bohr's Theory of Complementarity [...] explains that we do not study the world so much as study our interaction with it.' McEwan (1989: 13)
4 And 'she knows that at the heart of things there are limitations and paradoxes (the speed of light, the Uncertainty Principle) that prevent her from knowing or expressing everything; she has no illusions of her omniscience, and yet her power is limitless because it does reside in her alone' McEwan (1989: 15).
5 'The dominant theme would have to shift from violence to nurture. Children, not oil or coal or nuclear energy, are our most important resource [...]. Could we ever learn to 'live lightly on the earth', using the full range of

our technological resources, but using them in harmony and balance with our environment rather than in crude violation of it?' McEwan (1989: 16)
6 McEwan (2008).
7 McEwan (1998: 172).
8 Partly because of a perceived near exhaustion in the expressive intradiegetic novel, McEwan has also said that he is no longer interested in writing in the first person (*The Cement Garden*; *Black Dogs*; *Enduring Love*.) and this echoes an interest in the Universal alongside differences between individual circumstances. The closing section of *Atonement* is arguably less a postmodernist twist than a critique written in the first-person of the legacy of the modernist first-person novel and of the contemporary reader's rising desire for heritage realism. "I've lost all interest in first person narrative. [...] I want the authorial presence taking full responsibility for everything. Although the narrator of On Chesil Beach is not a character you could describe, or has any past or future, it is a presence which assumes the aesthetic task of describing the inside of two people's minds. Then the reader can make a judgement. Of course there is a way of loading a first person narrative voice with authorial insight, or brilliant turns of phrase, but most writers don't try for this – it's difficult." Cook et al (2009: 133).
9 Appleyard (2007: 2).
10 Appleyard (2007: 2).
11 This was the project that Professor Jocelyn Kale, Clarissa's godfather, was working on in *Enduring Love*.
12 McEwan (2006a: 58). The essay was first published in 2005 and is an expanded version of an essay first published in *The Guardian* as "The Great Odyssey" in 2001.
13 As Robin Headlam Wells and JohnJoe McFadden succinctly explain, "Modern humanists argue that, by enabling us to make imaginative contacts with other minds in worlds remote historically or culturally from our own, literature can help us to appreciate that our common humanity is more important than the ethnic and religious differences that create so much havoc in our lives [...] In that way, humanists believe, literature can encourage those central principles of Enlightenment thought – sympathy, understanding and toleration." Introduction to Headlam Wells and McFadden (2006: 5)
14 Functionalism sees mental states (beliefs and desires, etc.) constituted solely by their functional role and so able to be produced in non-human systems.
15 Huntington's disease is a progressive neurological genetic disorder, ascribed to one specific gene. Some cognitive abilities and psychomotor functions are affected progressively. An extensive discussion of the importance of Huntington's Disease in the understanding of genes can be found in Chapter Four, "Fate", of Matt Ridley's Genome (2000: 54-64).
16 Catherine Belsey, "Biology and Imagination: the role of culture", in Headlam Wells and McFadden (2006: 124-5).

17 Cook et al (2009: 124).
18 Theory of mind denotes the human ability to ascribe mental states, including beliefs, desires, and intentions, to oneself and to others, and especially to understand that others have different thoughts and feelings.
19 McEwan (2006a: 40)
20 Sandall (2008: 7). See Childs (2007).
21 Jean-Jacques Rousseau (1979: 222-23).
22 Phillips and Taylor (2009: 99)
23 Winnicott quoted Phillips and Taylor (2009: 97).
24 McEwan (2006a: 40-60).
25 Epigraph to McEwan (2005a). Further references are cited in the text.
26 Among many other writers, Conrad is an allusive touchstone for McEwan's fiction; for example, the conclusion of *Black Dogs* refers to the eponymous canines "crossing the shadow line and going deeper where the sun never reaches" McEwan (1998: 174).
27 Darwin (1968).
28 At the very start of Enduring Love, McEwan asks a fundamental question about human kindness: why do people rush to the aid of another. Adam Phillips and Barbara Taylor comment on the contrast between pagan and Christian understandings of such acts: "This joyous element in pro-kindness thought was suppressed by post-Augustinian Christianity. Kindness became linked, disastrously, to self-sacrifice, which made it a sitting duck for philosophical egoists such as Thomas Hobbes who could easily demonstrate that self-sacrifice was rarely practised, even by its most ardent proponents. Pagan kindness, by contrast, had no truck with self-sacrifice." Phillips and Taylor (2009: 19).
29 "With Hobbes, selfishness and aggression were transformed from moral vices into psychological facts." Phillips and Taylor (2009:25).
30 In his *Treatise of Human Nature* (1739-40), Hume compared feelings between people as akin to the vibration of violin strings. Sympathy and identification become the source of fellow feeling for Hume (see Theory of Moral Sentiments [1759]).
31 McEwan has an interest in this from the modern day perspective of Dawkins' selfish gene, which he believes stood at the beginning of a golden age of science writing. "With a fine sense of literary tradition, the physicist Steven Weinberg, in his book *Dreams of a Final Theory*, revisited Huxley's lecture on chalk in order to make the case for reductionism. Steven Pinker's application of Darwinian thought to Chomskyan linguistics in *The Language Instinct* is one of the finest celebrations of language I know. Among many other indispensable "classics", I would propose E. O. Wilson's *The Diversity of Life* on the ecological wonders of the Amazon rain forest, and on the teeming micro-organisms in a handful of soil; David Deutsch's masterly account of the Many Worlds theory in *The Fabric of Reality*; Jared Diamond's melding of history with biological thought in *Guns, Germs and Steel*; Antonio Damasio's hypnotic account of the neuroscience of the

emotions in *The Feeling of What Happens*; Matt Ridley, unweaving the opposition of nature and nurture in *Nature via Nurture*; and recently, the philosopher Daniel Dennett, conscious of Hume as well as Dawkins, laying out for us the memetics of faith in *Breaking the Spell*." McEwan (2006b), published on the thirtieth anniversary of Richard Dawkins's groundbreaking book *The Selfish Gene*.

32 Thus, at the moment of the accident, Perowne is thinking about the fragility of happiness. McEwan (2005: 81) The happiness that he thinks is hard to analyse and that is under-discussed in the academy: "for the humanities, generally, misery is more amenable to analysis: happiness is a harder nut to crack." McEwan (2005: 78)

33 McEwan, (2006a 50).

34 They are named perhaps for Edward and Florence Ashburnham, the protagonists of that other sad story of anomalous sexual codes and an un-consummated marriage, Ford Madox Ford's 1915 novel *The Good Soldier*. It is thus unsurprising that McEwan compares the 1910s and the 1960s in his essay and implicitly in his novel.

35 McEwan (2007: 7). Further page references are given in the text.

36 Edward wants to write bio-vignettes on "semi-obscure figures close to important historical events" McEwan (2007: 45).

37 He has said about On Chesil Beach: "Walking returns me to the essentials: we live on a giant rock hanging in sterile space. If you walk for several days, it's surprising how quickly everything else in your life drops away. And how quickly a long walk translates itself into metaphor – life's journey, if you like." Cook et al (2009: 134).

38 McEwan (2006a: 41. A key text in the debate over human nature is Steven Pinker's *The Blank Slate: The Modern Denial of Human Nature* (2002).

39 Brown (1991: 130). "UP faces show happiness, sadness, anger, fear, surprise, disgust, and contempt, in a manner entirely familiar from one society to another." Brown (1991: 134)

40 McEwan (2006a: 46).

41 McEwan (2006a: 48 and 49). McEwan says : "Huxley leads us, of course to Darwin. My particular favourite is The Expression of the Emotions in Man and Animals, in which he makes the case for emotions as human universals, shared across cultures. He also makes an anti-racist argument for a common human nature." McEwan (2006b). McEwan focuses on the unusual and the extreme, in order to explore the everyday and indeed the universal – from concern with the incest taboo and ordinary extraordinary incestuous Oedipal desire in *The Cement Garden* to its extraordinary ordinary opposite in *On Chesil Beach*, when inability to communicate about sexual fears in a repressed society at the precise moment when sex is socially required.

42 McEwan (2005b).

43 Edward has a fear of failure and "arriving too soon" McEwan (2007: 7), but the larger issues are his tendency to temper and anger, as when his Jewish friend seems appalled that Edward exhibits a tendency towards physical

retaliation. Edward's anger with Florence occurs frequently: McEwan (2007: 135; 148; 157).

44 She wonders, "Had it taken her this long to discover that she lacked some simple mental trick that everyone else had, a mechanism so ordinary that no one ever mentioned it, an immediate sensual connection to people and events, and to her own needs and desires?" McEwan (2007: 61).

45 She has "conflicted feelings about her father" McEwan (2007: 49), and the sailing journeys she takes with him suggest some possibility of abuse, McEwan (2007: 99 and 106). Oedipal feelings are also referred to more than once, McEwan (2007: 50, 153-4).

46 And of his "separateness" after he knows McEwan (2007: 74).

47 Cook et al (2009: 129).

Bibliography

Appleyard, Brian: "The Ghost in My Family" News Review Section, *The Sunday Times*, 25 March, 2007, 1-2.

Brown, Donald E.: *Human Universals*, New York, 1991.

Childs, Peter: "'Believing is Seeing': The Eye of the Beholder", in Ian McEwan's *Enduring Love*, ed. Peter Childs, London, 2007, pp. 107-121.

Cook, Jon, Groes, Seb & Sage, Victor: "Journey Without Maps" in Ian McEwan: *Critical Perspectives*, ed. Sebastian Groes, London, 2009, pp. 123-34.

Darwin, Charles: *On the Origin of Species*, Harmondsworth, 1968.

Headlam Wells, Robin & McFadden, JohnJoe (Eds): *Human Nature: Fact and Fiction*, London, 2006.

McEwan, Ian: *A Move Abroad*, London, 1989.

McEwan, Ian: *Black Dogs*, London, 1998.

McEwan, Ian: *Saturday*, London, 2005a.

McEwan, Ian: "Save the Boot Room, Save the Earth", *The Guardian*, 19 March, 2005b.

http://www.guardian.co.uk/artanddesign/2005/mar/19/art1 (accessed 11 August 2009).

McEwan, Ian: "Literature, Science and Human Nature", 2006a, in Headlam Wells and McFadden (Eds) (2006: 40-60).

McEwan, Ian: "A Parallel Tradition", *The Guardian*, 1 April, 2006b. http://www.guardian.co.uk/books/2006/apr/01/scienceandnature.richarddawkins (accessed 11 August 2009).

McEwan, Ian: *On Chesil Beach*, London, 2007.

McEwan, Ian: "The World's Last Chance", *The Guardian*, 19 November, 2008, http://www.guardian.co.uk/environment/2008/nov/19/global-climate-change-policy-obama (accessed 11 March 2009).

Phillips, Adam and Taylor, Barbara: *On Kindness*, London, 2009.

Ridley, Matt: Genome, New York, 2000.

Rousseau, Jean-Jacques: *Emile, or On Education*. [1762] Translated by Allan Bloom. New York: Basic Books, 1979

Sandall, Robert: "Interview with McEwan", Culture Section, *The Sunday Times*, 26 October, 2008, 6-7.

Walter, Natasha: "Young Love, Old Angst", Review Section, *The Guardian*, 31 March, 2007, 7.

Anja Müller-Wood (Mainz)

The Murderer as Moralist or, The Ethical Early McEwan

1. Introduction

Ian McEwan's short story "Butterflies" (in *First Love, Last Rites* [1975]) – in which a child murderer recounts how he meets, molests and kills a little girl – contains a puzzling and apparently gratuitous scene of violence. As they are walking along a filthy canal in a desolate, unidentified part of London, the narrator-protagonist and his victim pass a gang of adolescents "preparing to roast a live cat" (85)[1]. When the girl asks the narrator what the youths are doing with the animal, he – in what might be taken as a merciful lie – feigns incomprehension and wordlessly urges her away from the atrocity that is about to be committed. He comments in retrospect: "It was difficult to see what they were doing now because of the black smoke. We were leaving them far behind and our path was once more along the factory walls" (85).

Perplexingly incongruent though this scene may at first appear, it actually provides the key to understanding "Butterflies". The episode is illustrative of the violence of this story (as, indeed, of the violence of the collection as a whole); more importantly, however, it draws attention to the fact that this violence is narrated. What it thereby also suggests is that the information the reader receives is filtered through the eyes of the narrator, who may misperceive and/or misrepresent events. In thus pointing to the potential unreliability of this first-person account, the scene hints at the metareferential gist of this story, which appears to be a confession, but whose narrator ultimately refuses to admit anything. Just as the black smoke veils the torture of the cat, "Butterflies" can be seen to set up an extended narrative smokescreen to hide a real act of violence – the killing of a child.

Our awareness of the story's narratedness inevitably has an impact on the way we interpret the text, influencing our assessment of the narrator-protagonist as well as our own position *vis-à-vis* the story. As I will argue in the following, "Butterflies" raises crucial questions about the interaction between narrator, narrative and reader: How (and to which ends) does the narrator shape the self-image that he presents? What is the reader's function within this narrative choreography and which responses are expected from her or him? How much of the narrator's image are we willing to take at face value – and can we resist the information that he offers? These questions, I maintain, have clear ethical implications.

To speak about the ends and functions of literature as well as about readers' resistance to a text means adopting a pragmatic perspective that may go against the grain of the discursive and contextual interpretations that currently dominate literary scholarship. However, "Butterflies" clearly invites an interpretation in the light of these categories. Such a reading allows us to rethink not only the story in question, but also McEwan's early work more generally, where the confessional stance exemplified by "Butterflies" is often exploited to a very similar effect.[2] What it also allows us to reconsider is the relationship between literature and ethics. If "Butterflies" is an expressly ethical story, then we need to contemplate the question where the ethical dimension of literature is located in order to appreciate this quality. What the story urges us to do is to shift our attention away from its content towards its structure – that is, its functional arrangement. It is here – in the text's choreography of reader responses – that its true (and unsettling) ethical significance lies.

2. Towards a Functional Approach to Literary Ethics

McEwan's early "shock-lit"[3] has, for obvious reasons, been inspiring different kinds of ethical interpretations for quite some time. On the more conservative end of the critical spectrum, interpreters have tended to take his early work as triggering unambiguous moral responses.[4] Hence a first-person narrator like that of "Butterflies" might be considered a "mad monologist"[5] from whose ideas and attitudes readers need to distance themselves (for instance, by bestowing this convenient evaluative label upon him). Almost precisely the opposite interpretation is offered by more radical critics, who have applauded McEwan for confronting readers with their own "delight in degradation"[6]. Finally, those obviously informed by a postmodern scepticism regarding reality and truth have argued that the "unrelentingly moral"[7] quality of McEwan's early writing lies in its "radical uncertainty" (see Hanson, 142) and defiance of a definite ethical position.

Although superficially these readings appear to be worlds apart, their notion of literary ethics is essentially similar: all see literature's ethical dimension as located in its content – in *what* is being said rather than *how* it is being formulated. Such content-based ethics have characterised much of the work done in the wake of the "ethical turn" of the 1990s.[8] Ethical criticism of this kind typically takes it for granted that texts transmit a particular, usually transformative (and therefore didactic) message[9]; it is less interested in the specifics of these transmission processes. Even critics explicitly concerned with the "ethics of reading"[10], who acknowledge that individual texts may have specific effects upon the reader, tend to eschew detailed investigations of the methods and goals of such narrative choreography and instead base their interpretations on abstract ethical principles from outside of the text.

"Butterflies" quickly points up the limits of ethical readings conducted in this way, drawing attention to how the narrative's arrangement achieves its effects. Although the narrator has an appalling revelation to make, he does so in a way that diminishes any overt shock effect, mainly through misrepresentations that serve to distance him from the event. The scene in which he brings about the death of the child – as will become apparent, the way he frames this episode makes it difficult for us to call his actions "murder" – is a case in point. Although in this instance the narrator climactically reveals the events leading up to the death of the child (Jane), his narrative euphemistically veils the deed:

> Jane was almost out of the tunnel. When she heard my footsteps behind her she turned round and gave a kind of yelp. She started to run too, and immediately lost her footing. From where I was it was difficult to see what happened to her, the silhouette against the sky suddenly disappeared into the black. She was lying face down when I reached her, with her left leg trailing off the path almost into the water. She had banged her head going down and there was a swelling over her right eye. Her right arm was stretched out in front of her and almost reached into the

> sunlight. I bent down to her face and listened to her breathing. It was deep and regular. Her eyes were closed tight and the lashes were still wet from crying. I no longer wanted to touch her, that was all pumped out of me now, into the canal. I brushed away some dirt from her face and some more from the back of her red dress.
> 'Silly girl,' I said, 'no butterflies.' Then I lifted her up gently, as gently as I could so as not to wake her, and eased her quietly into the canal. (87)

Of particular significance here is the narrator's emphasis on his limited grasp of the event: his difficulty in seeing "what happened", the reduction of the girl to a "silhouette against the sky" and her sudden disappearance "into the black". The self-defensive vagueness of these formulations is echoed by the euphemistic analogy of death and sleep on which the paragraph closes, which – apart from affirming the narrator's cognitive limitations also serves to assert his fundamentally gentle nature.

Of course, this suggestion is preposterous: the only sane thing would have been to be rude and wake (and so save) the unconscious child. Yet the scene is of course not about *a priori* notions of rational sanity – in fact, it perverts such notions by showing how easily they can be exploited to exactly the opposite end. In so doing, it draws attention to the fact that the narrator is not only unreliable, but that this unreliability may serve strategic aims. It thereby raises uncomfortable questions: How much distance is there between the world and the man who causes the unconscious child to drown in the canal? Is the distance itself not part of his self-defence? In how far is this one of the veils anticipated in the cat-roasting scene quoted above?

The narratologist James Phelan offers a differentiated functionalist framework to understand the ethical implications of McEwan's story. For Phelan, literary texts are, above all, rhetorical and hence communicative: "somebody telling somebody else on some occasion and for some purpose that something happened" (2003 132). Far from merely being a formal feature, narrative technique is therefore a crucial *pragmatic* device to shape the reader's responses to a text. For that reason, Phelan argues, narrative technique has distinct ethical implications: "individual narratives develop their own sets of ethical issues" (2003 133). These are revealed in the way texts are constructed to engage both cognitively and emotionally with the reader through the different "ethical positionings" (2003 133) that result from the "dynamic interaction" between different textual and extratextual points of view. Amongst those ethical positionings is, importantly, that of the flesh-and-blood reader of a text, who is not only the recipient – and hence target – of the narrative construct, but also, ultimately, its judge.[11]

Locating a text's ethical significance in areas beyond its manifest content, Phelan's pragmatic perspective defies the notion that literary ethics can be separated from literary form. Indeed, what Phelan points out is not only that the discussion of literary ethics requires taking the representational dimension into account: for Phelan a text's ethics *lies in* its aesthetics (or vice versa). If the study of literary ethics can be rethought at all, then it is from this functionalist perspective, which – by radically expanding our notion of ethics – also explains why the kind of insights described by Phelan might be made most forcefully by texts that defy our own moral norms.[12] Phelan's particular concern with the ethics of overtly "unethical" texts is exemplified by his discussion of Vladimir Nabokov's infamous novel *Lolita*, whose paedophile narrator-protagonist is a captivating rhetorician; shamelessly boasting about his sexual triumphs with the juvenile Lolita, Humbert invites the reader into his mind and asks him not only to accept, but indeed to share his views and attitudes.

When investigated on the basis of its content alone, the novel has little ethical insight to offer. This kind of assessment would be in tune with the traditional critical suspicion of first-person narratives as simplistic and one-sided[13]; a closer look at Nabokov's novel reveals a far more sophisticated narrative situation, however. Phelan calls Humbert Humbert "an unreliable self-conscious narrator" (2003 136) because his retrospective narrative, rather than being a homogeneously gleeful report of his sexual exploits, is shot through with self-critical commentary. Such narrative subtlety is due to what Phelan calls instances of "dual focalisation" in the novel – moments, that is, in which the narrator-protagonist not only reports story-world events from within, as it were, at the moment as he is experiencing them – but also comments on them retrospectively and from an outside perspective. As a result, dual focalisation lends a text a potentially contradictory double-voicedness[14] to which the reader must respond in an equally differentiated way.

While on the whole, the narrator's subjective account invites the reader to take his position, signals that are identifiable as Nabokov's critical point of view "communicat[e] his ethical disapproval of Humbert and invit[e] the authorial audience to share in it" (135). According to Phelan, Nabokov's novel turns the readers simultaneously into the advocates for and critics of his protagonist: "before we can stand with Nabokov and away from his character, we have to stand with Humbert and share his perspective" (135). Nabokov's novel is disturbing not least because it reminds us of how hard it is to resist narrative manipulation – a difficulty magnified by the fact that this resistance is choreographed by the narrator in the first place.

The nameless narrator of "Butterflies" is Humbert's worthy successor not only thematically – because of the motif of paedophilia that connects both texts – but also because, like *Lolita*, his presumably simple account is complicated by moments of dual focalisation. These render both the narrator and our own view of him more complex. Rather than, as has been suggested, appealing to our darker impulses and desires[15], McEwan's story caters to our most worthy inclinations and attitudes, turning the readers into his defendants by harnessing their abilities to feel empathy and pity. It is the awareness of this narrative abuse, I argue, that constitutes the real, but usually underestimated, shock effect of this story.

3. Veiling the Truth

If "Butterflies" is probably the most unsettling text in McEwan's generally disturbing first short story collection *First Love, Last Rites*[16], this quality is due less to the story's graphic gruesomeness than to the monotonous impassivity with which the narrator recounts the fatal encounter with his victim. Almost elegiac in tone, the story creates a deceptive sense of calm, serenity and, indeed, honesty regarding the terrible event that is being described. Whether the narrator actually tells the truth cannot be determined, however: his perspective is subjective, limited and therefore inevitably unreliable (Stanzel 122). All we can ascertain with some reliability are the aims and principles according to which the narrative is choreographed to involve the reader.

The story's opening promises a narrative of utter transparency, as the narrator states calmly: "I had seen my first corpse on Thursday" (71). Yet, however candid this first statement might seem, it is already part of the text's distancing strategy. This pattern continues even after the narrator has identified the "corpse" as that of a child called Jane from his neighbourhood, drowned a few days previously in a nearby canal. He is the last to have seen the girl and is, at the beginning of the story, preparing to meet her parents. However, his depictions of the child are ambiguous to say the least. His repeated references to "Jane" or "little Jane" ("the canal little Jane drowned in [72]"; "Jane's corpse" [74]) suggest familiarity, yet they are intermixed with equally frequent impersonal references to "the little girl" (78) or "this one" (76). Although the narrator here takes two different perspectives towards the girl, these serve a similar aim. Speaking about her as if he were ventriloquising other people even when he uses her first name, the narrator here affirms his distance from the child, her death and his guilt.

In a similar way, the narrator seems to employ the words of others when he describes himself and his actions. For instance, he presents the statement that he makes at the police station in a way that makes it sound as if it had been made by someone else:

> Upstairs I signed the papers which said that I had been walking across the footbridge by the railway lines and that I had seen a girl, identified as the one downstairs, running along the canal towpath. I looked away and a little later I saw something red in the water which sank out of sight. Since I cannot swim I fetched a policeman, who peered into the water and said he could see nothing. I gave my name and address and went home. An hour and a half later they pulled her up from the bottom with a dragline. (75)

Depicting himself as the object of somebody else's account, the narrator emphasises his physical distance from the event that the statement documents. By the end of the story, of course, we know that exactly the opposite is true: far from being an unconcerned witness, the narrator is directly implicated in the child's by no means accidental death. Whatever sense of distance he creates with his account is as untrustworthy as it is strategic.

The narrator's disconnectedness from the world is offset by his far more direct and precise assessment of the behaviour of others, especially as it relates to him. In that way he presents himself as the only perceptive person in an otherwise ignorant environment. For example, when, at the beginning of the story, he meets his neighbour Charlie in the street, he claims to know that the older man, despite being already informed about the female corpse the narrator has not yet identified, still "wanted to hear my story" (71). During a second encounter, later in the day, he is convinced that "for some reason Charlie held [the girl's] death against me" (78). The narrator's suspicion dovetails with his interpretation of the office girls' behaviour at the police station when he had made his statement: "They glanced at me uneasily. They suspected me of something, they always do" (75). While the reference to an inborn female suspiciousness ("they always do") underlines the nagging gynophobia that colours the story, it does so by placing the women within the context of a larger power structure. They are satellites of a brutal police force, cogs in the wheels of an institution that asserts its power by intimidation. For instance, the narrator speculates that the physical contact sought by a policeman at the station where he had made his statement "could be a trick they learn at police school to give them the power they need" (73).

The inevitable verso of the narrator's paranoia is his isolation. Taken together, these characteristics interact to establish an attractive, potentially pitiable image – a mournful auto-portrait that exploits very basic human (and humane) emotions such as empathy, pity and compassion. We learn that when the narrator meets and kills the girl, he has not spoken with anyone for several days (77). He informs us about his looks – inherited from his equally isolated mother – which he claims are the reason for his loneliness and isolation: "My chin and neck are the same thing, and it breeds distrust" (74), with the result that "women […] won't come near me" (74).

The world's indifference and rejection is set off by his desire for friendship, which is encapsulated most strikingly in a brief encounter with a group of West Indian boys playing football in the street. His failure to use the stone they aggressively kick at him as a means to kick off a friendly conversation affirms his absolute isolation: "They all laughed at [his trapping the stone with his foot] and clapped and cheered me, so that for one elated moment I thought I could go back and join their game" (79). The boys immediately lose interest and return to their game, but in his imagination, in the final section of the story, the narrator takes up and expands upon precisely this optimistic scenario to emphasise his yearning for company. The effect is twofold: inspiring the reader's defensive sympathy while simultaneously blotting out the narrator's responsibility:

> I should have turned round then, slowly, acknowledging their applause with a faint grin. Then I should have kicked the stone back, or better, stepped over it and walked casually towards them, and then, when the ball came back, I would be with them, one of them, in a team. (88)

If we believe the narrator (which of course we should not), he is a pitiable zombie moving like an automaton in an alien world. Echoing *The Stranger* – Albert Camus's novel with which McEwan's story has a more than passing resemblance – he emphasises the heat on the day he narrates his story to explain his lethargy and passivity: "It was Sunday, there was nothing to do, it was too hot" (71)[17]. When, leaving Charlie after their first encounter, the narrator turns to the left simply "because that was the way I was facing" (72). Even his words seem to possess absolute autonomy: the word "butterflies" that he utters in order to lure the girl to the canal is "out before I could retrieve it" (82).

Within this narrative structure deliberately arranged to provoke reader empathy, through which the narrator portrays himself as a passive object reacting or being acted upon by external stimuli, the child comes to be firmly located on the side of a world seen as hostile and threatening. When narrator and girl meet, she initiates their conversation. Addressing him when he walks past her house – thereby abandoning the safety of her family's garden – she follows him. Her initiative causes him mixed feelings of subdued pleasure and stifling unease. In the course of their walk, she quickly loses all further inhibitions, asking personal questions ("Have you got lots of money already?" [80]), transgressing physical boundaries ("hanging" on his arm [80]) and beginning to nag, beg and make demands like an irritating girl friend: "Could you buy me something if you wanted to?" (80). The girl's agency is affirmed soon after she and the narrator have set out on their walk by the canal where she will eventually drown. Suddenly, it is she who seems to lead the way to the isolated spot where she will be abused and killed – in fact, what the narrator insinuates here is that it is she who guides herself to her own death.

The girl's ambiguous agency, responsibility – indeed: guilt – is further underlined by the innate sensuality that the narrator ascribes to her. Her opening line, as he claims to remember it, is her bluntly intimate reference to the scent of his soap: "You smell like flowers." (76) This statement conjoins her lack of distance and precociousness with a physicality the narrator seems to find frightening. Her touch, resembling that of the policeman at the station, is a genuine intrusion, causing vehement bodily reactions. When she is "hanging on" the narrator's arm begging him to buy her a treat, he comments: "No one had touched me intentionally like that for a long time, not since I was a child. I felt a cold thrill in my stomach and I was unsteady on my legs." (80)

The narrator's sustained denial of all responsibility for the death of the child is entwined with his complete denial of his own physicality. Throughout the story, he depicts himself as the one who sees, hears and observes, usually from afar, while others express their lack of distance by touching. His own body is as alien to him as other human beings, producing overwhelming somatic responses beyond his control. After wiping the girl's ice-cream stained lips with his finger, he reacts vehemently: "I had never touched another person's lips before, nor had I experienced this kind of pleasure. It rose painfully from my groin to my chest and lodged itself there, like a fist pushing against my ribs." (82-83) This visceral response anticipates the orgasm that he forces her to bring about: " 'Touch it, touch it.' She reached out her hand and her fingers briefly brushed my tip. It was enough, though. I doubled up and came, I came into my cupped hands." (86)

The body-mind distinction that underpins the narrator's self-image and his view of the world also explains other seemingly cryptic features of the story, which – when seen in this light – fuse into a larger meaningful and proleptic mosaic when seen in this light. For instance, when the child begs him to buy her "a small, pink, naked doll, moulded from one piece of plastic" (80), the obscenity of the toy – which the child forgets immediately – emphasises her precociousness and anticipates her sexual abuse. So does her red dress, which almost as if by itself "rides up over her backside" (83) when the narrator lifts up the girl when she (almost imperiously) demands to see the boats in the canal. These tokens, in turn, are echoed by the interest that his neighbour Charlie shows for the child, which the narrator foregrounds in a way that invites our suspicion. Seen in light of the girl's precociousness, the neighbour's concern becomes tinged with something more than innocent friendliness. By contrast, the narrator's passing references to fine art (comparing the child to a Modigliani painting [77]), classical music (recognising the Mozart piano sonata played by the ice-cream van [72]), as well as the overarching metaliterary reference to Camus's *The Stranger* affirm a sensitivity and sophistication that bespeak his innocence. Meanwhile, his passing hint at the skinheads beating up the sons of the Pakistani owner of the corner shop (78) and his interest in the West Indian boys playing football in the street mark him as more tolerant and open-minded than others in his environment.

This overt structural contrast between passivity and activity, between a narrator who depicts himself as innocent and a reputedly aggressive physical world – between, ultimately, the mental and the physical – ought to be enough to provoke the reader's suspicion. However, the text's underlying logic and function only emerge fully when seen within the narrative's larger structure of denial. As long as the reader has not completely understood the relationship between the narrator and the child – and realised that the world has every reason to "hold the child's death against him" – he or she is likely to find the former's self-defensive image plausible if not attractive. Only when we have fully understood the narrator's involvement in the death of the child do we realise that his black-and-white world view is part of a larger retrospective strategy to defend the speaker while vilifying all others. The aim of this strategy is to weaken the moral dismay the reader actually ought to feel. In the end, we are even unable to call the narrator a killer because with his depiction of his deed he denies us that label.

Yet because the apparently closed narrative proffered by McEwan's narrator is strategic, it raises a host of questions about the validity of his account: How intentional was the girl's first touch? How distanced was the narrator really? Did she really stumble or was she pushed? Arranged to evoke such doubts about the tale that we are told, the story affirms – and refines – the point that the narrator makes when emphasising the smoke-obscured maltreatment of the cat in the scene quoted at the outset: our view of reality is potentially obscured by the way we represent it. The story thereby highlights what the narrator conceals: namely that the screen that he acknowledges as an inevitable factor in our relationship with reality is created by himself.

4. The Duplicity of Confession

A treacherous confessional tale, McEwan's story illuminates the duplicity that seems to characterise all literary confessions: as retrospective assessments of a past event or experience, these are inevitably characterised by the double-voiced quality of dual focalisation.[18] For James Phelan, as we have seen, this double-voicedness is where the ethical dimension of dual focalisation lies. Dual focalisation, he argues, complicates readers' responses to a dubious narrator like Humbert Humbert not only by introducing a critical perspective into his subjective account, but also by forcing us to share the narrator's stance before we can criticise him. The ethical significance of *Lolita*, then, lies in our understanding this. And yet one wonders whether Phelan is here not a little too optimistic about both the inevitability and obviousness of this insight. Not only might a reader fail to detect the criticism that dual focalisation introduces into a text. We may also ask why the second perspective should be less strategic – and hence more reliable – than the first.

McEwan's story provides a somewhat more sceptical take on Phelan's view, using dual focalisation to defy whatever positive, self-defensive perspective this narrative stance helps to establish. This is illustrated in the following striking passage:

> To have someone walking along with me on Wednesday was something of an opportunity, too, even if it was only a little girl with nothing to do. Although I would not have admitted it at the time, I felt pleased that she was genuinely curious about me, and I was attracted to her. I wanted her to be my friend. (79)

The second sentence sets up a troubling tension between the narrator's past and present assessment of an event that he claims to be able (or willing) to view as pleasurable only in retrospect.[19] The positive tone of this passage is in stark contrast to the outspoken misanthropy that the narrator had expressed before; emphasising his ability to revalue his past, he suggests that he has undergone a marked psychological and moral development. The passage, then, is a bid for the reader's sympathy, understanding and forgiveness, encapsulating the aims of this narrative and identifying the readers' function within it. The manipulative intentionality of the account makes the fact that the narrator is preparing to visit the child's parents as he is telling his story all the more ominous.

And yet, in a way that anticipates later novels such as *Atonement*, the story also asks us to resist such manipulation by recognising and evaluating their rhetorical drift and pragmatic intention.[20] Just as in *Atonement*, in whose disruptive coda the narrator identifies the novel as a fictional transformation of her guilt, in "Butterflies" cues signalling the need for resistance are introduced by the narrator himself. He does so even in the scene of the killing. As the narrator is about to push the unconscious child into the canal after she has stumbled and fallen, he comments: "Silly girl [...] no butterflies." (87) This reference is duplicitous, pointing both to the promise the narrator makes in order to lure the child to the canal and to the child's own keenness to see the butterflies. The child becomes increasingly wary as she follows the narrator on the narrow towpath along the murky water; however, when she discovers a flowering weed in a tunnel, she literally urges them on by interpreting this as a proof of the presence of butterflies: "There have to be flowers [...] for the butterflies" (84).

However childlike this logic may seem at first sight, it already anticipates the end of innocence that finds its sad culmination in the girl's death. Her apodictic proclamation seals her fate, affirming what the narrative has been insinuating all along: that she is the driving force in this fatal encounter, while at the same time expressing a naïve trustfulness that questions that agency. After all, as the reader knows, the narrator makes his promise of butterflies in the full awareness that "the stench [by the polluted canal] would dissolve them." (82) The butterflies serve as a bait to which the girl not only rises, but which she paradoxically lays herself. The victim is the perpetrator – at least, this is what the narrator would like us to believe.

He, by contrast, emphasises his superior scepticism and ability to resists such cues. Although he dreams about friendship and company and expresses these dreams to garner the readers' sympathies, he also acknowledges that his dreams cannot be fulfilled. At the end of the story, even his own fantasy of playing football with the boys, thereby becoming part of a "team", ends with the concession that opportunities for such experiences "are rare, like butterflies." (88) Unlike the girl, then, he has learnt to interpret the signs that others send him correctly; he will not be fooled.

The narrator's assessment is a self-reflective signal hinting, not least, at the story's deceptive title. Like the real butterflies in the story, those in the title serve as a lure to lead the reader onto the wrong track. Through this echo, the narrator equates his readers and his victim, assuming that both share a fundamental desire to be entrapped by stories. Yet while for the girl the encounter is fatal, for the readers it is potentially morally meaningful. In confronting us with our own willingness to follow the leads placed by the narrator, McEwan's story ruthlessly uncovers our proclivity to condone, explain and tolerate human actions as long as they are presented through attractive stories – be they about beautiful insects or pitiable human beings. Hence the ethical significance of "Butterflies" does not lie in the way it triggers our own moral superiority regarding the narrator – which would allow us to judge his actions – but in the way it urges us to face up to our weakness in the face of his tale.

Notes

1 All references are to the 1997 Vintage edition.
2 Of the eight stories in First Love, Last Rites, six – including the one discussed in this article – are first-person narratives.
3 Head, 30.
4 This perspective is exemplified for instance by Jarfe.
5 The term was popularised by Ansgar Nünning, who also applies it to McEwan's work.
6 For instance, Kiernan Ryan emphasises that "the confessional posture of the first-person narratives [...] casts the reader as confidant, as the secret sharer of what is divulged". This, so Ryan, has disturbing results: "[t]he pleasure afforded both writer and reader is not confined to ironic superiority to the benighted narrator; it includes the vicarious pleasure of possession by one's own shameful double. Such fiction flagrantly panders to people's worst instincts, but its alertness to depravity's seductive appeal challenges its readers to come clean about the scale of their own capitulation. For as long as we keep fencing off the perverted and barbaric, the murderous and revolting, as unfathomably alien to us, the secret grip of

these proclivities on our hearts only tightens. To admit the delight we take in degradation, to find our own buried fantasies mirrored in the outcast's eyes, is to begin slackening the noose of blind compulsion" (Ryan 15).
7   This is how Walter Evans (140) judges McEwan's writing. For a similar view, developed on the basis of different literary examples, see C. Namwali Serpell. Problematically, the critical emphasis on ambiguity and openness does not so much provide an alternative to other, normative notions of ethics, as turn ambiguity into yet another (unambiguous) norm.
8   Representative samples of ethical criticism are collected in Davis & Womack. Although, as they point out in their Introduction to the volume, ethical criticism is an inevitable and enduring critical stance, represented by such names as F. R. Leavis and Northrop Frye, it nevertheless gained momentum during the era of poststructuralist critique of subjectivity and its implied critique of subjective ethical faculties.
9   Wayne C. Booth emphasises "the power of narrative to change our lives, for good or ill": "The essential issue for critics [...] is not whether some part of a given story violates this or that moral code; rather, it is the overall effect on the ethos, the character, of the listener. And that effect is not to be measured by some simple study of overt behaviour after listening: it must include the very quality of the life lived while listening." (18)
10 For instance, according to Derek Attridge (1999) "an essential part of a full response to a text that strikes me with the force of the new [...] is a deduction of its modus operandi, an accurate understanding of the repeatable rules according to which the text operates as a meaningful entity" (25). This encounter, he argues, can trigger a response on the part of the reader that "will involve a suspension of my habits, a willingness to apprehend the text's inaugural power" (25), and this in turn constitutes a "nonmoral" form of ethics (29) based not so much on an implied morality, but on the terms of engagement that guide the encounter between text and reader.
11 Phelan, 2005 325.
12 See James Phelan's emphatic assessment: "individual narratives explicitly or more often implicitly establish their own ethical standards in order to guide their audiences to particular ethical judgments. Consequently, within rhetorical ethics, narrative judgments proceed from the inside out rather than the outside in. It is for this reason they are closely tied to aesthetic judgments. The rhetorical theorist, in other words, does not do ethical criticism by applying a pre-existing ethical system to the narrative, however much he or she may admire the ethics elaborated by Aristotle, Kant, Levinas, or any other thinker; instead, the rhetorical theorist seeks to reconstruct the ethical principles upon which the narrative is built. To be sure, the rhetorical theorist does bring values to the text, but he or she remains open to having those values challenged and even repudiated by the experience of reading." (2005 325)

13 In his seminal study The Craft of Fiction, Percy Lubbock dismisses first-person narratives for their psychological limitations: "But when the man in the book is expected to make a picture of himself, a searching and elaborate portrait, then the limit of his capacity is touched and passed; or rather there is a better method, one of finer capacity, than ready to the author's hand, and there is no reason to be content with the hero's mere report." (Lubbock 140)

14 This double-voicing resembles the Bakhtinian concept of heteroglossia, as Phelan points out in his essay "Why Narrators Can Be Focalizers – and Why It Matters" (2001) 60.

15 As exemplified by Kiernan Ryan's assessment of McEwan's early stories: "McEwan is playing games – sometimes sardonic, sometimes dangerous games – with his and our addiction to sensationalized sex and violence, with our craven demand to be excited by garish transgressions. Sex and violence: the ubiquitous tabloid twins have become fetishized objects of consumer desire, and too many of us have acquired a taste for the illicit fix they deliver, whatever we may publicly and piously avow to the contrary. The pornographic is no longer skulking elsewhere, but happily tapdancing inside our heads. It has long since turned whole populations into voyeurs of staged and screened atrocities, greedy parasites on others' furtive pleasures, fatally deluding themselves that they are not answerable for the images on which they feed. Many of McEwan's stories are out to expose this insidious scenario by rattling the chains of complicity which bind writer and reader. They meet our demand for something shocking and salacious, but in a fashion which invites us to acknowledge our affinity with their estranged narrators and unhinged protagonists." (Ryan 14)

16 As McEwan states about the story: "I couldn't possibly write that story now, it would frighten me too much. As children come more into your life the possibility of their death is not something you can play with lightly." (John Haffenden, Novelists in Interview (London, 1985) 173)

17 Camus's novel opens with the words: "It was a blazing hot afternoon" (4).

18 This duplicity is discussed by Breuer and Foster, who both emphasise that the confessional intention is undermined by the fallibility of the means of representation available to the confessor.

19 Once it has been established who is the perpetrator here, the events take on a distinct inevitability, although the narrator evaluates his deed: "It had become a necessity to persuade her to walk along the canal with me. I sickened at the idea." (82)

20 On resistance and Atonement, see Müller-Wood.

Bibliography

Attridge, Derek: "Innovation, Literature, Ethics: Relating to the Other", *PMLA* 114:1, 1999, 20-31.
Booth, Wayne C.: "Why Ethical Criticism Can Never Be Simple". – In Todd F. Davis and Kenneth Womack (Eds.): *Mapping the Ethical Turn. A Reader in Ethics, Culture, and Literary Theory*, Charlottesville and London, 2001, pp. 16-29.
Breuer, Ulrich: *Bekenntnisse. Diskurs – Gattung – Werk,* Frankfurt *et al.*, 2000.
Camus, Albert. *The Stranger*. Trans. Stuart Gilbert, London, 1946 [French original: 1942].
Davis, Todd F. & Kenneth Womack (Eds.), *Mapping the Ethical Turn. A Reader in Ethics, Culture, and Literary Theory*, Charlottesville and London, 2001.
Evans, Walter: "The English Short Story in the Seventies". – In Dennis Vannatta (Ed.), *The English Short Story. A Critical History*, Boston, 1985, pp. 120-72.
Foster, Dennis A.: *Confession and Complicity in Narrative*, Cambridge, 1987.
Jarfe, Günther: "Experimental Aspects of Ian McEwan's Short Fiction". – In Anja Müller-Wood (Ed.): *Texting Culture/Culturing Texts. Essays in Honour of Horst Breuer*, Trier, 2008, pp. 15-24.
Haffenden, John: *Novelists in Interview*, London, 1985.
Hanson, Clare: *Short Stories and Short Fictions, 1880-1980*, London, 1985.
Head, Dominic: *Ian McEwan*, Contemporary British Novelists, Manchester, 2007.
Lubbock, Percy: *The Craft of Fiction*, London, 1921.
McEwan, Ian. "Butterflies". – In Ian McEwan: *First Love, Last Rites*, London, 1997 [First edition: 1975].
Müller-Wood, Anja. "Enabling Resistance: Teaching *Atonement* in Germany". In Steven Barfield, Anja Müller-Wood, Philip Tew & Leigh Wilson (Eds.): *Teaching Contemporary British Fiction*, Anglistik & Englischunterricht, Heidelberg, 2007, pp. 143-58.
Nünning, Ansgar: "Kurzgeschichten von Ian McEwan in einem Englisch-Leistungskurs: Darstellung grotesker Welten aus der Perspektive des 'verrückten Monologisten' ", *Literatur in Wissenschaft und Unterricht* 23, 1990, pp. 36-50.
Phelan, James: "Narrative Judgments and the Rhetorical Theory of Narrative: Ian McEwan's Atonement". – In J. P. & Peter J. Rabinowitz (Eds.): *A Companion to Narrative Theory*, Oxford, 2005, pp. 222-36.
---: "Dual Focalization, Retrospective Fictional Autobiography, and the Ethics of Lolita". – In Gary D. Fireman, Ted E. McVay, Jr. & Owen J. Flanagan (Eds.): *Narrative and Consciousness: Literature, Psychology, and the Brain*, Oxford, 2003, pp. 129-45.

---: "Why Narrators Can Be Focalizers – and Why It Matters". – In Willie van Peer & Seymour Chatman (Eds.): *New Perspectives on Narrative Perspective*, New York, 2001, pp. 51-64.

Ryan, Kiernan: *Ian McEwan*, Writers and Their Work, Plymouth, 1994.

Serpell, C. Namwali: "Mutual Exclusion, Oscillation, and Ethical Projection in *The Crying of Lot 49* and *The Turn of the Screw*", *Narrative* 16:3, 2008, 223-55.

Stanzel, Franz: *Theorie des Erzählens*. 6th ed. Göttingen, 1995.

Roland Weidle (Bochum)

The Ethics of Metanarration: Empathy in Ian McEwan's *The Comfort of Strangers*, *The Child in Time*, *Atonement* and *Saturday*

"[T]o know the boundaries, is the essence of sanity" (*S* 4), says the narrator at the beginning of Ian McEwan's *Saturday*, referring to the fact that Henry Perowne, the protagonist of the novel, has not quite transgressed the line between sleeping and waking. The interference, the conflation and mixing of separate ontological layers, is not only a prominent issue in *Saturday* but also a recurring theme in McEwan's oeuvre. Moreover, it is also a topic that has undergone considerable change in his work since the publication of his first novel, *The Cement Garden* in 1978. In his treatment and presentation of alternative, imaginary worlds, be it in dreams, daydreams, memories, embedded stories etc., McEwan attaches particular importance to the act and concept of narration. This paper will focus on some of these "metanarrative" structures and strategies and comment on their functions in selected novels and key-passages. I will argue that by employing metanarrative strategies, the implied author expresses a certain moral view that is in line with some of McEwan's own moral tenets, yet also proves to be problematic.

1. Metafiction vs. Metanarration

In the past, McEwan has been repeatedly categorized as a typically postmodern writer who plays with the boundaries of fact and fiction and draws our attention to the "fictionality, […] the constructed nature, of his writing" and to the "narrative creation of the world"[1] by introducing protagonists who are narrators and/or authors. Such a view would automatically lead to defining McEwan as an author of metafiction, a term coined by Patricia Waugh in 1984 to describe

> fictional writing which self-consciously and systematically draws attention to its status as an artefact in order to pose questions about the relationship between fiction and reality. In providing a critique of their own methods of construction, such writings not only examine the fundamental structures of narrative fiction, they also explore the possible fictionality of the world outside the literary fictional text.[2]

The defining features of metafiction are self-reflexivity and the highlighting of the constructed and textual character of the world, both of which undermine the boundaries between reality and fiction. If the world is conceived in textual terms, if it can be written, re-written, narrated and read like a literary text, then the differences between literature and reality disappear. Metafiction "enacts a disturbingly sceptical triumph over our sense of reality"[3]. One of the most popular examples of British metafiction is Martin Amis' *London Fields* (1989) which by means of its many metalepses, its highly selfreflexive stance and opaque narrative and focalizing structures, achieves this unsettling and destabilizing effect on the reader and radically questions the concept of reality and its representation in literature.

With the exception of the early collections of short stories *First Love, Last Rites* (1975) and *In Between the Sheets* (1978) all of McEwan's novels contain, to varying degrees, self-reflexive elements. The homodiegetic narrator in his first novel, *The Cement Garden* (1978), comments on his own narrative function: "I am only including the little story of his death to explain how my sisters and I came to have such a large quantity of cement at our disposal" (*CG* 13); in his second novel, *The Comfort of Strangers* (1981), every night the couple Colin and Mary tell each other stories and the act of story-telling performs a central function in the plot. The novels of the middle period, the late 1980s and early 1990s, also abound with allusions to writing, narrating and authoring. Stephen in *The Child in Time* (1987) is an author of children's books and in his daydreams reinvents and rewrites reality; in *The Innocent* (1990) protagonists and readers become sharers in secrets and are referred to as "author-figures" (*I* 17) of possible worlds; Jeremy in *Black Dogs* (1992) writes and narrates the story of June, his mother-in-law. Protagonists in the later works are often authors (*Enduring Love*, 1997; *Atonement*, 2001) or (incompetent) readers (*Saturday*, 2005; *On Chesil Beach*, 2007). The question remains, however, to what extent McEwan's novels are really metafictional in the sense that they blur the boundaries between reality and fiction.

In this respect Ansgar Nünning's differentiation between metafiction and metanarration proves helpful. Metafiction, according to Nünning,

> refers to comments on the fictionality of the narrated text of the narrator [...and metanarration] concerns the narrator's reflections on the discourse or the process of narration [...] Metanarration refers more to those forms of self-reflexive narration in which aspects of narration (and not the fictionality of the narrated) become the subject of the narratorial discourse.[4]

Where metafiction radically undermines our notions of stable realities, metanarration confines itself to thematizing and reflecting upon narrative processes and structures. And where metafiction always works against illusion, metanarration works both against, and contributes to the building of illusion.[5] Both genres, metafiction and metanarration, however, are characterized by a high degree of self-reflexivity.

2. The Nature of Empathy: McEwan's Ethics

In an essay entitled "Literature, Science, and Human Nature," McEwan expresses his belief in a "universal human nature"[6], a "human essence"[7] that connects all humans and finds its true expression in "human literature"[8]. Although he remains conspicuously vague about what that essence actually is,[9] he becomes more specific at one point:

> We have, in terms of cognitive psychology, a theory of mind, a more-or-less automatic understanding of what it means to be someone else. Without this understanding [...] we would find it virtually impossible to form and sustain relationships, read expressions or intentions, or perceive how we ourselves are understood. (ib. 5)

According to McEwan it is our capacity and ability to put ourselves in the minds of others that constitutes the basis of human interaction and sociability. One of McEwan's most well-known statements illustrates this point even more poignantly. Five days after the terrorist attacks on the World Trade Center he writes in *The Guardian*:

> This is the nature of empathy, to think oneself into the minds of others. […] If the hijackers had been able to imagine themselves into the thoughts and feelings of the passengers, they would have been unable to proceed. It is hard to be cruel once you permit yourself to enter the mind of your victim. Imagining what it is like to be someone other than yourself is at the core of our humanity. It is the essence of compassion, and it is the beginning of morality.[10]

"Empathy" and "imagination" are, for McEwan, "prerequisite[s] of human solidarity"[11], the necessary conditions, but also the means, of an interpersonal moral consciousness. One is reminded here of 18th-century discourses on sympathy, and in particular of Adam Smith's view that sympathy and sympathetic interaction form the basis of moral judgment:

> By the imagination we place ourselves in his [the sufferer's] situation, we conceive ourselves enduring all the same torments, we enter as it were into his body, and become in some measure the same person with him, and thence form some idea of his sensations, and even feel something which, though weaker in degree, is not altogether unlike them. […] And hence it is, that to feel much for others and little for ourselves, that to restrain our selfish, and to indulge our benevolent affections, constitutes the perfection of human nature; and can alone produce among mankind that harmony of sentiments and passions in which consists their whole grace and propriety.[12]

McEwan's view on ethical behaviour is closely linked to our narrative capacity of imagining the feelings and thoughts of our fellow human beings. In the following it will be argued that McEwan in some of his novels subjects this narrative power of imagination to close scrutiny; that the reader is presented with cases of self-indulgent, a-social empathy and imagination, and that this in turn makes McEwan not a postmodern but a 'pre-postmodern' writer.

3. The Comfort of Strangers

McEwan first two novels, *The Cement Garden* (1978) and *The Comfort of Strangers* (1981), are usually regarded to belong to the oeuvre of "Ian Macabre"[13] due to the violent and cruel contents of his first writings, especially his early collections of short stories, *First Love, Last Rites* (1975) and *In Between the Sheets* (1978). It can be argued, however, that even the violent and the macabre aspects at this early stage in his writing career serve a moral purpose. *The Comfort of Strangers* will serve as a case in point.

The unmarried couple Colin and Mary spend their vacation in a city, whose identity is not disclosed, but which closely resembles Venice. Although they spend their evenings going to restaurants and bars, their relationship and their sexual life are trapped in routine. One evening they meet the uncanny stranger Robert, who exerts a compelling influence over them with his dark childhood-stories. After a second meeting Robert invites the couple to his home to meet his wife Caroline, whom he apparently physically abuses. During their visit Colin and Mary experience the violent and menacing side of their host. The visit, however, seems to have a somewhat cathartic effect because after returning to their hotel they spend the following days in a state "of gratifying physical and spiritual intimacy, somehow caused by their meeting with Robert and Caroline"[14]. After a renewed visit to Robert and Caroline's house, the hosts impart to their guests that they are planning to move to Canada. While Robert takes Colin out for a walk, Caroline tells Mary about her sado-masochistic relationship with her husband. Caroline then drugs Mary who after the men return is made to watch Robert kill her husband by cutting his arteries. When Mary wakes up the hosts have disappeared and the novel ends with Mary identifying her dead husband at the local police station.

This brief synopsis already points to the prominent role that narrativity plays in the novel. Narrative acts are not only to be found on the extradiegetic but also on the diegetic level in the shape of various intradiegetic narrators. The couple's favourite pastime, for example, is the telling and re-telling of dreams to each other: "Each evening, in the ritual hour they spent on their balcony before setting out to find a restaurant, they had been listening patiently to the other's dreams in exchange for the luxury of recounting their own" (*CS* 1). But not only acts of narration are the subject of the book. Other narrative facets and aspects, such as narrative conventions, narrative competence and the unreliablity of narrations[15] are also repeatedly addressed and reflected upon as can be seen, for example, in the following passage where Colin tries to recount to Mary a scene he just witnessed from the balcony:

> Colin immediately set about recounting the little drama in the street below. [...] Colin could not reproduce the vague misunderstandings that constituted, according to him, the main interest of the story. Instead, he heard himself exaggerate its small pathos into vaudeville, perhaps in an attempt to gain Mary's full attention. He described the elderly gentleman as "incredibly old and feeble", his wife as "batty beyond belief", the men at the table were "bovine morons", and he made the husband give out "an incredible roar of fury". In fact the word "incredible" suggested itself to him at every turn, perhaps because he feared that Mary did not believe him, or because he did not believe himself. (*CS* 6-7)

Likewise, the sinister Robert is introduced as someone who "was preparing the way to telling his story" (*CS* 18). During his first encounter with the couple he tells them his childhood-story which in fact consists of four episodes, or rather mini stories. These serve as evidence for his menacing character, but they also openly reveal themselves as unreliable narrations.[16] Given this unreliability it is even more suprising what effect these stories have on Colin and Mary after they leave the restaurant: They get lost and have to spend the night on the streets. On the following day, Robert testifies to the disturbing and irritating force of his own stories the previous night: "'This is my fault,' Robert cried. 'I kept you late with wine, and my stupid stories.'" (*CS* 39). During the ensuing visit at Robert's house the two couples tell each other stories from the past and Robert shows Colin around, pointing out "various aspects of his father's and grandfather's possessions" (*CS* 53). The intense narrative exchange and the menacing atmosphere during the visit have a cathartic effect on Colin and Mary that not only leads to a revitalisation of their sexual relationship but also to a heightened narrative awareness that constitutes in some sense a rebirth, a "renewal" (*CS* 62) of themselves and their lives. To put it differently: Robert's narrations prove to be contagious and trigger in Colin and Mary narrative and metanarrative energies.

> They sat on the balcony late into the night [...] and talked again of childhood, sometimes remembering events for the first time, formulating theories about the past and about memory itself. [...] all speculation, all anxieties and memories were marshalled into the service of theories about their own and each other's character as if, finding themselves reborn through an unexpected passion, they had to invent themselves anew, name themselves as a newborn child, or a new character, a sudden intruder in a novel, is named. (*CS* 60-61)

Clearly recognizable is the characters' narrative perception (both of themselves and of the other) and how – sheltered by the exclusively private interaction of their room – they reinvent, rewrite and change their own biographies. After the encounter with Robert (another "intruder in a novel") the couple experiences a narrative freedom that seems to enable them to transgress the boundary that separates reality from fiction. This liberating effect of storytelling and self-invention, however, also has its downside, because the stories Mary and Colin tell each other evoke the image of the sinister story-teller Robert:

> They took to muttering in each other's ear as they made love, stories that came from nowhere, out of the dark, stories [...] that won from the spellbound listener consent to a lifetime of subjection and humiliation. Mary muttered her intention of hiring a surgeon to amputate Colin's arms and legs. She would keep him in a room in her house, use him exclusively for sex, sometimes lending him out to friends. (*CS* 62-63)

Colin on the other hand phantasises about a machine that would disembowel Mary like an animal and how he would afterwards sexually abuse her.[17] These hypodiegetic narrations thus mirror the events on the diegetic level. Robert, too, is a violent sadist and psychopath, who abuses his wife and eventually kills Colin in the presence of Mary. The critic Charles Forceville argues that the couple is to some extent jointly responsible for the tragic ending. In fact, there were enough signals to warn them of Robert and Caroline's sinister intentions.[18] There is "a disturbing conspiracy between 'agents' operating at two fundamentally different narrative levels, namely the external narrator, an agency that is by definition extradiegetic, and the diegetic characters".[19] Also, the frequent use of free indirect speech makes it difficult for the reader to decide whether he is sharing the extradiegetic narrator's or Mary's and Colin's thoughts.[20] Mary and Colin not only turn out to be incompetent 'readers' of the world as text, they are also unreliable, and irresponsible narrators who play with the boundaries between reality and fiction. The couple's narrative excesses that predominantly take place in the isolated setting of their hotel room (and bed), and which are centred on the fictionalization of their lives, are the products of misguided imagination. Instead of increasing empathy and thereby furthering human solidarity, Colin and Mary's narratives lack a social function and reach their 'climax' in sado-masochistic sex phantasies. The ending of the novel establishes some sort of "poetic justice": attracted by Robert and Caroline's stories, unable to see through their narrative strategies and unreliablity as narrators, and 'infected' by their hosts' misguided imagination, both steer toward the final catastrophe.

4. Child in Time

The novel *Child in Time*, published in 1987, is regarded by some as the turning point in McEwan's writing career, a change from the previous "literature of shock [...] into a more socially conscious literature"[21]. Others go even further and diagnose an "ethical turn in McEwan's writing career"[22]. Notwithstanding the fact stated above, that even the early 'shockers' prove to some extent to propagate a moral view, ethical issues in fact seem to play a more important role in the novels written after *The Comfort of Strangers*. *The Child in Time* is about the author of children's books Stephen Lewis who tries to come to terms with the disappearance of his 3-year old daughter, the subsequent break up of his marriage and the ensuing identity crisis. He constantly succumbs to daydreams in which he tries to rewrite the past or create possible and alternative scenarios of the future. It soon becomes clear, that these daydreams develop into an obsession that slowly gain control over their 'author' Stephen:

> Much later he was to realise that he never really thought about his situation at all, for thought implied something active and controlled; instead images and arguments paraded in front of him, a mocking, malicious, paranoid, conradictory, self-pitying crowd. [...] He was the victim, not the progenitor, of his thoughts. They washed over him [...]. (*CT* 148)

Stephen's imagined stories are what the narrator calls "compulsive" (*CT* 5), "without control, almost without consciousness" (*CT* 7). He "could not help drifting off, could not prevent himself reflecting" (*CT* 22).[23] *The Child in Time* shows in an even more striking manner than *The Comfort of Strangers* the destructive effects of an uncontrolled narrative imagination that tries to dissolve the boundaries between different ontological levels. The more Stephen gives in to his fantasies, the more his life and his identity disintegrate. He is "unhealthily stuffed up with his recent past, like a man with a cold. If he could only live in the present he might breathe freely" (*CT* 110-111).

It is, ironically, a particularly grave 'narrative' mistake – he substitutes another girl for his daughter – that triggers Stephen's liberation from his compulsive narrativising and thus clears the way for his recovery. After the intense and upsetting experience of 'writing' someone else as his daughter, Stephen feels "purged" (*CT* 121) and he finally realizes that he has to stop confounding dreams with reality. He finally learns to separate fact from fiction and to accept the loss of his daughter.[24] *The Child in Time* underlines, even more so than *The Comfort of Strangers*, the implicit author's criticism of an imagination turned inward, which, instead of furthering "human solidarity,"[25] proves to be, in the words of the narrator, "unhealthy" (*CT* 110).

5. *Atonement*

Atonement, published in 2001, describes the attempts of the protagonist and author Briony Tallis to atone for her lying in the past. The book is about her attempts to atone in a literary fashion for her rewriting of past events (i.e. falsely accusing her sister's fiancé, thereby sending him to prison for three and half years and the subsequent invented reconciliation between her, Robbie and her sister). It is, however, an attempt that does not succeed.

Atonement is McEwan's most metanarrative novel. It treats the act of narration in various ways. On a paratextual level it quotes from Northanger Abbey at the beginning of the book, on the diegetic level it is above all the teenage Briony who is obsessed with literature, and on the extradiegetic level the sudden shift from a heterodiegetic to an autodiegetic narration draws attention to the act of narration. In addition, the repeated and long reflections on the narrative act and process generate in the reader a heightened narrative consciousness:

> I've been thinking about my last novel, the one that should have been my first. The earliest version, January 1940, the latest, March 1999, and in between, half a dozen different drafts. The second draft, June 1947, the third ... who cares to know? My fifty-nine-year assignment is over. (*A* 369)[26]

This, however, does not make *Atonement* a metafictional work. The reader is not confronted with confusing metalepses that in a typical postmodern fashion play with and confuse the various narrative levels (as for example in the works of Amis, Auster and Pynchon), nor is the reader made to believe that there is basically no difference between textual artefacts and the world as text. On the contrary, the novel insists on a precise definition of the line that separates social reality from fiction. Even Briony realizes in the end that her fictional atonement was "an impossible task" (*A* 371). The final message of the novel is then, that the world is not a text that can be written or re-written. *Atonement* shows how by trying to fictionalize life on the one hand, and by treating fiction as reality on the other, our foundations for moral behaviour are questioned and undermined.

6. Saturday

Saturday's Henry Perowne, unlike the protagonists in McEwan's previous novels, does *not* suffer from a compulsive narrative urge. On the contrary, he is presented as a literary ignoramus. Names like

Fenton, Hughes and Motion "mean nothing to Perowne" (*S* 130) and it is inconceivable to him that one could devote one's life to literature as his daughter Daisy has.[27] Perowne's decisively antiliterary stance is further accentuated in his and the narrator's reflections[28] on the purpose of literature and the relationship between reality and fiction. Perowne only reads occasionally and when he finds the time he appreciates literature that strives to capture 'reality':

> Henry has read the whole of *Anna Karenina* and *Madame Bovary*, two acknowledged masterpieces. At the cost of slowing his mental processes and many hours of his valuable time, he committed himself to the shifting intricacies of these sophisticated fairy stories. […] The details were apt and convincing enough, but surely not so very difficult to marshal if you were halfway observant and had the patience to write them all down. These books were the products of steady, workmanlike accumulation. (*S* 67)

While realistic novels barely meet Perowne's standards and demands for "a recognisable physical reality", the "so-called magical realists" and their "irksome confections" that are actually meant "for children" (ib.) are met with outright derision. For Perowne "fiction [… is] too humanly flawed" (*S* 68) and Daisy's claim that one cannot live without stories is "simply not true" (ib.).

Does McEwan then present us after all with an 'ideal' protagonist who does not conflate the realms of life and fiction? Perowne seems to be a figure firmly rooted in reality, a neurosurgeon and not a dreamer/writer like Colin, Stephen or Briony, who, misguided by a too vivid narrative imagination, attempt to narrativize their lives. In the end, however, Perowne has to realize that the division of life and art is not as clear as he thought it to be. When Daisy recites Matthew Arnold's "Dover Beach" to the thugs, Baxter and Nigel, the poem has such a strong effect on the intruders that they do not carry out their original intention to rape her. "'You wrote that. You *wrote* that'. […] 'It's beautiful.'" (*S* 222), Baxter keeps saying.[29] Not only does the poem 'convert' Baxter and lead to the final happy ending, it also generates understanding, compassion and empathy in Perowne for Baxter and his plight: "[…] it's through Baxter's ears that he hears the sea's 'melancholy, long withdrawing roar, retreating, to the breath of the night wind, down the fast edges drear and naked shingles of the world.'" (*S* 221f).[30] In an interesting twist McEwan allows Perowne to do something that Briony in *Atonement* is criticized for: conflating the literary and the 'real' world. The intention and message, however, remains the same. Narrativising your surroundings and allowing literary patterns to influence your life is only permissible if it serves a social and moral purpose, if it generates empathy which McEwan understands as "the building block of our moral system".[31] Briony in *Atonement* attempts to rewrite her past in order to elude moral responsibility but in the end she has to acknowledge that this narrativisation has failed. Perowne on the other hand does not believe in the interdependence of reality and fiction, but realizes in the end that narratives can have a decisive and wholesome influence on life, as long as they are grounded in socially responsible empathy.

It follows then that the supposedly clear divide between the 'Ian Macabre' of the early novels and the moral writer of the later works is not as evident as many assume it to be. McEwan has always been a writer with a moral agenda, and his belief in empathy and imagination as the building blocks of our moral system attest to this. What makes McEwan's case so interesting is that this moral agenda comes in postmodern disguise. His metanarratives abound in self-reflexive elements but they lack the radical and destabilizing impetus of metafiction. McEwan is therefore not a postmodern writer who wishes to comment on the textual character of the world. On the contrary, in his novels the different ontological layers always remain clearly identifiable[32] and the boundaries between them stay intact. McEwan's model of empathy, the 'narrative imagination' discussed in this paper, is loaded with social and moral responsibility and has a clear moral purpose.

The nature and validity of such a moral perspective on empathy, however, remains problematic. McEwan's belief in "universal expressions of emotion", a "universal human nature"[33] and a fixed "human essence"[34] contradicts his concept of empathy which equates more or less – as shown above – with Adam Smith's notion of sympathy. Smith's concept is at heart interactional and pre-supposes a self which is not fixed and always re-negotiating its own boundaries by way of reflection and using the other as a mirror in the "process of self-formation"[35]. Imagination in this sense has a destabilising effect on the self. As David Marshall has pointed out:

> For Smith, the imagination seems to have all of these powers: it can convert us into another person and transport us back and forth, offering both identity and difference. Sympathy seems to blur the boundaries of the self while somehow maintaining the integrity of the self.[36]

Novels like *The Comfort of Strangers, Child in Time*, *Atonement* and *Saturday* may show how 'responsible empathy' might work in fiction and to what effects. McEwan's differentiation, however, between 'good' and 'bad' variants of narrative imagination oversimplifies the issue. Moreover, his view of a self that is fixed and universal while at the same time engaging in empathy is contradictory and at odds with current discourses on subjectivity and the self.

Notes

1 Schemberg, *Achieving 'at-one-ment'* 32.
2 Waugh, *Metafiction* 2.
3 Butler, *Postmodernism* 70.
4 Nünning, "On Metanarrative", 16. Cf. Also Dose, "Grenzen des *Storytelling*".
5 Cf. Nünning, "On Metanarrative" 17.
6 McEwan, "Literature" 10.
7 McEwan, "Literature" 10.
8 McEwan, "Literature" 12.
9 At one point McEwan describes the "instinct for language [as] a central part of our nature" (McEwan, "Literature" 17).
10 McEwan, "Only Love and then Oblivion". McEwan has repeatedly made statements to this effect. Cf. Schemberg, *Achieving 'at-one-ment'* 87.
11 Schemberg, *Achieving 'at-one-ment'* 88.
12 Smith, *Theory of Moral Sentiments* 9, 25 (I.i.1.2, I.i.5.5).
13 Cf. Dose, "Grenzen des *Storytelling*" 244.
14 Forceville, "Conspiracy" 120. Cf. *CS* 59 et sqq.
15 For an exhaustive discussion of metanarrative features and categories cf. Nünning, "On Metanarrative".
16 Cf. For example the repeated use of "perhaps" in Robert's hypodiegetic narratives (*CS* 20, 21, 23).
17 Cf. *CS* 63.

18 Forceville, "Conspiracy" 121. Cf. For example the episodes on their first visit to Robert and Caroline's, where Robert punches Colin and where the hosts hide their guest's clothes.
19 Kiernan Ryan (*Ian McEwan* 34) also argues that Colin and Mary are "strangely compliant" and involved in a "passive collusion".
20 Forcevill, "Conspiracy" 125.
21 Slay, *Ian McEwan* x.
22 Schemberg, *Achieving 'at-one-ment'* 28.
23 "Stephen sinks into the mire of introspection" (Ryan, *Ian McEwan* 49).
24 For Slay (*McEwan*, 120) this episode (mistaking another girl for his daughter) and the sixth birthday 'party' Stephen gives for his absent daughter mark the beginning of the protagonist's recovery and his acceptance that his daughter is irrevocably lost.
25 Schemberg, *Achieving 'at-one-ment'* 88.
26 For further aspects of narration *Atonement* reflects upon cf. Dose ("Grenzen des *Storytelling*") and Finney ("Briony's Stand Against Oblivion").
27 Perowne has also never heard of the Newdigate Prize, let alone the fact that Fenton and Wilde – like his daughter Daisy – were awarded with it (cf. *S* 135).
28 Very often it is not very clear whether events and thoughts are focalized internally or externally, whether we are witnessing the narrator's or Perowne's thoughts and opinions.
29 Cf. Also: "'How could you have thought of that? I mean, you just wrote it.' And then he says it again, several times over. 'You wrote it!'" (*S* 223).
30 Also Perowne's father in law, Grammaticus, on hearing the poem recited by Daisy and witnessing Baxter's reactions, develops compassion and sympathy for the almost-rapist of his granddaughter: "You know, it sounds completely mad, but there came a point after Daisy recited Arnold for the second time when I actually began to feel sorry for that fellow. I think, my dear, you made him fall in love with you." (*S* 229).
31 Dawkins, "Interview". Cf. Also McEwan's comment in the same interview that we "need that instinctual imagination that carries us into the minds of others".
32 McEwan stresses his preference for "some kind of balance between a fiction that is self-reflective on its own processes, and one that has a forward impetus too, that will completely accept the given terms of the illusion of fiction" (Reynolds/Noakes, *Ian McEwan* 20).
33 McEwan, "Literature" 10.
34 McEwan, "Literature" 19.
35 Seigel, *The Idea of the Self* 144.
36 Marshall, *The Figure of Theatre* 179.

Bibliography

Butler, Christopher: *Postmodernism: A Very Short Introduction*, New York: Oxford University Press, 2002.
Dawkins, Richard: "Interview with Ian McEwan", *YouTube*, 21 July 2009 <http://www.youtube.com/watch?v=o7LjriWFAEs>.
Dose, Gerd: "Die Grenzen des *Storytelling*: Ian McEwan's *Atonement* (2001)", *Cool Britannia: Literarische Selbstvergewisserungen vor der Jahrtausendwende*. Eds. Norbert Greiner and Roland Weidle. Trier: Wissenschaftlicher Verlag, 2006. 243-58.
Finney, Brian: "Briony's Stand Against Oblivion: The Making of Fiction in Ian McEwan's *Atonement*", *Journal of Modern Literature* 27.3 (2004): 68-82.
Forceville, Charles: "The Conspiracy in *The Comfort of Strangers:* Narration in the Novel and the Film", *Language and Literature: Journal of the Poetics and Linguistics Association* 11.2 (2002): 119-35.
Marshall, David: *The Figure of Theatre: Shaftesbury, Defoe, Adam Smith, and George Eliot*, New York: Columbia Press, 1986.
McEwan, Ian: *Atonement*. [*A*]. 2001. London: Vintage, 2002.
---. *Black Dogs*. 1992. London: Vintage, 1998.
---. *The Cement Garden*. [*CG*]. 1978. New York: Vintage, 1994.
---. *The Child in Time*. [*CT*]. 1987. London: Random House, 1997.
---. *The Comfort of Strangers*. [*CS*]. 1981. New York: Random House, 1997.
---. *Enduring Love*. 1997. London: Vintage, 2004.
---. *First Love, Last Rites*. 1975. New York: Anchor, 1994.
---. *In Between the Sheets*. 1978. London: Vintage, 1997.
---. *The Innocent*. [*I*]. 1989. London: Vintage, 2005.
---. "Literature, Science, and Human Nature." *The Literary Animal: Evolution and the Nature of Narrative*. Eds. Jonathan Gottschall and David Sloan Wilson. Evanston, Ill.: Northwestern University Press, 2005. 5-19.
---. *On Chesil Beach*. 2007. London: Cape, 2007.
---. "Only Love and then Oblivion: Love Was All They Had to Set Against Their Murderers", *The Guardian Online* 16. September 2001. 28. Januar 2006.
<http://books.guardian.co.uk/departments/politicsphilosophyandsociety/story/0,,555258,00.html>.
---. *Saturday*. [*S*]. London: Vintage, 2005.
Nünning, Ansgar: "On Metanarrative: Towards a Definition, a Typology and an Outline of the Functions of Metanarrative Commentary", *The Dynamics of Narrative Form*. Ed. John Pier. Berlin: de Gruyter, 2004.
Reynolds, Margaret, and Jonathan Noakes: *Ian McEwan: The Essential Guide to Contemporary Literature*, London: Vintage, 2002.
Ryan, Kiernan: *Ian McEwan*, Plymouth: Northcote House, 1994.

Schemberg, Claudia: *Achieving 'at-one-ment': Storytellying and the Concept of the Self in Ian McEwan's* The Child in Time, Black Dogs, Enduring Love, *and* Atonement, Frankfurt/M.: Lang, 2004.

Seigel, Jerrold E: *The Idea of the Self: Thought and Experience in Western Europe Since the Seventeenth Century*, New York: Cambridge University Press, 2005.

Slay, Jack: *Ian McEwan*, New York: Twayne, 1996.

Smith, Adam: *The Theory of Moral Sentiments*. 1759. Eds. D. D. Raphael and A. L. Macfie. Indianapolis: Liberty Fund, 1982.

Waugh, Patricia: *Metafiction: The Theory and Practice of Self-Conscious Fiction*, London: Routledge, 1984.

Katherina Dodou (Uppsala)

Dismembering a Romance of Englishness.
Images of Childhood in Ian McEwan's *The Innocent*

1. Introduction

This article proceeds from a query regarding the persistent appearance of childhood imagery in Ian McEwan's *The Innocent* (1990). Unlike so many of McEwan's other works, *The Innocent* has very little to do with the lives and experiences of children; it does not contain child characters on the level of plot, nor does it thematise the configuration of childhood or of "the child" in the ways of, for instance, *The Child in Time* (1987). And yet, images of childhood innocence and play recur with such frequency and in such instances that they give pause: when the protagonist walks the devastated streets of post-war Berlin, when he inspects the centre of a major Anglo-American Cold War operation, when he sexually attacks his fiancée-to-be. What does the inclusion of this imagery do for the novel?

In addressing this question, I seek to exemplify a recurring practice for McEwan of employing the meanings attached to childhood – among them, moral innocence and virtuousness, naivety and weakness – in order to explore post-war British society. The appearance of childhood figurations in the absence of child characters is a prevalent feature also in such novels as *The Comfort of Strangers* (1981), *Saturday* (2005) and *On Chesil Beach* (2007), in which features of "childlikeness" and "childishness" are similarly attached to adults. A study of the ways in which McEwan employs childhood in *The Innocent* constitutes a starting point from which to consider this practice. At the same time, the examination serves to throw light on a hitherto unacknowledged political dimension of the novel.

I want to propose that far from only functioning as an embodiment of the innocence that the title indicates, or as a sign of the protagonist's psychological regression, of his inability to cope with his circumstances (Head 2007), the appearance of childhood images and figurations is rooted in McEwan's interrogation of a mythologised narrative of Englishness. Even though McEwan criticism has recognised that *The Innocent* addresses the "condition of Britain" in the aftermath of the Second World War (Ryan 1994, Brown 1994), McEwan's critique in this novel of a distinctly "English innocence" has yet to be fully appreciated. Indeed, *The Innocent* comprises an important example of how the perception of Englishness and the waning of the British Empire have been treated in the contemporary British novel. Published at a time when a politically-engineered vision of national greatness was being revived in Britain (Webster 2005), *The Innocent* brings images of childhood into play to call into question a story of national identity and history that amounts to a romance; a story in which decency, civilization and heroism are the main constituents.

2. The Critique of Englishness

Not surprisingly, the recurring images and figurations of childhood in this novel coalesce around innocence, the idea upon which the novel hinges. On the simplest level, McEwan explores innocence as the thorn in the protagonist's sense of identity: as the "childlikeness" which he needs to shed in order to attain "civilised" maturity. After all, it is a sense of being "an initiate, a truly mature adult at last" that concerns the protagonist Leonard foremost (56). Against a condition of "childlikeness" which belongs to the past and which he understands as weakness, incompetence and non-agency – and against such monuments of his "former self" as the "childish chocolate" bars lying on his kitchen table – the protagonist can think of himself as more adult, more mature. (75)

Innocence in the novel emerges also as a particularly English quality, rooted in its social decorum and professional ethos. McEwan offers a satirical take on "English innocence" that taps into the convention of representing English reticence or ineptitude as childlike. Invoking an image of the British officers as the silly gentlemen with their milk teeth and virginities intact, playing at espionage as they would with their toy trains, McEwan employs the "trope of 'the innocent abroad'" – the amateur that so often populates the British spy novel (Denning 1987: 67) – to depict a vision of English amateurism in a world of professionals. The mockery is sustained by such examples as the American CIA agent Glass's dismissal of the work that the SIS officer MacNamee does for the Berlin tunnel. Emphasizing American ascent to political dominance, and drawing attention to the antagonisms characterising the Anglo-American cooperation, Glass effectively relegates the Englishman to the inconsequential world of the nursery:

> This joker MacNamee. He should be at home with his train set. You know where he did his calculations for the heat output? On the back of an envelope. An envelope! We would have had three independent teams. If they hadn't come up with the same result, we would have wanted to know why. How can the guy think straight with teeth like that? (111)

Proclaiming the Englishman's incompetence and, by extension, declaring the British government unfit to be a leading global power, Glass's infantilising impulse hits the mark with the mentioning of MacNamee's teeth. The reference here is to an earlier episode where the Englishman explains that he still uses his milk teeth: "The other lot never came through. I think perhaps I never wanted to grow up." (66) The allusion to J. M. Barrie's Peter Pan, that emblem of perpetual childhood, supports the perception of the British as overgrown children to the American "adults." In view of the personal-national dynamic of the novel, in which individual characters also become representatives of their respective countries, an episode such as this serves to re-define "English innocence" as a national predicament following the eclipse of British imperial power by the Americans.

More significantly, and this is what I will be focusing on here, McEwan examines "English innocence" as an alibi in a spiral of increasing brutality. At stake here is partly what Robert Young calls the "idea of Britain as a moral nation," whose "particular power, responsibility and burden was the creation of global order and the administration of an impartial justice, based on a belief in fundamental English decency: *Pax Britannica*" (Young 2008: 233).

Relying on this vision of national supremacy and exceptionality – which in "popular imperialism" since the nineteenth century has defined the Englishman as the morally justified and "high-minded hero" (Dawson 1994, Webster 2005) – Leonard manages to push aside any reflection of concern about his violent impulses. He imagines brutality as existing outside of him and his identity. He declares his rape fantasies, for example, "alien to his obliging and kindly nature, they offended his sense of what was reasonable" (77). Indeed, Leonard is so convinced of his moral stature as an Englishman that he transforms his sexual violence into a language of unfairness and innocence. Upon finally realizing that his fiancée-to-be Maria is terrified by his assault, he thinks that:

> It was unjust this unspoken blame. He appealed to an imaginary court. If this had been anything other than playfulness, if he had meant her harm, he would not have stopped when he did, the very moment he saw how upset she was. She was taking it literally, using it against him, and that was quite unfair. [...] There came to him an image of a blue clockwork locomotive, a present on his eighth or ninth birthday. It pulled a string of coal trucks round a figure-of-eight track until one afternoon, in a spirit of reverent experimentation, he had overwound it. (82)

Constituted as an icon of moral blamelessness, harmlessness of intention and lack of guilt, the image of a child at play appears at the moment when Leonard's "exhilarating game" has tipped over into brutality. Leonard's memory reveals, on the one hand, his desire to rid himself of his inexperience and ineptness, and, on the other, his longing to remain morally blameless. A childhood image brings this dynamic of innocence into relief. At the same time, it problematizes the protagonist's frame of reference, since what for Leonard constitutes a sensual game, for Maria brings back memories of witnessing the rape of a wounded German civilian by a Russian soldier whose division reached Berlin at the end of the Second World War. Maria, McEwan makes sure to point out, also "had a memory, but only ten years old and more burdensome than a broken toy train." (82)

The question that Leonard's memory raises acutely comprises the problem of accountability. In longing to hold on to a sense of guiltlessness, Leonard seeks to usurp the place of victimized suffering and relocate the blame for the rift in his and Maria's relationship onto her. The image of play and harmlessness suggests that Leonard idealises childhood as a state of imagined innocence. The image that occurs to him as he silently professes his blamelessness – and the language of unfairness in the passage echoes the childhood image – indicate Leonard's attempt to exonerate his crime by associating himself with this vision of childhood as a time of no responsibility. The problem of accountability culminates with Otto's manslaughter and dismemberment. As in the case of sexual violence, Leonard converts his brutality into a logic of innocence: "He was innocent, that he knew." (201)

McEwan's concern with a specifically "English innocence" here emerges in the overtones that mark Leonard's violence. On several occasions before attacking Maria, for example, Leonard's rape fantasies end with him craving to eat something English: "he thought about food, about sausages. Not Bratwurst or Bockwurst or Knackwurst, but an English sausage, fat and mild, fried brownish-black on all sides, and mashed potatoes, and mushy peas" (78). His impulse to feast on English cuisine after enacting a fantasy of conquering the German "defeated enemy" reverberates with Leonard's response upon first seeing Berlin to revel in a sense of national supremacy before the German wasteland. Yet another image of childlikeness underscores the ethical implications of what Leonard regards as an innocent fantasy. During the assault, it seems to him that Maria "gave off a childish smell of toothpaste and soap." (80) Embodying a sense of weakness and vulnerability to physical abuse, cleanliness and purity against the corruption of adult actions and particularly against sexual assault, the figuration of Maria as childlike in this instance invokes the image of a violated nursery. Leonard invades and sullies a protected realm, as the representative of a military power seeking to assert national and cultural control over an individual whom he claims to love and wishes to care for. All the while, he ratifies his actions with respect to the idea of his own decency.

The deeper implication in *The Innocent* is that what is perceived as English innocence generates a fantasy of harmlessness. Reverberating on the professional and political level in the novel this notion of harmlessness renders the *Peter Pan*-image of the insulated adventure the model for the Englishman's endeavours. In relation to the professional sphere of activity, this image emerges when Leonard descends into the Berlin tunnel for the first time:

> It was a toytown, packed with boyish invention. Leonard remembered the secret camps, the tunnels through the undergrowth he used to make with friends in a scrap of woodland near his house. And the gigantic train set in Hamleys, the safe world of its motionless sheep and cows cropping the sudden green hills that were no more than pretexts for tunnels. Tunnels were stealth

and safety; boys and trains crept through them, lost to sight and care, and then emerged unscathed. (66)

The passage conveys the Englishman's sheltered childhood from the horrors of the Second World War, to be sure. Yet, in Leonard's rehearsal for the stealth and manoeuvring of intelligence, McEwan portrays a vision of war that approximates a risk-free and harmless enterprise. The equation between espionage and an "extravagantly playful" boyhood escapade can also be seen as bringing into relief Leonard's investment in an ideology of Englishness and its imperial venture that compares imperialism with a heroic, if not boyish, adventure. It is not merely that Leonard's understanding of espionage alludes to Rudyard Kipling's designation in *Kim* (1901) of the business of spying as "the Great Game". His memory also recalls Robert Baden-Powell's popular manual for Scouts, *Scouting for Boys* (1909), and its invitation to early-twentieth-century English boys to "find a 'backwoods' for themselves, and go adventuring" in preparation for the business of defending the British Empire (Boehmer 2005: xiv). Leonard's frame of reference with regard to the tunnel operation and likewise to the Second World War – in conjunction with Leonard's first walk in Berlin the novel evokes the image of the thirteen-year-old protagonist pretending to be a bomber plane destroying the city below – suggests that an adventure or game logic of imperialism which was disseminated in "boy culture" throughout the twentieth century is formative for how Leonard perceives Englishness and, with it, Britain's imperial project (Dawson 1994).

The problem, as it were, arises in that Leonard seems unable to distinguish between an ideal of masculine imperial adventure and reality. The vision of espionage and war as make-believe is transposed onto his acts of violence, so that Leonard views his attack on Maria as "a game, an exhilarating game" that she merely "mistakes" for the real thing (81). McEwan's novel, in this respect, scrutinises a perception of Englishness that reconciles imperial brutality with boyish high-mindedness.

While revealing the ethical limitations of the notion of innocence, the violence Leonard exerts on Maria's, and likewise on Otto's, body criticises a vision of Englishness configured as civilized, powerful and heroic. It is important here that Leonard imagines Maria as the casualty of his conquest, his by "right of unimaginable violence and heroism and sacrifice." (77) The features of English heroism and dominance that he draws upon to justify his violence are central to what Wendy Webster has called "empire stories" – narratives of "power and conquest" that stress "the manliness and militarism embodied in the soldier hero" – narratives that ratified an imperialist ideology in Britain during the height of its colonization and that were transposed upon the end of Empire onto narratives of greatness in the Second World War (Webster 2005: 3). Bringing into play this vision of Englishness as heroic and righteous at the moment of military and national glory, Leonard's rape fantasies and his assault enact a version of the manly hero who liberates Europe. In attacking Maria, he specifically casts himself as "*a soldier*, weary, battle-marked and bloody, but heroically rather than disablingly so" (78, original italics). His assault thus interweaves sexual dominance with notions of imperial conquest and the idea that violence is justified as a "right" of victory.

Leonard's treatment of Otto similarly calls upon this idea of the "soldier hero", the decent and triumphant Englishman fighting for his country (Dawson 1994). The description of the dismemberment is suggestive in this respect. "What was on the table now was no one at all," McEwan writes, "It was the field of operations, it was a city far below he had been ordered to destroy. Solingen. The gin again, the sticky Beefeater, then the big one, the thighs, the big push, and that would be it, home, a hot bath, a debriefing." (166) The account of the corpse and the dismemberment alludes to Leonard pretending to be a bomber plane destroying the German landscape below. It invokes the figure of the Beefeater as the guard of the British head of state and as the spirit Leonard consumes to manage the act of dissection. The reference to the "big push" – ambiguously bringing into play the bloody 1916 Battle of the Somme and to the 1945 Allied advances to the German capital – is similarly a part of the "empire stories" of national greatness that were attached to Britain's role in the two World Wars. The fact that the protagonist recuperates the violence done on Otto's body in a romance of virility and power – "This was the order of things, the order of battle" Leonard imagines as he anatomises his German rival (166) – further emphasises the fact that a deep-seated narrative of national heroism and triumph over an enemy is at stake in his brutality.

It is part of McEwan's deflation of this myth of national greatness – and likewise of the masculine ideal that inhabits the spy thriller genre – to present Leonard in ironic terms as an anti-hero. Even as he identifies himself with the British subject who tackles issues of national consequence, Leonard is hardly a central agent in the project of national dominance. He is not merely dispensable in the tunnel as a technician installing recording equipment, his championship of British interests as a mole on the American base are pitiable at best – he had only "tried a couple of locked doors, that was all" (98). His negligibility in the business of espionage is confirmed in his trifling role in the betrayal of the Berlin tunnel. At the end of the novel McEwan discloses that it is in fact the double agent George Blake – making a cameo appearance as Leonard's neighbour – who tips off the Russians: on this point McEwan remains true to what is known about the Berlin tunnel (Martin 1981).[1] The confined and self-serving span of his actions and motivations provides further evidence of his failure as a driving force for the fortification of the imperial project. The "soldier hero" fantasy is called upon at moments of violence as a justification for his private purposes and comprises alongside his conviction of his decency a cover for his solipsistic brutality.

Ultimately, the novel calls into question a narrative of the "civilising" and "benign" mission of the *Pax Britannica* – so central to the ratification of imperial politics and, for that matter, for the spy novel (Denning 1987). McEwan employs a genre whose very existence, as Denning has shown, is entrenched in an ideology of national heroism, competence and power. Rather than sensationalise violence as part of sanctioning an imperialist ideology of British supremacy, however, he offers a vision of gruesome violence and exploitation thinly veiled behind a myth of English "civilised" decency. Indeed, the sheer detail with which he describes the protracted scene of the dismemberment and disposal of Otto's body at the climax of the novel devastates the fantasy of political and moral innocence. It collapses a vision of English innocence and heroic dominance into a trajectory of increasing brutality and moral culpability. Thereby, it brings, not merely Leonard's claims to innocence, but a narrative of Englishness into a crisis.

3. The Trouble with Nostalgic Memory

The crisis in the protagonist's identity as an innocent and as an Englishman is part of a wider ambition in the novel: to address a series of questions regarding the remembrance and the re-writings of history. This ambition is brought to the fore by the coda of *The Innocent* which gestures towards a management of the past through Maria's 1987 letter, and, likewise, Leonard's return to Berlin, "where old matters could be unearthed" (218). The post-script itself has a framing function and as such it is important to the overall meanings of the novel. In the coda, an image of childhood is once again brought into play after having been absent in the novel during the encounter between Leonard and Otto. Even though it makes but a single appearance in the postscript, I propose that it serves to articulate a form of nostalgia which suggests a management of the past outside the ethics of accountability.

A vision of childhood appears in the letter that brings Leonard back to Berlin thirty years after he fled from his crimes. Reviewing her years with Leonard, Maria explains that:

> When I think of you, I don't only think of the terrible thing with Otto. I think of my kind and gentle Englishman who knew so little about women and who learned so beautifully! We were so easy together, it was such fun. Sometimes *it's as if I'm remembering a childhood*. I want to ask you, do you remember this, do you remember that? When we biked out to the lakes at weekends to swim, when we bought my engagement ring from that huge Arab (I still have that ring) and when we used to dance at the Resi. How we were the living champions and won a prize, the carriage clock that's still up in our attic. (223, emphasis added)

Maria's evocation of the past in terms of a childhood suggests a Golden Age of pre-lapsarian innocence – of uncomplicated joy and intimacy, of being carefree and in love – before the fall to corruption and guilt. That childhood offers a model for perceiving the past is a practice traceable to what is often called "Romantic historicism" (Chandler 1998). Towards the end of the eighteenth century, a new sense of history emerged in which, Carolyn Steedman has shown, the child and childhood became a means of configuring the past (Steedman 1995). Nostalgia was central to this view which located personal history inside the individual, in her memories, and which imagined individual and collective history in the shape of childhood, as that which is irrevocably lost to the adult and to society. Maria's letter makes this model operative when she sets up "the terrible thing with Otto" – which remains unnamed – as the definitive break that marks the loss of moral and legal innocence.

Her version of the past is carefully cleansed of unpleasantness. It wilfully omits Otto's abuse, his regular visits to verbally and physically assault Maria after their separation. Likewise, it disregards the sense that "Otto was always with them," even before the couple discover him hiding in Maria's closet on the night of their engagement (117). More importantly, Maria's nostalgic re-imagining "dis-remembers" Leonard's attempted rape and the rift his attack created in their relationship. It excludes Leonard's secret life at the tunnel, the tensions and double-dealings in Cold War Berlin and even the ruins of the city. The entire political backdrop and material setting of the plot is obscured, and replaced by an idealised fantasy.

This vision of the past plays into Leonard's romance of innocence; the narrative he formulates in the aftermath of the sexual assault: "He had to remind her [Maria] who he was really, the young innocent she had sweetly coaxed and brought on." (101) Re-emphasizing his identification as an innocent, Maria's memory suggests redemption thirty years after the fact, and allows Leonard to restore the narrative he hung on to from the start: that his violent fantasies were "misunderstood" and that his crimes were circumstantial (94). Leonard's response to Maria's letter sponsors her nostalgic and selective vision of their past. Convinced that the ruins of the tunnel have enabled him to finally understand Maria's letter and to know "what he was going to do," Leonard envisions travelling to Maria's current US residence to pick up their relationship where they left off (225).

In relation to the British nineteenth-century novel, Nicholas Dames has described the mechanics of nostalgia as a narrative end point in terms of offering "a retrospect that remembers only what is pleasant, and only what the self can employ in the present" (Dames 2001: 4). This form of remembrance which depends upon selective forgetting is descriptive of the protagonists' forgetting in *The Innocent*. For all the urges to unearth that past, the impetus of Maria's letter and likewise of Leonard's reaction in the coda is to reconfigure their personal histories according to the logic of nostalgic amnesia.

The thematization of amnesiac memory in the novel identifies a broader problem of historiography, a question that has preoccupied McEwan, prior to *The Innocent*, in his screenplay *The Ploughman's Lunch* (1983) and in relation to the orchestration of history in his television play *The Imitation Game* (1981). The re-creation in *The Innocent* of the past as a childhood – cleansed of unpleasantness – points towards McEwan's treatment also of a selective and idealising accommodation of a national history. His treatment of the topic, I propose, is rooted in discourses of national greatness that emerged in Britain in the late twentieth century.

In the 1970s and 1980s, as Webster and Dawson have explicated, conservative voices in Britain, in particular from the Thatcher administration, revived a politically charged story of national greatness. A central feature of this "epic" was the perception of the "'wartime spirit' of Churchill, Dunkirk, the Battle of Britain and the Blitz, as embodying the essential, valued qualities of national character" (Dawson 1994: 14). In this narrative, Britain's last moment of greatness was the Second World War, before the turning point of the Suez crisis in the mid-1950s, the loss of Empire and the perceived "permissiveness" of the Labour governments and the post-war "welfare consensus" made a detrimental impact on the nation's moral and economic development. Beyond the recuperation of the "high-minded soldier hero" for narratives of glorious nationhood, Webster identifies, in particular, the ways in which Winston Churchill came to be used in the promotion of the myth of national greatness and so ratify the Falklands war of 1982.

This narrative of English valour and victory associated with the Second World War is repeatedly called upon in *The Innocent*. Upon his first walk in his new hometown, McEwan makes sure to point out, Leonard made his way through a pleasant residential district of Berlin "with a certain proprietorial swagger, as though his feet beat out the rhythms of a speech by Mr Churchill." (5) This reference to Churchill comprises the culmination of a passage that articulates Leonard's sense of national pride about British military supremacy in the Second World War: "It was impossible for a young Englishman to be in Germany for the first time and not think of it above all as a defeated nation, or feel pride in the victory." (5) That McEwan includes this image of Churchillian national "spirit" is not merely a result of his interest in the details of history, of giving his character thoughts corresponding to the perceptions of the time, as David Malcolm has suggested (Malcolm 2001: 20). This reference to Churchill is also part of McEwan's critique of the revival of a British wartime ideal which was promoted in the 1980s for political and military purposes.

That McEwan wishes to deflate a mythologised narrative of the Second World War as a moment of greatness is evident from the opening of the novel. It is not merely that McEwan punctures Leonard's narrative of English heroism by casting it in irony: Leonard, we find out, "spent the war with his granny in a Welsh village over which no enemy aircraft had ever flown. He had never touched a gun, or heard one go off outside a rifle range" and, in fact, "it had been the Russians who had liberated the city" (5) so the narrative of triumphant Englishness is as romanticised as it is unsubstantiated. McEwan also calls the idea of greatness and heroism into question primarily by having it anticipate Leonard's impulse to "conquer" Maria and later to dismember Otto. *The Innocent* suggests that the impulse to revel in the devastation of the city, or, for that matter, to exert violence onto a body is rooted in the notion that, as an Englishman, Leonard has a right of access and property to a "defeated" country.

More importantly, to return to the question of nostalgic forgetting, this violence, justified via the British "solider hero" fantasy and ratified by Leonard's belief in his essential innocence, is what Leonard chooses to forget in the coda when thinking back on his past. McEwan's revisiting in this historical novel the mid-1950s – a moment defined as marking Britain's imperial descent – in the 1980s when British national self-perception was being re-defined is of consequence. In so far as McEwan's thematization of imperialist Englishness, memory and history is shaped by the British political scene in the 1980s, by what he has referred to as "the thunderous Churchillian rhetoric which was so readily available to politicians of all persuasions" at this time (McEwan 1989: 28), his treatment of nostalgia in *The Innocent* comprises a novelistic equivalent of what Paul Gilroy has called "postimperial melancholia" (Gilroy 2005). Aligning melancholia with a form of collective amnesia, Gilroy's account of Britain's inability to "face, never mind actually mourn," the dramatic events of the past is also descriptive of the forgetfulness that characterises the protagonists' history-making, an amnesia that the coda ultimately dramatises.

At stake in the retrospective vision that the post-script offers is a repressed history of violence and a failure to take moral responsibility for a series of brutal acts. From addressing the political and ethical implications of the Cold War, a history of treachery and violence, the thrust of the novel in and through the coda shifts to conveying a story of love that survives against all odds. The postscript, in this respect, enacts on the level of narration the protagonists' unsettling nostalgic impulse to forget. The stark contrast between the re-creation of the past as a time without responsibility in the coda and the sixty-page description of manslaughter, dismemberment and betrayal immediately preceding it is testimony to this.

Of *The Ploughman's Lunch* McEwan has explained that he wished to explore "the uses we make of the past, and the dangers, to an individual as well as to a nation, of living without a sense of history" (McEwan 1989: 26). In that screenplay and his introduction to it, McEwan calls into question what he identified as contemporary "fabrications of the past" which aimed to shape, for political purposes, national identity. Like *The Ploughman's Lunch*, *The Innocent* functions as a fictional commentary on the redefinition of the nation and of national self-perception in the 1980s with its sharp questioning of narratives of national greatness that repress a violent imperialist past. McEwan examines the portrayal of the British eclipse by America, the depiction of a changing national self-perception, and the configuration of childhood as a space of innocence and vulnerability in *The Innocent*. Ultimately, however, he also critiques a narrative of Englishness that romanticises the historical past as a time of national glory, heroism and benevolence.

By way of concluding, I want to return to my initial conjecture: that McEwan draws on the meanings attached to childhood – from its designation as a position of weakness to its identification as a time of innocence – to treat issues that lie at the heart of his political project. A close examination of the usage of the idea of childhood in the novel reveals a repeated and specific rooting of the protagonist's actions, and in particular his brutality, in a complex vision of Englishness that joins the ideal of the innocent boyish amateur with the ideal of the "soldier hero". While it reveals the limits of innocence, childhood imagery in the novel calls into question a deep-seated myth of national greatness.

Note

1 McEwan has acknowledged his debt to David C. Martin's record of Operation Gold, *Wilderness of Mirrors*, in the "Author's Note" to *The Innocent* (227).

Bibliography

Boehmer, Elleke: "Introduction," *Scouting for Boys: A Handbook for Instruction in Good Citizenship*, Robert Baden-Powell, Oxford, 2005.
Brown, Richard: "Postmodern Americas in the Fiction of Angela Carter, Martin Amis and Ian McEwan", *Forked Tongues? Comparing Twentieth-Century British and American Literature*, London, 1994.
Chandler, James: *England in 1819: The Politics of Literary Culture and the Case of Romantic Historicism*, Chicago, 1998.
Dames, Nicholas: *Amnesiac Selves: Nostalgia, Forgetting, and British Fiction, 1810-1870*, Oxford, 2001.
Dawson, Graham: *Soldier Heroes: British Adventure, Empire and the Imagining of Masculinities*, London, 1994.
Denning, Michael: Cover Stories: Narrative and Ideology in the British Spy Thriller, London, 1987.
Gilroy, Paul: Postcolonial Melancholia, New York, 2005.
Head, Dominic: Ian McEwan, Manchester, 2007.
Malcolm, David: Understanding Ian McEwan, Columbia, 2001.
Martin, David C.: Wilderness of Mirrors, New York, 1981.
McEwan, Ian: The Innocent, or The Special Relationship, London, 2001.
---. "Introduction to The Ploughman's Lunch," A Move Abroad: Or Shall We Die? and The Ploughman's Lunch, London, 1989.
Ryan, Kiernan: Ian McEwan, Plymouth, 1994.
Steedman, Carolyn: Strange Dislocations: Childhood and the Idea of Human Interiority 1780-1930, London, 1995.
Young, Robert C.: The Idea of English Ethnicity, Oxford, 2008.
Webster, Wendy: Englishness and Empire 1939-1965, Oxford, 2005.

Lynn Guyver (Warwick)

Post-Cold War Moral Geography.
The Politics of McEwan's Poetics in *The Innocent*

It has been suggested that McEwan's novel *The Innocent* (1990) marks both "a stylistic departure" in its reference to the cold-war spy thriller, and the beginning of "a significant phase of political writing" in which McEwan ventures beyond his focus on the private sphere to engage with the legacy of major twentieth-century social and political upheavals.[1] While those features signal important departures for McEwan in his personal trajectory as a writer, they nevertheless represent continuities within intellectual and literary traditions that, for a variety of reasons, were falling out of fashion by the late 1980s. In taking on the bigger historical questions that have shaped our understanding of Britain's place in the world, and writing within humanist literary traditions, McEwan's work could also be regarded as going against the grain of what dominated western intellectual and cultural debates at that time. As Marc Delrez observes, McEwan "appears to turn his back on postmodernism […] to concentrate on the more unpalatable business of looking the beast of history straight in the eye."[2]

In addition to reviewers' admiration for McEwan's clever manipulation of the spy novel,[3] much of the critical interest in *The Innocent* focuses on the novel's insight into the period of post-war history it depicts, as well as the moral ramifications of narrative events and what motivates the choices made by characters represented in the novel to act in the way they do.[4] Dominic Head, for example, makes a compelling case for the novel as a work of political allegory that sheds light in particular on the power relations between the USA and Britain in the early post-war years, and suggests that the novel "invites an equation between individual action and international politics".[5] The tension that is created between the "sexual, emotional and political" challenges to the innocence of the young Englishman Leonard Marnham[6] serves to expose human brutality not only at private and public levels, but also as existing deep in the English psyche.

My concern is less with the historical significance of the novel's geopolitical context. I am interested more in what that context and – equally importantly – the particular means used to represent it, contribute to our understanding of the *post*-cold war period in which the novel was conceived and written; in other words, the focus is on McEwan's late 1980s' choices for what motivates his 1950s characters, whereby the narrative's overt political subject matter is shaped by the implicit politics of McEwan's poetics. It is significant that McEwan returns in his narrative to the early phase of the cold war in 1950s divided Berlin precisely at the moment when the cold-war political narrative is coming to an end. Moreover, he adopts the conventions of the realist spy thriller in combination with that genre's classic cold-war setting in divided Berlin at a time when anti-realism in fiction is in mode and the cold-war espionage narrative is expected to lose its resonance.[7]

In attempting to account for what McEwan achieves by siting his *Bildungsroman* in the nexus of those British historical and literary traditions, my analysis draws on Pierre Bourdieu's notion of the 'field of cultural production' and the idea that the competition for different ways of understanding human relations has a great deal to do with gaining recognition for the manner in which a particular way of seeing is organised in individual works.[8] According to Bourdieu, the author's anticipation of beneficial returns[9] from the reception of a work is a determining factor in that author's choice of a work's form and content. The choice is not arbitrary or unlimited, but necessarily delimited by the existing conditions and relations of production in the field, and to its framing power structure in the wider social formation. The work is an expression of those conditions as its particular organisation of ideas represents a combination of choices made in relation to available resources. Although we do not conventionally expect literary works to make claims to historical truth, insofar as an author employs his/her own distinctive ways to make particular sense of human relations, they implicitly claim the truth of their organising forms to do that work. Striving for distinctiveness in that endeavour, as well as recognition for it, are, I believe, intrinsic to literary practice. The literary means used to represent the way people live could be said to constitute its ultimate subject, or, as Bourdieu puts it: "the true subject of the work of art is nothing other than the specifically artistic manner in which artists grasp the world".[10]

While the focus of this inquiry is on how McEwan's distinctive choices are manifested in the novel itself, the author's own account of the work's origins is also revealing, not least since the thoughts given to Leonard in the final sentence of the novel would appear to have been inspired by the experience McEwan describes in his interview with Rosa González-Casademont published in 1992. He explains that the idea for the novel emerged in 1987 when he was visiting West Berlin following a recent trip to the Soviet Union where he was given good reason to believe that the cold war would soon be over. Looking eastwards from a viewing platform across the Wall and the 'death strip' that was once Potsdamer Platz, he reflected on how that might all eventually vanish. Instead of writing about the end of the cold war (an idea he later returns to, of course, in his next novel *Black Dogs* (1992)), he says he wanted to base his novel on a true story set in Berlin at the height of the cold war, and for a long while he imagined that story would be "about an escape from the East". He settled instead on a spy story about a tunnel being constructed in the opposite direction – from West to East.[11]

Edward Said's study of the western intellectual tradition of 'orientalism'[12] and related work in the fields of postcolonial studies and cultural geography have argued that those compass directions are far from being neutral, innocent or stable markers of political and geographical fact that can claim simply that East is East etc..[13] They can instead be regarded as signifiers of relational distinctions that draw on common conceptions about East and West that have been reproduced and continually reworked in long traditions of cultural representation, in which the particular interests of the perspective from which they are viewed are also registered. Those binary distinctions are meaningful not merely in terms of the geopolitics they represent, but for the value judgements associated with the existence of a boundary as a marker of division, as well as of difference in value that can be measured in different ways. Our understanding of human relations depends to a great extent on the way we distinguish between such categories of difference, and the terms employed to represent them; whether they express notions of continuity/discontinuity, convergence/divergence, superiority/inferiority, progress/backwardness, maturity/childishness, and so on. Works of literary representation contribute to the reproduction of those distinctions insofar as they draw on assumptions about human relations that are in common currency. They simultaneously rework them according to the particular conventions and formal organisation of the text, and feed them back into the historical imagination.

At the time McEwan was writing *The Innocent*, the antagonistic configuration of the cold-war boundary between East and West that had been a self-evident fact of life for over forty years was suddenly foremost in western consciousness since it was in the process of being dismantled from the 'other' side. McEwan's two Berlin novels *The Innocent* and *Black Dogs* are in many ways complementary and straddle that period of transformation with the benefit of hindsight in both cases: the former revisiting its origins in anticipation of imagining something humanly better, the latter reluctantly acknowledging the difficulty of that task. Neither novel, however, is necessarily 'about' Berlin or East-West relations per se, but the binary moral geography of Berlin is represented as the symbolic space in which ideas of difference in human relations in general (and British relations in particular – as a universal model) can be re-examined in response to the shift in the balance of world power precipitated by developments throughout Eastern Europe at that time.

The representation of divided Berlin is complemented by McEwan's exploitation of generic conventions of the cold-war spy thriller that lends the novel its seemingly authentic atmosphere of post-war paranoia. It does indeed seem that "*The Innocent* is in some ways an uncomplicated spy novel, a thriller written in straightforward prose",[14] thanks to McEwan's clever mimicry of the kind of conventions one would normally expect of the genre. However, a closer inspection of the traditional formulas and functions of the spy thriller in relation to McEwan's actual use of the form (for representing 1950s Berlin in late 1980s Britain) suggests that McEwan has different ambitions for the genre: he would appear to be exploiting the familiar conventions of both literary and historical traditions in order to demolish the expectations their collective moral geography commands over certain ways of understanding human relations. In that sense, *The Innocent* could be described as

McEwan's attempt to dismantle the boundary from the western perspective in order to open up a better space for the new world order to occupy in the no-man's land between the past and future.

In his study of the genre, Michael Denning suggests that the British spy thriller:

> is ostensibly one of the most 'political' of popular fiction genres. Its subject is global politics: the Empire, fascism, communism, the Cold War, terrorism. Yet its political subject is only a pretext to the adventure formulas and plots of betrayal, disguise, and doubles which are at the heart of the genre and of the reader's investment.[15]

According to Denning, those formulas and plots embody the ideological function of the genre in the way in which they structure their different political 'cover stories'. That function is to keep symptoms of uncertainty and powerlessness at bay by retaining faith in the virtue of human agency to restore order and a sense of rectitude to a troubled world in which Britain remains centre stage. The thriller's origins lie in the fate of the British Empire, and it emerges out of the adventure stories of the late nineteenth century as Britain's position in the world comes increasingly under threat from rival powers. The spy story chronicles Britain's steady decline and compensates for the sense of loss of its power and status on the world stage in terms of rivalry and betrayal. In that sense, it is one of the most compensatory and ambivalent of literary forms that has evolved over time to account for political and social change.

Denning suggests it distinguishes itself from the traditional novel's focus on the individual's psychological development in relation to society by reappropriating older allegorical devices to account for what is perceived to be a collective condition conceived in individual terms. Using a kind of reversal of the biographical novel's formula, the spy thriller explains the contradictions of British social relations in terms of the actions and guises of the secret agent who is licensed with the ambivalent freedom to cross the boundaries it is his task to secure. The spy is the vehicle for that imaginary operation which enables a totality to be explained (reductively) in complementary ethical binary terms.[16]

From Denning's use of the words "rival", "boundary", "other", "alien" and "betrayal", it is clear that the spy thriller's ethical code rests on the recognition of a distinct complementary binary formula of inclusion and exclusion, which is also antagonistic in its complementarity. Thus, irrespective of the specific (complex) nature of the historical 'pretext' (e.g. Empire, fascism etc.), the spy thriller transforms that specificity into a simplified adversarial pattern in accordance with its own binary ethical terms. The symbolic struggle for the supremacy of one half of that dichotomy over the other – for waging and winning a moral war by restoring things which have been temporarily displaced to their rightful places – provides the 'thrill' of the genre.

The traditional narrative syntax the thriller adapts to this end is that of the romance heroic quest with its masculine gendered emphasis. According to Denning, the distinctiveness of the genre is historical rather than simply formulaic; it lies in "[t]he syntax of plot, the way the permutations of mission, hunt, and investigation are worked, the way the hunter/hunted dialectic is articulated in varieties of what we might call masculine romance".[17] Those permutations and varieties accommodate changes in the relations of social reproduction of the specific period in question and provide us with comparative 'readings' of the current state of the nation, who is responsible for that state, which virtues are worth preserving or salvaging, and in which social grouping those virtues are best represented.

If we accept Denning's explanation, the 'surface' story of Operation Gold and Leonard's role in it constitute the pretext for McEwan's deployment of the genre's binary formula and the expectations it creates for the restoration of moral order in the post-cold war period. McEwan certainly avails himself of multiple series of the spy thriller's dual levels, not least those of secrecy, rivalry and deception, to tell the story of the 'amateur' Leonard, the classic 'innocent abroad' figure.[18] However, as will be discussed in relation to textual examples below, it would seem that rather than using those levels for the purpose of short-cut solutions and simplification, McEwan actually increases the complexity of the narrative of Leonard's progress by maintaining the ambiguity of those binary devices, by refusing to resolve contradictions, and depriving his narrative of any moral high ground.

In the traditional thriller, the tension is produced between dual narrative levels which serve to explain causality. They afford the reader a privileged perspective on the progress of the hunt from the point of view of both the hunter and the hunted. McEwan departs from the tradition by maintaining the narrative viewpoint almost exclusively from Leonard's third person perspective, thereby confining the reader's levels of knowledge to the range of his unfolding experience, his suspicion and fear, and producing tension in that sense of psychological confinement. Never quite knowing enough is the dilemma of the innocent, and the reader is rendered a hostage to Leonard's growing confidence and secret uncertainty. Leonard is shown to be his own worst enemy, and is effectively hunting himself.

The way in which McEwan formally controls the reader's access to information complements the narrative organisation of the dangerous quest for knowledge. This takes Leonard through different stages of private and public induction at the hands of those whose knowledge, at least initially, is greater than his: his German lover, Maria, and his American colleague, Bob Glass. Leonard's quest for knowledge involves recognising boundaries as points of convergence and divergence. His relationship with Maria, for example, is first based on his recognition that "there were so many points of contact"[19] between them, and that Maria herself embodies contradictory characteristics of both "womanly power" and "childlike dependency" (p. 47). As the novelty of exploring those points of contact wears off, Leonard learns how to distinguish between points of connection, and reverses the perspective to explore the possibilities of viewing their relationship in terms of difference and separation. Hence, he later acts upon his formerly innocent intimation that Maria "had the sort of face, the sort of manner, onto which men were likely to project their own requirements" by attempting to rape her (p. 47).

Conversely, he believes that childhood is a separate realm of being which is irrevocably lost when one arrives at manhood until he discovers, to his initial scorn and then to his delight, that Americans have the knack of combining the two. On the one hand, he rediscovers boyish pleasures in his employment in the serious adult business of the US surveillance operation located in a tunnel. On first viewing, he is given to observe with some ironic prescience of his own fate, and oblivious of the significance of this tunnel's dangerous connection with the enemy camp:

> It was a toytown, packed with boyish invention. Leonard remembered the secret camps, the tunnels through the undergrowth

> he used to make with friends [...]. And the gigantic train set in Hamleys, the safe world of its motionless sheep and cows cropping the sudden green hills that were no more than pretexts for tunnels. Tunnels were stealth and safety; boys and trains crept through them, lost to sight and care, and then emerged unscathed. (pp. 71-72)

On the other hand, he develops a "disgusted fascination" for the fact that grown American men can be "so publicly playful" in indulging in childish ball games, drinking chocolate milk and jumping around to music (p. 16). From his immersion in American culture, especially the infectious rock and roll music of the era, he discovers an unexpectedly frivolous side to himself.

Before Leonard is introduced to covert means of scrutiny which offer him simultaneously greater freedom and greater anxiety, he first has a lesson in overt observation when his new American companions introduce him to different forms of Berlin nightlife. His primary education into contrastive ways of seeing and behaving prepare him for graduation to the discovery of their secret possibilities. Above all, for Leonard it is a first-hand education in American culture, for which the screen version has prepared him. Glass and Russell provide the running commentary which instructs their eager pupil how to understand what he is seeing, and confirm what he already anticipates of his first adventure "deep in the Communist camp" (p. 32). Leonard is informed:

> 'we're starting you in the East so you can enjoy the contrasts later. We're going to the Neva Hotel.' [...] 'It used to be the Hotel Nordland, a second class establishment. Now it has declined further, but it is still the best hotel in East Berlin.' (p. 31)

The commentary complements McEwan's narrative viewpoint from Leonard's perspective which confirms the cultural preconceptions of Communist terrain he has presumably gleaned from images in wartime propaganda or US popular culture; the sinister and tawdry nature of those images is illustrated by the adjectives with which he recreates the gothic atmosphere of his surroundings: "dim", "dark", "deserted", "silent", the "well-fingered pink" quilting of the bar, the "unlit" chandeliers and the "chipped gilt-framed mirrors" (p. 31). Leonard also learns by his companions' example a sense of licence that can be exercised in relation to the enemy in his companions' ostentatious, supercilious behaviour in ordering large quantities of Russian champagne, and speaking loudly and critically of their hosts, crucially, without fear of contradiction:

> 'What the Commies are selling is miserable, miserable, and inefficient. [...] Boy, have they found a way of minimizing happiness! [...] I mean, look at this place! Leonard, we brought you to the classiest joint in their sector. Look at it. Look at the people here. Look at them!' Glass was close to shouting. (p. 35)

By inference and example, Leonard becomes rapidly aware that the USA not only boasts the monopoly on happiness, but maximising self-gratification is the good-life creed for everything it stands for – from the lavish expenditure on Operation Gold to the generous size of canteen portions "which seemed at one with the whole enterprise" (p. 124). The USA can afford not to fear contradiction because it has the power to turn contradiction to its own ends.

Leonard's violent and deceptive thoughts and behaviour reflexively illustrate the moral limitations of the way in which antagonistic political narratives frame private lives. The tensions they produce in ordinary individuals like Leonard are woven ever more intricately back into the social fabric of the times by means of "those quiet, forceful conventions that keep men and women in their tracks" (p. 117). That is not to suggest that Leonard is merely a passive victim of his times, but rather that he is shown to be both the conductor and emitter of its forces in how and why he thinks and chooses to act in the manner he does. The dilemma in which Leonard finds himself is produced by the choices he makes from the range of contradictory options available to him in the circumstances of his time and place: in a sense, he has been 'framed' by the political and moral codes of his era and location when he and Maria decide it is easier to dismember and dispose of Otto's body than to inform the authorities. By constructing a character who makes choices which place him outside the governing mores, McEwan invites closer inspection of the validity of the kind of codes that are antagonistic to Leonard's aspirations. We are forced to reappraise the ethics of a system which demands conformity to a particular type of behaviour, but thereby produces dissent.

Leonard is McEwan's device for explaining the forces which control the limits of individual and collective knowledge. Learning how to recognise boundaries and their contradictions, and to exploit their claims to power in order to maximise his own happiness, signals the end of his innocence. Leonard's fall from grace is precipitated by his discovery of hierarchies of binary distinctions embodied in those boundaries, especially in the various 'clearance levels' he encounters in the workplace, and their transferable distinctions of power to other areas of social life.

Awareness of the relational nature of national identities, and of his own in particular, marks the beginning of that process. He first becomes conscious of his Englishness outside the social confines which afford him that identity. The move abroad to the ruined heart of Germany ten years after its defeat at first gives Leonard a sense of national superiority, which he goes on to exert over his German lover in brutal sexual fantasies (in which she represents the defeated enemy, his spoil of war, and the proof that "he was victorious and good and strong and free" (p. 83)), as well as in the butchery of her ex-husband's body. As he walks the streets of Berlin "with a certain proprietorial swagger" on his first evening, noting the restoration of ruined buildings, and conveniently forgetting that "it had been the Russians who had liberated the city", he is given to reflect: "It was impossible for a young Englishman to be in Germany for the first time and not think of it above all as a defeated nation, or feel pride in the victory" (p. 5). The certainty of that defeat (and hence, of victory) is shaken when his poor comprehension of spoken German leads him mistakenly to interpret the banter of a group of elderly drinkers as brazen boasting of Nazi acts of genocide.

On the other hand, his personification of Britishness is a source of anguish in relation to the Americans. He already has "an intimation of the power of American style", and the way in which Americans "seemed utterly at ease being themselves" from his exposure to American culture back home. His apprehension of the risible image he will present to Glass as the stiff Englishman – as he attempts to affect the casual look from his wardrobe of grey suits – is also an intimation of his awareness that being casual and at ease with yourself comes with the style and confidence of affluence and political power which Britain has lost. Leonard is of the generation whose inherited sense of nationality is worn with as much self-conscious unease as clothing representing their parents' sense of style: "His Englishness was not quite the comfort it had been to a preceding generation. It made him feel vulnerable" (p. 8).

Leonard's new circumstances heighten his awareness of the inadequacy of being British, but in particular, of being a British male, in a period of US cultural and political ascendancy, and above all in a new era of warlike conditions. He is doubly displaced publicly and privately as an Englishman and as a man. Having been coopted as a token British technical footsoldier in a war which ultimately serves to endorse American expansion, Leonard is obliged to prove his worth publicly by being loyal to his country's subordinate role in the 'special relationship', and privately by being loyal to the tradition of gendered social roles. But above all, he is obliged to do so on American terms, in relation to the Soviet threat. In that sense, McEwan's use of the spy thriller form turns the masculine romance quest into Leonard's unheroic search for his own masculinised national identity. He performs being an Englishman in the antagonistic space of former enemy territory and between two cultures hostile to his ambitions.

At the same time, Leonard acquires the transferable survival skills learnt in that contested space. In particular, he learns the contradictory value of the concept of secrecy which alerts him to the possibilities and pitfalls of the dual levels of identity represented by being and seeming. His awareness that how things appear is not necessarily how they are in reality is both useful and dangerous knowledge. The way in which he applies that knowledge to violent ends raises the novel's central issue of what constitutes human morality at public and private levels.

The proximity of the boundary with the zone of Soviet control provides the geopolitical pretext for exploring the different levels at which not only the public and private spheres, but also international human relations in general are inextricably interconnected. It reveals how competition for control over the terms of connection involves the construction of arbitrary, and therefore contestable, boundaries which serve to assert and protect individuated claims to power, above all those of the USA. Knowledge is a commodity whose exchange value confers power on the beholder. The dividing line between East and West Berlin represents the fundamental spatialised terms which determine all other symbolic crossing points in the thoughts and actions of characters in the novel. The border at that time was still open and yet we feel the presence of the Wall six years before it was constructed. Readers' imaginative access to the nearby Soviet zone is confined to the manner in which it is perceived at an objective distance from the detached, subjective perspective of western intelligence. That way of seeing constructs a defensive wall in the minds of western observers who need to preserve a privileged sense of their own subjectivity in relation to their invented object of scrutiny. That object is denied any means of self-presentation on its own terms. McEwan ensures that the terms of representation remain the preserve of his western characters. Material that is authentically Soviet (such as the information obtained from tapping Soviet lines of communication) has to be processed as a means of authenticating different forms of western identity.

The postscript to *The Innocent* returns an elderly Leonard to the scene of his crime in 1987. Now marked by the presence of the Wall, he revisits the boundary where the tunnel was sited to regain a sense of connection. In anticipation of being reunited with Maria, he also anticipates political reunification: a time when the Wall would be "all torn down" (245). The imagery of broken masonry evokes the memory of the torn body with which McEwan torments us at the heart of the novel. The most significant stage of Leonard's education is autodidactic: the dismembering of Otto instructs Leonard in the dreadful knowledge that undermines every distinction he has learnt to make – namely, that there is ultimately no difference between himself and the man he is in the process of hacking to pieces. One is led to assume that the tearing down of the Wall may afford a similar revelation about human relations.

McEwan's novel was received with great acclaim for its unique treatment of the spy thriller. But as has been suggested here, McEwan's use of the genre is unorthodox and partial, insofar as his 'cover story' and its setting raise expectations for the genre, but the formal means used to organize that narrative do not meet those expectations in the traditional way. This is evidently not regarded by McEwan's readers and reviewers as a failure on his part, but one wonders what a spy thriller aficionado would make of it.

If, as suggested above, striving for distinctiveness and distinction is intrinsic to literary and cultural production as Bourdieu claims, what terms of recognition could McEwan be hoping to elicit by means of this novel? He would certainly not appear to be seeking recognition for his mastery of the spy genre's binary ethics. It would seem that he is more interested in showing how the genre's reductive morality formally complements his own critique of the cold-war political narrative. Contrary to restoring binaries and their boundaries, it would appear to be part of McEwan's ambitions for his use of the spy thriller form in that spatial and temporal context to overcome the conventional demands of each to restore boundaries to particular notions of identities, especially those of Britishness. He does this by exploiting the ambivalence of the form to regain a sense of the complexity of human responses which binary systems inhibit and distort. He reveals the unpredictability of human morality which refuses to be bound by simplistic formulas and reduced to convenient explanations – literary or political – and which forces a way through those structures, not obeying but bending or breaking the rules. McEwan's transgression of the conventions of the thriller complements his narrative representation of what is extraordinary about human behaviour in transgressing convention. In that way, he takes formal responsibility for a humanism in which "the subject is always that which is radically irreducible, that which will seep through the cracks of your categories and play havoc with your structures".[20] In that way, he salvages a sense of universal human potential by demolishing the authority of hierarchical oppositions and their forms of representation in which many other writers find themselves enmeshed.

At the same time, I feel obliged to question how politically useful such a stance is that implicitly defends a view of human freedom and equality that is premised not only on uncertainty, but on the type of uncertainty that is most commonly associated with *anti*-humanist arguments for the virtues of indeterminacy, relativism and contingency. That is of particular concern if we consider that McEwan's work can be regarded as a contribution to the debate about the kind of world we would like to make in the aftermath of the cold war. The contradiction, I believe, reveals a wider cultural dilemma of representation that registers the problem for writers like McEwan searching for ways of making qualitative distinctions of human value in a field dominated by either the principles of exchange value or of relativism.

Relatedly, the model of reconciliation McEwan offers in his postscript repeats the pattern Marc Delrez has observed about *Black Dogs* and some of the other novels; namely, that when it comes to the bigger questions, the only political solution McEwan can ultimately come up with is the retreat into the consoling yet guilt-ridden space of the private sphere.[21] Again, this would appear to be a problem of representation that betrays a cultural inability to conceive the large-scale picture of social relations. Ironically, that was being performed on the other side of the Wall just as McEwan was writing his novel. The result, though, as we know with hindsight, was that both the sense of uncertainty and forced retreat into the private sphere of the kind that are implicit in McEwan's formal analysis, were in fact universalized following the end of the cold war when the opportunity to imagine something better than what had gone before was effectively lost. In that sense, *The Innocent* and its 'sequel' *Black Dogs* would at least seem to resonate with their post-cold war structures of feeling.

Notes

1. Dominic Head: *Ian McEwan*, Manchester, 2007, pp. 91-92.
2. Marc Delrez: "Escape into Innocence: Ian McEwan and the Nightmare of History", *Ariel* 26, 2 (1995), 7.
3. For example, John Carey writes in his review in the *Sunday Times*, quoted on the back cover of the Picador 1990 edition of the novel: "To call *The Innocent* a spy novel would be like calling *Lord of the Flies* a boy's adventure yarn [...] [the] plot crackles like thin ice with dread and suspense."
4. A comprehensive examination of critical accounts of the novel is provided in: Peter Childs (Ed.): *The Fiction of Ian McEwan*, Basingstoke, 2006.
5. Dominic Head: *Op. cit*, p. 93.
6. *Ibid.*, pp. 92-93.
7. For example: "Ironically, he has celebrated the obsequies of the East-West spy thriller by writing one of the subtlest". David Hughes, review in *The Mail on Sunday,* quoted on the back cover of the Picador 1990 edition of the novel.
8. Pierre Bourdieu: *The Field of Cultural Production: Essays on Art and Literature*, Ed. Randal Johnson. Cambridge, 1993.
9. This refers to the type of reward the writer aspires to in order to achieve what they perceive to be the work's 'surplus value' – be it financial, praise from their peers/the general public/politicians, or merely the pleasure of creating – in terms of recognition for the work's contribution to the symbolic economy.
10. Pierre Bourdieu: *Op. cit.*, p. 118.

11 Rosa González-Casademont: "The Pleasure of Prose Writing vs Pornographic Violence: An Interview with Ian McEwan", *The European English Messenger*, 1:3, 1992, 42-43.
12 Edward Said: *Orientalism: Western Conceptions of the Orient*, London, 1995 [originally published 1978].
13 See, for example: Larry Wolff, *Inventing Eastern Europe: The Map of Civilization on the Mind of the Enlightenment*, Stanford CA, 1994; Stuart Hall, "The Local and the Global: Globalization and Ethnicity" in Anthony D. King (Ed.), *Culture, Globalization and the World System*, Basingstoke, 1991; Nigel Thrift, "Literature, the Production of Culture and the Politics of Place", *Antipode*, 15, 1983, 12-24; Peter Jackson, *Maps of Meaning*, London, 1992; James Duncan & David Ley, *Place/ Culture/ Representation*, London, 1993.
14 Peter Childs (Ed.): *Op. cit.*, p. 76.
15 Michael Denning: *Cover Stories: Narrative Ideology in the British Spy Thriller*, London, 1987, p. 2.
16 *Ibid.*, p.14.
17 *Ibid.*, p.13.
18 Denning identifies the characters in Eric Ambler's early novels especially. See the section 'Innocents abroad' in *Ibid.*, Chapter 3, "Epitaph for an amateur". pp. 67-80.
19 Ian McEwan: *The Innocent, or The Special Relationship*, London: Picador, 1990, p. 56. Further page references to this edition will be included in the text.
20 Terry Eagleton: *The Illusions of Postmodernism*, Oxford, 1996, p. 131.
21 Marc Delrez: *Op. cit.*, 18, 20.

Dr. Lars Heiler [Universität Kassel]

Unleashing the Black Dogs.
Cathartic Horror and Political Commitment in *The Innocent* and *Black Dogs*[1]

In his essay "On Truth and Lies in a Nonmoral Sense", written in 1873, Friedrich Nietzsche makes the following observation:

> What does man actually know about himself? Is he, indeed, ever able to perceive himself completely, as if laid out in a lighted display case? Does nature not conceal most things from him – even concerning his own body – in order to confine and lock him within a proud, deceptive consciousness, aloof from the coils of the bowels, the rapid flow of the blood stream, and the intricate quivering of the fibers! She threw away the key. And woe to that fatal curiosity which might one day have the power to peer out and down through a crack in the chamber of consciousness and then suspect that man is sustained in the indifference of his ignorance by that which is pitiless, greedy, insatiable, and murderous – as if hanging in dreams on the back of a tiger.[2]

Nietzsche uses this paragraph in order to state an epistemological problem about our inability to glimpse truth because the condescending rationalism which guides our presuppositions prevents us from understanding the course of nature, including our own, and it is only through the illusion of an ostensibly transparent language that we seem to understand the world, ourselves, and the relationship between them.

I would like to use Nietzsche's contention as a starting point for a discussion of Ian McEwan's novels *The Innocent* and *Black Dogs* because it seems to be dealing with issues that we find in McEwan's unsettling narratives all the time: the antagonism between reason and emotion, the thin dividing line between civilization and savagery, and the inability of the mind to become fully aware of what motivates the individual's actions.

Moreover, Nietzsche refers to the human body in its concrete physicality when he expatiates on "the coils of the bowels, the flow of the blood stream, and the quivering of the fibres". These aspects of the body which usually remain invisible and are shut out by human consciousness, are appositely demonstrated in Ian McEwan's spy novel *The Innocent*, which is set in 1950s Berlin and in which the young English technician and would-be secret agent Leonard Marnham dismembers the corpse of Otto Eckdorf and catches a disturbing glimpse of what is ordinarily obscured. In a novel like *The Innocent*, which deals with initiation on many different levels, Leonard's insight into the details of human anatomy is coupled with an insight into the darker sides of human nature, a nature that is dominated by violence and aggression. It is this shock of recognition, the discovery of his own violent personality, which he has never admitted to himself before, that seals the end of Leonard's relationship with his fiancée Maria Eckdorf, Otto's ex-wife.

As many critics have emphasised, the union between the two lovers, and its subsequent failure after they have carved up Otto, can be read in terms of political allegory, because the relationships between the main characters are indicative of the links between their countries of origin. According to Jack Slay, Maria and Leonard are "emblematic of their cultures". Their love is a

> symbolic political union, a reuniting of forces torn asunder by the upheavals of the twentieth century. [...] In *The Innocent*, then, McEwan presents politics as love, individual union as the derivation for transcultural pacification and acceptance.[3]

Likewise, the dismemberment of Otto Eckdorf finds its political correlative in the division of Berlin, Germany and Europe after World War II. And finally, the fact that Leonard eventually loses Maria who seeks refuge in the arms of American agent Bob Glass are indicative of Britain's fading influence in the postwar world order. The analogy between private lives and world politics is sustained until the very end, because there is a glimpse of hope for a reunion of Maria and Leonard as well as for a new Europe after the anticipated collapse of the Berlin wall, an event which is imagined by Leonard in 1987. As Kiernan Ryan states: "The final sentence looks forward to a transfigured future in which mutual absolution and political deliverance converge."[4]

These metaphorical and metonymical links between the private and the political in *The Innocent* are evident, although one could ask the question whether the two spheres dovetail as neatly as a first reading seems to imply. The main objective in the first part of this essay is, however, to elucidate how Leonard's very private and intimate moment of horror and his loss of moral innocence provide a form of catharsis and whether this leads to a call for political commitment or rather subverts such a call.

By catharsis I mean a strong emotional reaction to a horrifying event which challenges a character's understanding of oneself and the world. Leonard's violent reaction at the sight and smell of Otto's dissected body represents such a moment. Disgusted and overwhelmed by nausea he hastens to the bathroom:

> The insult was, Leonard had time to think, as he stepped hurriedly round the up-ended halves of the torso that were still joined, that all this stuff was also in himself.
> As if to prove it, he gripped the edges of the lavatory bowl and brought up a mouthful of green bile.[5]

On the one hand, the dismemberment of Otto Eckdorf represents the last and most incisive in a series of events which shatter Leonard's ignorance of, and innocence in, matters sexual, emotional, moral and political. His initiation is not a smooth process, but a rather bumpy road leading towards an increasing awareness of his own limits and his helplessness in the face of the complexity of personal relationships and of post-war politics. Through the labyrinthine private and professional links between himself, Maria Eckdorf, Bob Glass and others, Leonard's life becomes politicised in a very tangible manner, a strategy which the novel continues to pursue during Leonard's great moment of horror.

The cutting up of Otto's corpse is depicted in minute detail and accompanied by Leonard's thoughts and feelings in the face of an unprecedented personal crisis. His main strategy to cope with this crisis is to read Otto's dead body as a sign of a defeated Germany: "They were not killing anyone here. Otto was dead. Solingen. They were dismantling him. Solingen. Nobody was missing. Solingen. Solingen. Otto is disarmed." (165) The grotesque tension between

Leonard's gruesome task and the abstractions he deploys to block it out culminates in the assertion: "What was on the table now was no one at all. It was the field of operations, it was a city far below he had been ordered to destroy." (p. 166)

By mentally objectifying Otto and turning him into a 'body politic' which symbolizes the defeat and division of Germany, Leonard manages to complete his bloody business. One could read this analogy as a mere defence mechanism which does not bring about a significant change in Leonard's attitude towards politics, but helps him to concentrate on the chaos in his private affairs. It is true that in trying to dispose of the cases into which the body parts are packed Leonard subsequently develops a certain proficiency in appropriating the language of espionage which helps him to fool British and American agents and to participate in the rather absurd game involving state secrets and clearance levels. On the other hand, even his betrayal of the joint British and American tunnel, known as 'Operation Gold', and the storage of Otto's remains in the tunnel may have certain diplomatic repercussions, but in effect they distance Leonard even further from politics and precipitate his return to a private and apolitical existence in London.

In his recent study on Ian McEwan (2007) Dominic Head presents a nuanced and sophisticated reading of Leonard's initiation and its potentially cathartic effects. He uses Julia Kristeva's theory of abjection in order to highlight the function of Otto Eckdorf's corpse for Leonard's process of development. According to Kristeva the corpse as the ultimate representation of the abject challenges notions of self and social stability and questions the production of meaning within the symbolic order. As Head explains:

> The 'insult' Leonard feels at the sight of Otto's innards [...] opens him up to an appreciation of the breakdown of meaning in abjection, where the threatened collapse of 'borders, positions, rules' emphatically 'disturbs identity, system, order'.[6]

If one accepts this hypothesis then Leonard's experience of the corpse as the site of the abject, the other of social order, also generates doubts about the validity of political orders and value systems. Leonard's betrayal of the tunnel operation could then be seen as a logical consequence of his disbelief in the meaning and significance of spying as a necessary practice of political entities in order to secure their hegemony in the global power game.

The cases which contain Otto's body parts develop an almost magical quality when used by Leonard in the spying game. While he tries to dispose of the cases in order to cover up the killing and mutilation of his rival he half-consciously employs them in order to eradicate the principles of the new world order by making everyone believe that they contain a great secret – that this secret is irrelevant for the course of international politics is of no importance. Once Leonard understands the rules of the game he realizes its absurdity. The depiction of the agents as players of games and of the tunnel as a "toytown, packed with boyish invention" (66) has alerted the reader to the ludic and regressive character ascribed to the spy world in *The Innocent* before Leonard becomes fully aware of it.

When Leonard is haunted by a Frankensteinian nightmare in which he restores Otto's dismembered corpse to physical integrity again, Head construes this scene as an indication of Leonard's desire to return to the supposedly safe haven of stable meanings and identities: "the apparent workings of a guilty conscience might also be read as a denial of the abject, as a reassertion of stable identities that are being effaced in the reaction to the corpse."[7] The validity of this interpretation is confirmed by Kristeva's meditations on the elements which are apt to counter the forces of abjection and "to save me from death: childhood, science, among other things."[8] Interestingly, scientific abstraction and childish adventurousness are the two spheres or modes which dominate the spy world and 'Operation Gold', therefore Leonard's decision to hide the cases containing Otto's corpse in the tunnel appear like a wish to ban abjection by containing its material evidence in a place which seems to promise an end to the powers of horror, before the novel exposes the operation's political significance as a chimera and the tunnel as a hotbed of abjection. In the words of Claire Colebrook:

> However, the supposed position of mastery that the tunnel would enable is exposed, at the end of the novel, to have been always already redundant. Politics takes on the structure of the open secret; nothing is truly held apart, and there is no ultimate sense or truth that is contested. What must be maintained, though, is the fantasy of communication – that tunnels, codes, passages and networks are ultimately subtended by a prior truth.[9]

In the novel's postscript which reveals the whole extent of the political intricacy and futility of the tunnel operation Leonard comes to see the prospect of a union with Maria in conjunction with a potential fall of the Berlin Wall, and he imagines taking Maria to Berlin in order to "take a good long look at the Wall together before it was all torn down." (226) There is no talk anymore of actively building a new Europe, instead, the process of history is taken in by Leonard from a distance, as a passive observer. This new attitude, which is sharply contrasted with the frantic activity of the secret services in post-war Berlin, may strike the reader as disturbingly apolitical, as a regressive withdrawal into cosy privacy and inner emigration, a retreat from the "vandalized, garbage-strewn arena of politics".[10]

On the other hand, an insight into the limited options of the individual subject in highly complex political situations might be a more realistic stance than narcissistic self-delusions about the opportunity for political agency. This may be seen as a starting point for a more sceptical political commitment which abandons claims to universal solutions, but is able to focus on the particular without losing the universal out of sight. McEwan's own reflections about the relationship of the novelist's art and politics seem to tie in with such a demystification of official and institutionalised politics:

> The successful or memorable novels we think of as 'political' are always written *against* a politics. Satire, mockery, reduction to absurdity, direct attack or simply the detailed, remorseless naming of what is there, these are the novel's weapons against political, or for that matter, military or religious systems which restrict or deny human possibility.[11]

Focussing on the individual is therefore not necessarily an indication of silent resignation on the part of the novelist, but the only possible point of departure: "By measuring individual human worth, the novelist reveals the full enormity of the State's crime when it sets out to crush that individuality."[12]

Nevertheless, it would be rather short-sighted to see the end of the novel as an affirmation of Leonard's new political awareness and as a celebration of an individuality which has not been "crushed" by the machinations of the authorities. As Christoph Schöneich has shown in a study on the post-war English *Bildungsroman*, one is well-advised to differentiate between the character and reception perspectives of the novel in order not to miss an important point: inspired by Maria's letter, an older and superficially more mature Leonard again indulges in fantasies of childhood and innocence as if he had never stared into the abyss of abjection. The postscript is redolent of a nostalgic sentimentality which Schöneich does not ascribe to the novel in its entirety, but to Leonard's character perspective which is enmeshed in forms of romantic misrecognition all over again.[13] The cathartic effects of the dismemberment scene on Leonard, as flimsy as they may have been in the first place, seem to have washed away completely and his narcissistic delusional fantasies of a reunion with Maria are once more short-circuited with naïve hopes for political renewal. As Claire Colebrook has recently argued it is ultimately the reader's insight into the impact of such regressive desires for the establishment of power structures and into the mechanisms of *méconnaissance* which represent a keen political edge in McEwan's works:

> Images of children dominate McEwan's fiction precisely because he sees that desire for perfect stillness and self-enclosure as ultimately political: it charges all our images of humanity, of communication, of self-hood and time. […] True radicalism would not be the simple opposite of this illusory closed and self-perfecting wholeness; radicalism would not be the emergence from childhood into a position of mastery, progression, pure becoming and knowledge. Instead, mastery may be more radical – closer to the root of the political – by examining the fantasies of power, wholeness, domination and mastered time. Similarly, at the level of form, it might be more radical to present and render explicit the drive to conservation, the drive to remain a world unto oneself. This would yield a fiction that could be read at one and the same time as the most alluring and seductive of narratives, while also presenting the politics and desire of being seduced into the image of organic wholeness.[14]

Eventually, horror does provide cathartic effects for Leonard but, ironically, catharsis also has new horror in store for him – the horror of disorder, instability and a sustained loss of faith in the viability of political and individual identities. Therefore, he continues to seek refuge in a form of pseudo-adolescent identity moratorium which also precludes him from developing a 'mature' concept of the political and a more circumspect political awareness, a task which is ultimately left to the reader's activity.

Ian McEwan's next novel, *Black Dogs*, published in 1992, covers similar ground as *The Innocent*. As in the previous novel, World War II as the pivotal event in 20th century history is shown in its impact on the private lives and political attitudes of the central characters. And it is again the private experience of violence which puts world politics into a completely new perspective.

When June Tremaine is attacked by two black dogs in the south of France in 1946, she interprets this encounter as the ultimate turning point in her life which radically challenges her individual and political identities. After it, she leaves the Communist Party, falls out with her husband Bernard and leaves England to spend her life in search of spiritual enlightenment in the south of France.

The novel's narrative structure is non-linear and fragmented, which is why June's near-death experience with the black dogs, which were supposedly left there by Gestapo forces after the war, is alluded to as early as chapter I, but never fully revealed until the novel's final pages. This analytical structure intensifies the impact of the black dog episode as a moment of vision and catharsis which re-shapes June's view of life and her attitude towards religion:

> I met evil and discovered God. I call it my discovery, but of course, it's nothing new, and it's not mine. Everyone has to make it for himself. People use different language to describe it. I suppose all the great religions began with individuals making inspired contact with a spiritual reality and then trying to keep that knowledge alive.[15]

June's view of the central importance of this episode for her life is repudiated by her rationalist husband Bernard who dismisses the conclusions his wife draws from the alleged encounter with the animals as irrational. What is more, he deems June's retreat from life in her French hermitage socially and politically irresponsible.

Apart from Bernard it is June's son-in-law Jeremy who has to come to terms with the interpretation of the black dog episode, writing, as he is, a memoir of June's life, a memoir in which the black dogs are supposed to form the centrepiece. His response to June's narrative is ambivalent, he is "both beguiled and sceptical" (50) and observes:

> Turning-points are the inventions of story-tellers and dramatists, a necessary mechanism when a life is reduced to, traduced by, a

> plot, when a morality must be distilled from a sequence of actions, when an audience must be sent home with something unforgettable to mark a character's growth. Seeing the light, the moment of truth, the turning-point, surely we borrow these from Hollywood or the Bible to make retroactive sense of an overcrowded memory? (Ibid.)

Jeremy's self-referential comment on the constructive character of life narratives expresses his doubts about the function of the encounter for June, but there are other open questions: what exactly are the dogs supposed to represent? On the one hand, June insists on their physical reality: "'No, you clot. Not symbolic!' I hear her correcting me. 'Literal, anecdotal, true. Don't you know, I was nearly killed.'" (28) Despite June's insistence on the physical reality of the dogs they gain an undeniable metaphorical quality in both her own and Jeremy's narratives. By challenging a symbolic reading of the dogs it is June herself who provides the necessary cues for their intertextual and mythological interpretation:

> I'm not saying these animals were anything other than what they appeared to be. Despite what Bernard says, I don't actually believe they were Satan's familiars, Hell Hounds or omens from God, or whatever he tells people I believe. […] I haven't mythologised these animals. I've made use of them. They set me free. I discovered something (59).

Although June lives like a recluse in France, the novel goes out of its way not to portray her embrace of religion as a complete withdrawal from political responsibility. Instead, her experience of horror and the lessons she draws from it serve as a comment for the entire novel, which can be read as a history of violence in the private and public spheres since World War II and the Holocaust. June is acutely aware of the connections between minor acts of violence and the atrocities committed in the name of political ideologies, connections which in her view are located in the human psyche:

> The evil I'm talking about lives in us all. It takes hold in an individual, in private lives, within a family, and then it's children who suffer most. And then, when the conditions are right, in different countries, at different times, a terrible cruelty, a viciousness against life erupts, and everyone is surprised by the depth of

> hatred within himself. Then it sinks back and waits. It's something in our hearts. (172)

According to June, political commitment cannot be realized within the confines of ideologies or party politics. Like *The Innocent*, *Black Dogs* denies a view of the political which can be fitted into simple and straightforward binary terms.

It is Jeremy's function as narrator and judge of Bernard and June's competing testimonies which intensifies the reader's impression that the construction of stable oppositions will simply not do as an explanation of the world, let alone provide a solution to its problems. As many critics have pointed out, neither June and Bernard's nor Jeremy's accounts of the past are completely reliable, and coherence and closure are qualities which this novel does not possess in abundance.[16] How, then, does the novel's relativism allow for the construction of political commitment or a clear-cut political conviction? David Malcolm's question "How does all this connect?"[17] reflects the novel's elusive character:

> Perhaps it does not do so as clearly as one might hope. [...] But perhaps the novel does achieve a kind of coherence by suggesting that both rationality and non-rationality can lead to violence and the breakdown of civilized norms. [...] The problem is that the black dogs will return, mysterious metaphors of individual human wickedness and of European madness, or horribly rational products of that madness.[18]

But if the black dogs are construed in the novel as mythical creatures which cannot be eliminated, if their return is inevitable, does that not invite a reading which advocates an apolitical fatalism as the main response to the hovering shadows of evil? This is not necessarily the case. One could also read the novel as a powerful reminder of the need for political commitment which has to originate in the individual but must not stop there. The connections that the novel establishes between the private and the public, the individual and the collective, between biography and history, create a frame of reference which defies simple approaches to political action (as advocated by the early Bernard), but does demand forms of political commitment.[19]

Despite his doubts about his mother-in-law's spiritualism Jeremy notices that June has stared evil straight into the eye and has been transformed by that experience: "In repose her face had a chiselled, sepulchral look; it was a statue, a mask carved by a shaman to keep at bay the evil spirit." (28) Just as her face seems to be invested with an apotropaic quality, June's narrative provides Jeremy and, by extension, also the reader, with a strong antidote with which to confront the evil in the world and in themselves. Maybe it is June who has seen the truth about human nature, who can alert us to its dangers and who can warn us, as Nietzsche did, not to be "hanging in dreams on the back of a tiger."[20]

The novel's claim for the necessity of individual acts of retracing the horrors of history in order to make cathartic use of them is emphasised during Jeremy and Jenny's visit to Majdanek concentration camp. This visit represents one of the crucial scenes in *Black Dogs* because it illustrates how horror and violence are unable to affect the individual when they are rendered in abstract and anonymous terms, thereby overwhelming our emotional and moral sensibilities:

> The extravagant numerical scale, the easy-to-say numbers – tens and hundreds of thousands, millions – denied the imagination its proper sympathies, its rightful grasp of the suffering, and one was drawn insidiously to the persecutor's premise, that life was cheap, junk to be inspected in heaps. As we walked on, my emotions died. There was nothing we could do to help. There was no one to feed or free. We were strolling like tourists (110-111)

The well-meaning educational strategy of shaping a political and moral consciousness by simply presenting the plain and horrible facts backfires and produces both emotional distance and ethical indifference in Jeremy.[21] It is only through the individual confrontation with horror that a form of political activity, understood as a reflection on the nature of evil and how to deal with it, is conceivable in the novel. Jeremy comes face to face with his own propensity for violence in France when he beats up an abusive father who has hit his own child in a restaurant. His outrage erupts in an act of brutality which leaves him "horrified with myself" (131)[22] because it warns him of his own destructive potential and lays bare the ambiguity of his own moral frame of reference. It is this event which constitutes his own personal moment of catharsis and enables him to see the connections between individual and collective forms of violence and the problem of controlling them.

As I have shown, *The Innocent* and *Black Dogs* both construct turning points which provide forms of catharsis through the experience of horror for their protagonists. Leonard Marnham's dismemberment of Otto Eckdorf and June Tremaine's encounter with the black dogs are located at the intersection of the private and public spheres, creating a contact zone for the individual and the political, or, more precisely, an interstitial zone in which both spheres are merged and become inseparable. McEwan's use of cathartic horror in the two novels is reminiscent of Jacques Derrida's discussion of the *pharmakon*, which can be understood as poison and remedy at the same time[23]: the protagonists of both novels have to experience the raw dynamics of violence and the horrible face of death in order to appreciate life and to reconsider their social and political convictions, albeit with different long-term effects.

At the same time, Mc Ewan symbolically unleashes the black dogs for the reader, who is invited to share the fate of the literary characters and to develop altered perceptions of social and political orders and their claims to universal validity. Both narratives seem to stage a withdrawal from the overtly political, but in effect they manage to bring in a claim for political commitment and ethical awareness which displays a good deal of scepticism, but invites us to question the false promises of narrow political ideologies and grandiose doctrines of salvation.

Both texts "remain [...] open-ended voyage[s] of exploration of experience; and not only the experience of the victim, but of his oppressor, too. Tyranny has its roots and causes in human nature and this is the essential subject matter of the 'political' novelist."[24] Thus, the two novels incorporate the political in a manner which Derek Attridge has described in the following terms:

> [A]cts of literature do not operate directly upon the political realm. [...] But literature can act powerfully to hold the political and the ethical up for scrutiny by momentarily dissociating them from their usual pressing context, *performing* the ethical decision and the political gesture. Literature – when it is responded to as literature – is not a political instrument, yet it is deeply implicated in the political.[25]

"After such butchery, what better time?" asks a female character in McEwan's libretto for Michael Berkeley's opera *For You* (2008).[26] Considering that she refers to the cancer surgery she has just come out of this question seems inappropriately melodramatic, her own post-operative depression notwithstanding. The phrase does sound like an ironic echo, though, of McEwan's earlier fictions such as *The Innocent* and *Black Dogs*, in which 'butchery' changes the trajectories of the characters' lives and renders innocence and 'better times' impossible for them. Nevertheless, the butchery they either suffer or commit offers them and the reader forms of catharsis which broadens the scope of their responses to politics and history.

Notes

1   I would like like to thank my colleagues Stefan Glomb and Don Lowman for proofreading this essay. Any mistakes are entirely my responsibility.
2   Friedrich Nietzsche: *Philosophy and Truth: Selections from Nietzsche's Notebooks of the Early 1870s*, ed. and transl. Daniel Breazeale, Atlantic Highlands, N.J., 1979, p. 80.
3   Jack Slay: *Ian McEwan*, New York, 1996, p. 136.
4   Kiernan Ryan: *Ian McEwan*, Plymouth, 1994, p. 60.
5   Ian McEwan: *The Innocent*, London, 2005 [1990], p. 169. Further references to this edition will be included in the text.
6   Dominic Head: *Ian McEwan*, Manchester, 2007, p. 95 [Julia Kristeva: *The Powers of Horror, An Essay on Abjection*, transl. Léon S. Roudiez, New York, 1982, p. 4]). Cf. Peter Childs: *The Fiction of Ian McEwan*, New York, 2005, p. 88: "The dead, dissected body is the point where signifying halts and hermeneutics ends, where the final ground of meaning is unmasked and metaphysical delusions implode. Hence the simultaneous horror and liberating gusto with which *The Innocent* assaults and defiles the human form."
7   Head 97.
8   Kristeva 4.
9   Claire Colebrook: "*The Innocent* as Anti-Oedipal Critique of Cultural Pornography". – In: Sebastian Groes (Ed.): *Ian McEwan*, London, New York, 2009, p. 54.
10 Ian McEwan: *A Move Abroad*, London, 1989, p. xi.
11 Idem.
12 Ibid. xii.

13 Cf. Christoph Schöneich: *Edmund Talbot und seine Brüder. Englische Bildungsromane nach 1945*, Tübingen, 1999, pp. 186-187.
14 Colebrook 56.
15 Ian McEwan: *Black Dogs*, London, 1993 [1992], p. 60. Further references to this edition will be included in the text.
16 Cf. Jago Morrison "Narration and Unease in Ian McEwan's Later Fiction", *Critique*, 42:3, Spring 2001, 267: "On a variety of levels, McEwan's text bears witness not to that process of coherence but rather to the insecurity or discordance of the biographical, historical, and metaphysical themes of which it is woven. Whether its central narrative motif of the black dogs is able to transfigure that discordance into a moment of durability or encapsulating meaning remains radically in question." Cf. also Marc Delrez: "Escape into Innocence: Ian McEwan and the Nightmare of History", *ARIEL* 26:2, 1995, 17 and Head 116.
17 David Malcolm: *Understanding Ian McEwan*, Columbia, 2002, p. 153.
18 Idem.
19 For an analysis of the role of narrative strategies for the novel's ethical dimension cf. Lars Heiler "The Holocaust and Aesthetic Transgression in Contemporary British Fiction". – In: Stefan Horlacher, Stefan Glomb & Lars Heiler (Eds.), *Transgression and Taboo in British Literature From the Renaissance to the Present*, New York, forthcoming spring 2010, pp. 311-313.
20 Cf. note 2.
21 Cf. Philip Griffiths: *Externalised Texts of the Self. Projections of the Self in Selected Works of English Literature*, Tübingen, 2008, p. 142: "[...] the concentration camp itself directly incorporates the potential for cruelty it was designed to guard against after the Second World War; as a marker buoy of the grand narrative of history [...] it smothers the emotional impact of personal histories – the *petites histoires* – on the collective imagination and is turned into a living symbol of humantiy's potential for cruelty and violence, an ahistorical anthropological constant that undermines the ideology of progress and the belief in a 'We Shall Overcome'." Cf. also Anja Müller-Wood and J. Carter Wood "Bringing the Past to Heel: History, Identity and Violence in Ian McEwan's *Black Dogs*", *Literature & History* 16:2, 2007, 49-50.
22 It is not until a young French woman stops him from his uncontrolled rage by saying "Ça suffit" (131) that he is able to realize what he has done.
23 Cf. Derrida's characterisation of the *pharmakon* as "that which, presenting itself as a poison, may retrospectively reveal itself in the truth of its curative power" (Jacques Derrida: *Dissemination*, transl. Barbara Johnson, Chicago, 1981, p. 128).
24 McEwan 1983: xii.
25 Derek Attridge: *The Singularity of Literature*, London, 2004, 119-120.
26 Ian McEwan: *For You*, London, 2008, p. 42.

Bibliography

Attridge, Derek: *The Singularity of Literature*, London, 2004.
Childs, Peter: *The Fiction of Ian McEwan*, New York, 2005.
Colebrook, Claire: "The Innocent as Anti-Oedipal Critique of Cultural Pornography". – In: Sebastian Groes (Ed.): *Ian McEwan*, London, New York, 2009, 43-56.
Delrez, Marc: "Escape into Innocence: Ian McEwan and the Nightmare of History", *ARIEL* 26:2, 1995, 7-23.
Derrida, Jacques: *Dissemination*, transl. Barbara Johnson, Chicago, 1981.
Griffiths, Philip: *Externalised Texts of the Self. Projections of the Self in Selected Works of English Literature*, Tübingen, 2008.
Head Dominic: *Ian McEwan*, Manchester, 2007.
Heiler, Lars: "The Holocaust and Aesthetic Transgression in Contemporary British Fiction". – In: Stefan Horlacher, Stefan Glomb & Lars Heiler (Eds.): *Transgression and Taboo in British Literature From the Renaissance to the Present*, New York, forthcoming spring 2010, 307-328.
Kristeva, Julia: *Powers of Horror. An Essay on Abjection*, transl. Léon S. Roudiez, New York, 1982.
Malcolm, David: *Understanding Ian McEwan*, Columbia, 2002.
McEwan, Ian: *A Move Abroad*, London, 1989 [1983].
---: *Black Dogs*, London, 1993 [1992].
---: *For You*, London, 2008.
---: *The Innocent*, London, 2005 [1990].
Morrison, Iago: "Narration and Unease in Ian McEwan's Later Fiction", *Critique*, 42:3, *Spring 2001, 253-268.*
Müller-Wood, Anja, and J. Carter Wood: "Bringing the Past to Heel: History, Identity and Violence in Ian McEwan's Black Dogs", *Literature & History* 16:2, 2007, 43-56.
Nietzsche, Friedrich: Philosophy and Truth: *Selections from Nietzsche's Notebooks of the Early 1870s*, ed. and transl. Daniel Breazeale, Atlantic Highlands, N.J., 1979.
Ryan, Kiernan: *Ian McEwan*, Plymouth, 1994.
Schöneich, Christoph: *Edmund Talbot und seine Brüder*. Englische Bildungsromane nach 1945, Tübingen, 1999.
Slay, Jack: *Ian McEwan*, New York, 1996.

Elsa Cavalié (Université de Toulouse)

"She would rewrite the past so that the guilty became the innocent": Briony's House of Fiction

It may seem unusual to compare Henry James and Ian Mc Ewan, but both of them built a novel or a house of fiction which began with a chance meeting with their heroine, as it were: in the preface to *the Portrait of a Lady*, James describes how his novel originated in the "sense of a single character, the character and aspect of a particular engaging young woman, to which all the usual elements of a 'subject', certainly of a setting, were to need to be superadded"[1] while in an interview McEwan declared that *Atonement* started with:

> a paragraph out of nowhere about a girl with some wild flowers in her hand, coming into a rather elegant room, aware of a young man gardening outside [...] and when I finished these six hundred words I thought 'I need to know more about this, I want to know who she is, when this is and where this is [...]' and then sort of started again this time inventing Briony who seemed to appear 'ready-made'.[2]

Then, constructing the novel consisted in, so to speak, 'building a Jamesian house' around Briony, finding the story and the place that could hold the "sense of her character". Such a house of fiction must be taken literally; McEwan's rewriting of the thirties revolves around a central country house, a place which stands at the crossroads between literary and architectural traditions, where, as Linda Hutcheon puts it: "All must be used; all must also be put into question, as architecture 'writes' history through its modem re-contextualizing of the forms of the past." (29)

Tallis House is indeed perceived as an ambiguous symbol, poised between modernity and decay – referring to modernist literary houses, not as hypotextual models, but rather as a means to enter into a conversation with tradition. The novel thus uses the artistic tradition, whether it be literary or architectural, to make a political point and indict Englishness as an 'invented tradition'. Furthermore, the geography of the house itself functions as a metaphor of the 'disorderly' quality of its inhabitants that sheds light on Briony's attempt to come to terms with the chaos of existence and to confront Otherness. Then, by the means of the artistic recreation of the past, an intricate web of spatial and architectural resonances unfolds, allowing for the need to 'go over' what happened. However, the elusive figure of the Other always escapes Briony, and the novel hints at the fact that her true atonement may lie in renouncing control.

The first part of the novel is set at Tallis House – a country house which appears to be very much part of the English architectural tradition, albeit not in a positive way. Indeed, the architecture of Tallis House ironically illustrates the fin-de-siècle departure from classicism that saw several country house owners develop what Mark Girouard calls architectural 'elephantiasis'[3], that is to say a frenetic rebuilding of country houses in the Gothic fashion:

> Morning sunlight, or any light, could not conceal the ugliness of the Tallis home – barely forty years old, bright orange brick, squat, lead-paned baronial Gothic, to be condemned one day in an article by Pevsner, or one of his team, as a tragedy of wasted chances, and by a younger writer of the modern school as "charmless to a fault." An Adam-style house had stood here until destroyed by fire in the late 1880s. What remained was the artificial lake and island with its two stone bridges supporting the driveway, and, by the water's edge, a crumbling stuccoed temple.[4]

Built in order to offer a suitable seat for the new money of the Tallis family, "a Gothic house stood for good principles as well as good cheer"[5] Girouard notes, the house seems to be lost in time, stranded as it is between the beautiful house that once was, the ugly house that is and the impressive house that could have been. Still, mentioning Pevsner is not only to be taken as a scholarly "effet de reel" and the reference to a potential article by a renowned theorist of Englishness draws attention a paradox: what is considered as "essentially English" in the architecture of Tallis House is, in fact, "essentially fake" (one may notice the lexical field of fallacy in the passage, with words like "stuccoed" or "artificial"). Englishness is thus likened to a social construct, or Barthesian "myth". Indeed, when Mrs Tallis thinks of the house, she remembers that "her father-in-law's intention [...] was to *create* an ambience of solidity and family tradition." (145, italics mine) The idea that tradition might be a deliberate, socially-orientated creation, likens the English country house to an 'invented tradition', to borrow Hobsbawm's word[6], and quite a successful one at that, for the house does provide the viewer with "an impression of timeless, unchanging calm" (145) although it was only built forty years before.

With *Atonement*, McEwan wanted to "enter a conversation with modernism and its dereliction of duty" (Interview Silverblatt). Critics often locate the heart of that conversation in Cyril Connoly's letter warning Briony against the dangerous attractions of "the crystalline present moment" and "the techniques of Mrs. Woolf" (312). However, it could be argued that the dialogue with modernism is also carried on through the numerous references to famous 'literary' houses which, like Tallis House blossomed in the first half of the twentieth century.

Let us recall, for instance, the emblematic *Howards End* and *Brideshead Revisited*, whose temporal and geographical framework are very close to that of *Atonement*, signaling the transition from innocence to bitter experience, from idealistic pre-modernism to reactionary nostalgia. Both novels claim that an 'English *genius loci*' inhabits the country house but question its survival when faced with industrialisation and modernity. In *Atonement*, the small temple near the house signals the remains of the religious within both the estate and the novel, so that the spirit of the place is embodied both by the domestic and mundane country house, and by the decorative temple, built in 1780 to connote some kind of spiritual presence. This dual presence may recall the house and tree in Forster's *Howards End* where "house and tree transcended any similes of sex. [...] Yet they kept within limits of the human. Their message was not of eternity, but of hope on this side of the grave"[7]. However, McEwan's novel offers a much darker take on the presence of the spiritual within the English country house, for whatever remains of the original spirit of the house is in an advanced state of decomposition. The temple is soiled by "moisture", "mould" and "the droppings of various birds and animals" (72). The windows of the temple have even "been smashed by Leon and his friends in the late twenties" (72): for McEwan the message seems to be of a 'lack of hope on this side of the grave'.

So that McEwan may be closer to *Brideshead Revisited* and its chapel which offers a vision of in betweenness in a world believed to be slowly decomposing because of the absence of God. As in *Atonement*, the chapel is simultaneously old and new – "rebuilt with the old stones behind the old walls; it was the last of the new house to come, the first to go."[8] But once again, the relationship to the intertext is one of subversion: while Brideshead's chapel was a beacon helping Lady Marchmain not to yield to her husband's lapse in morality, the island temple is the very place where Lola is raped. McEwan thus uses the architectural tradition to make a political point: the reader is not encouraged to have a nostalgic reading of that architectural emblem of Englishness, nor to interpret its decayed appearance as a sign of decaying moral values, but rather as an indictment of the myth of Englishness.

This ambiguous relationship of *Atonement* to the literary canon entails a questioning of the status of the interrelated notions of 'fake' and 'parody' in the novel. Like the "Surrey Hills transformed into a roasting Savannah" (38) in the novel, is *Atonement* only written as an antithesis to *Howards End*? Does McEwan's self-confessed use of "slightly mannered prose, slightly held in, little formal, tiny bit archaic" (Interview Silverblatt) only aim at creating a more realistic 'literary setting'? Or does it operate a systematic subversion of the Edwardian/Georgian novel that could liken it to what Jameson calls pastiche – "a neutral practice without any of parody's ulterior motives"[9]?

To go back to the image of the temple, it may work as a punctum in the landscape but it has indeed always been fake, since it "was intended as a point of interest, an eye-catching feature to enhance the pastoral ideal, and had of course no religious purpose at all" (73). It corresponds to what Jameson disparagingly defines as "historicism" in architecture "the random cannibalisation of all the styles of the past"[10]. This architectural trend is later epitomized by the transparent transformation of Tallis House into a luxury hotel "not unpleasant in itself, if you did not know what had once been there" (363), emphasizing the fact that, to quote Jameson again, "aesthetic production today has become integrated into commodity production generally"[11]. Yet, despite its very obvious status as a symptom of a bygone era, the temple cannot be discarded as mere simulacrum, to use Baudrillard's definition – "a question of substituting the signs of the real for the real"[12]. The dynamics of bereavement and loss resemiotize pastiche and its mechanical, purposeless quality, to acknowledge the humane dimension of loss and disconnectedness:

> The idea that the temple, wearing its own black band, grieved for the burned-down mansion, that it yearned for a grand and invisible presence, bestowed a faintly religious ambience. Tragedy had rescued the temple from being entirely a fake. (73)

Then, just like in *Brideshead* and *Howards End*, the country house in *Atonement* seems to evoke the in betweenness of a changing world and its ambiguous relationship with loss and nostalgia. Perhaps we should not speak so much of hypotext and hypertext, the one influencing the other, but rather see it as a case of "refraction" – defined by Susana Onega and Christian Gutleben as "involv[ing] the assumption of a dialectic relation between the canonical and postmodernist texts, affecting the result as well as the source, the new text as well as the old one, the modern product as well as the original prototype."[13] Then, one might argue that reading *Atonement* offers a new perspective on the previous 'countryhouse novels' and redefines the ambiguous relationship between nostalgia and Englishness thus making it a parody in Linda Hutcheon's sense – "repetition with critical distance that allows ironic signalling of difference at the very heart of similarity"[14]. The novel is then placed in a dialectic relationship to the artistic canon that sheds lights on the contemporary temptation to nostalgia.

However, Tallis House is not only a powerful symbol of the English tradition: in the first section of the novel, the reader thus discovers a series of habited spaces (often bedrooms) conveying a sense of their owners' personalities. Then a second topography of the building, mapping the intimate space, may be detected. Indeed, one can see in each of the characters' bedrooms a relatively straightforward correspondence between their characterisations and the descriptions of the rooms. The remote quality of Mrs Tallis's relationship to her family may for instance be detected in her familiar environment:

> She would soothe the household, which seemed to her, from the sickly dimness of the bedroom, like a troubled and sparsely populated continent from whose forested vastness competing elements made claims and counterclaims upon her restless attention. (70)

The hypallage – "sickly dimness" – encapsulates the essence of Mrs Tallis, whose life seems to be a long succession of migraines and bedrest. Somewhat like Mrs Ramsay in *To the Lighthouse* (1927) the matriarch represents the centre of the house, a protecting force which takes care of her husband and children, while remaining, in McEwan's novel, a disincarnate presence, powerless when it comes to influencing the course of events. Hiding in the shadows of her bedroom, her last decision in this scene – refusing to open the curtain and putting her sunglasses on – represents an apt metaphor of her refusal to commit herself emotionally.

Likewise, the twins' bedroom offers a warped image of their own personalities: "Their room was a pitiful mess of clothes, wet towels, orange peel, torn-up pieces of a comic arranged around a sheet of paper, upended chairs partly covered by blankets and the mattresses at a slew" (99-100). The orange peel cannot but remind the reader of the Quincey children's vivid hair colour ("Her cousins' colouring was too vivid – virtually fluorescent! – to be concealed", 10) and the phrase "pitiful mess" evokes the boys' bewilderment regarding their parents' divorce and their exile at Tallis House. Similarly, the wet towel might bring to mind the boys frequent tears and the fact that Pierrot often wets his bed. The general impression of the bedroom is one of messy proliferation, quite in keeping with the boys' states of mind, that one might read as a proleptic hint of their subsequent escape from Tallis House. In that description, the relationship of the characters to their daily environment is, according to Philippe Hamon's terminology, "semio-logic"[15]: "for the character entertains a relation of 'resemblance' to its environment and can almost be described in the same way" (my translation, E.C.).

Similarly, the description of Robbie's and Cecilia's bedrooms is made on an 'archeological mode' as each strata of personal belongings represents an era of their lives. Thus, Robbie's bedroom allows McEwan to subtly represent the past of his character through the items scattered around his room: his "hiking gear – boots, alpenstock, leather knapsack" (81), the anatomy textbook ("*Gray's Anatomy* was open by a folio pad of his own drawings", 82), his favourite novels and poems ("Beyond the compass were his copies of Auden's Poems and Housman's *A Shropshire Lad*", 82) and the typewriter (82) endow Robbie with what E.M. Forster would call a "roundness of character"[16]. Yet, the almost photographic impression of Robbie's bedroom is not limited to figuring his past. There also is a proleptic dimension to his untidiness: "The unmade bed, the mess of discarded clothes, a towel on the floor, the room's equatorial warmth were disablingly sensual" (81). One may read those as a hint of the coming love scene with Cecilia. Then the photographic vision of Robbie's bedroom might remind one of Barthes' comments about photography – "there is a superposition here: of reality and the past"[17] – insofar as it gives a perspective on what "has been"[18] and what is.

The treatment of Cecilia as a character is indeed quite close to Robbie's. Her room evokes her years at Cambridge and the undecided state of mind:

> Cecilia knew she could not go on wasting her days in the stews of her untidied room, lying on her bed in a haze of smoke, chin propped on her hand, pins and needles spreading up through her arm as she read her way through Richardson's Clarissa. (21)

Like Robbie, her position in her bedroom – an intimate space – both gives information about her past and her future, for the "pins and needles" she feels while reading seem to suggest that she is not cut out for a career as an intellectual, or even a passive existence like her mother's, but rather the more active part which she will take as a nurse during the war.

Still, although the kaleidoscopic vision of the various bedrooms may convey a sense of chaos, because of the unifying force of "disorder", a unity of vision is paradoxically achieved. Whether it be the twins, Cecilia, Robbie or even Mrs. Tallis, the common element between all the characters' 'intimate spaces' indeed seems to be disorder. Briony, the only character who values order, is particularly bemused by her sister's untidiness:

> What was the impulse that prevented Cecilia from replacing the caps and lids and screwtops of her makeup and perfumes? Why

125

> did she never empty her stinking ashtray? Or make her bed, or open a window to let in the fresh air? The first drawer she tried opened only a couple of inches – it was jammed, crammed full of bottles and a cardboard package. Cecilia might have been ten years older, but there really was something quite hopeless and helpless about her. (177)

It is striking to notice how, in Briony's mind, the order/disorder dichotomy is associated with the opposition between open and closed spaces. Screwtops have to be replaced, the bed made (and thus closed), the drawer closed, maybe betraying Briony's urge to 'contain the present' as a child and later attempt at encapsulating the past into a narrative when she has become a writer. Indeed, unlike her sister and the other members of her family, Briony lives in a completely ordered space:

> She was one of those children possessed by a desire to have the world just so. Whereas her big sister's room was a stew of unclosed books, unfolded clothes, unmade bed, unemptied ashtrays, Briony's was a shrine to her controlling demon. [...] Her straight-backed dolls in their many-roomed mansion appeared to be under strict instructions not to touch the walls; the various thumb-sized figures to be found standing about her dressing table – cowboys, deep-sea divers, humanoid mice – suggested by their even ranks and spacing a citizen's army awaiting orders (4-5)

One may notice that in both excerpts, Cecilia's bedroom is described through privative suffixes: "quite hope*less* and help*less*" and then "*un*closed books, *un*folded clothes, *un*made bed, *un*emptied ashtrays" (italics mine, E.C.). In the same manner "disorder" is linguistically derived from "order" – a value she cannot think away from – her description of Cecilia's room appears to be the photographic negative of her own, emphasizing the things that should have been. Order is furthermore associated with rigidity, "*straight*-backed dolls" obey "*strict* instructions" (italics mine) in a sentence where the alliteration in "str" conveys a sense of awkwardness. From the very first pages of the novel, it is clear for the observant reader that the young girl's relationship to order is problematic, and the use of the word "demon" can even be interpreted as a proleptic hint of her future "crime". According to Dominic Head:

> The young Briony's wish for a harmonious, organised world is a mark of her immature inability to accept contingency and the randomness of experience. This is also the source of her 'crime'.[19]

For it is Briony's irresistible attraction towards a world 'according to her image', that is to say ordered, that provokes Robbie's false accusation and, paradoxically, the resulting chaos in hers and her family's lives.

However, the disorder that prevails in the different rooms of the country house may also be interpreted as a metaphor of Briony's literary project. One can re-interpret the order/disorder dichotomy as emblematic of the difficulty in knowing the Other that might echo Keats' negative capability: "I mean Negative Capability, that is when a man is capable of being in uncertainties, mysteries, doubts, without any irritable reaching after fact and reason"[20]. Disorder may therefore be construed as pertaining to the proliferation of identities that cannot be encapsulated through/by the means of writing. According to Levinas:

> A human life – being born, dying – can be written by someone else, by the one who is not dead and that you call the 'survivor' or the 'historian'. But everybody perceives that there is an inescapable difference between the course of one's life and what will be kept of it in the chronological succession of events of history and the world.[21]

The first part of *Atonement* presents a narrative framework that may be likened to a classical tragedy: unity of time (a day), of place (Tallis House) and action – the mounting tension leading to Lola's rape and Robbie's arrest. Yet, the apparent smooth linearity is an elaborate illusion. The narrative framework, alternating between the different characters gives a kaleidoscopic, postmodern feeling to the story, the same events being described several times. Moreover, the revisiting of the same crucial places imbues those places with a particular intensity. Thus, the setting of the first encounter between Cecilia and Robbie – the library – becomes a space staging the process of rewriting, as the physical space also becomes a literary space.

The anamnesis seems to be likened to the presence of a chiaroscuro of light and darkness. Then the meeting between Robbie and Cecila in the library, as it is told through a focalisation on Robbie, is experienced as a call towards darkness/obscurity: "He followed her across the hall into the library which was in darkness, and waited by the door while she searched for the switch of a desk lamp" (132). An amorous dance between the two lovers soon starts, where Cecilia seems to disappear from Robbie's field of vision and to vanish into the darkness: "She moved beyond the light, down past the shelves. He stepped further into the room, not quite following her, but unwilling to let her out of close range." (132) Before Robbie finally finds Cecilia, the darkness intensifies and it is in a corner that the couple meets: "She was moving further away, toward the corner, into deeper shadow" (132) Choosing a corner to shelter their encounter is significant, for, according to Bachelard: "An imaginary room rises up around our bodies, which think that they are well hidden when we take refuge in a corner"[22]. The corner is a "haven that ensures us one of the things that we prize most highly – immobility"[23]. Cecilia and Robbie indeed experience their meeting as a moment out of conventional time. In that "sort of half-box, part walls, part door"[24] the play between light and shadows may be construed as symbolic of the awkward discovery of sexuality by the young couple – an ineffable moment not unlike D.H. Lawrence's *Lady Chatterley's Lover*. Earl Ingersoll indeed considers that scene as a pastiche of Lawrence: "The very same scene in the library, [...] screened by Robbie's memory, [offers] one of the most powerful pastiches of Lawrence's erotic representation in recent fiction."[25]

However, keeping in mind that Robbie's memory of the scene is still an emanation of Briony as the narrator, it is also possible to interpret this progression towards obscurity as another aspect of Briony's literary kaleidoscope – her attempt to enter the mind of the other in order to atone for her guilt, thus using art in order to confront Otherness. Then the library is not to be considered only as the setting for Robbie and Cecilia's lovemaking, but also as a metaphor of Briony's literary endeavour. Representing space and symbolically crossing the threshold of the room becomes a way to see the Other's truth and try to dissipate the shadows of Otherness.

When Briony revisits the same scene through a focalisation on the young girl that she was, darkness seems to dominate the scene. The threshold therefore becomes, as Philippe Hamon explains it, a variation of the window motif used to "frame" the description[26]:

> At first, when she pushed open the door and stepped in, she saw nothing at all. The only light was from a single green-glass desk lamp which illuminated little more than the tooled leather surface on which it stood. When she took another few steps she saw them, dark shapes in the furthest corner. (123)

Briony's crossing the threshold is far from a cognitive epiphany. She cannot see anything – a blindness that might hint at her inability to identify Lola's 'real' attacker a few hours later. As she gets nearer to the corner of the room, Robbie and Cecilia eventually take shape. The narrator's refusal to identify them by their first names and the emphasis on vague signifiers such as "them", "dark shapes" underline Briony's lack of visual and intellectual lucidity. That first vision of one of the crucial scenes of the novel is indeed dominated by the blur of optical illusion:

> The scene was so entirely a realization of her worst fears that she sensed that her overanxious imagination had projected the figures onto the packed spines of books. This illusion, or hope of one, was dispelled as her eyes adjusted to the gloom. (123)

The irony is telling: although Briony seems to realize that there is no visual illusion here, she is still tricked by her imagination into the wrong interpretation of what she sees. The striking image of Robbie and Cecilia as projected figures on the spines of books is both proleptic and metafictional: it announces the discovery, at the end of the novel, of Briony's authorship, for the young couple is nothing but the projection of Brionyvs psyche throughout the novel. Thus, the reader is tricked into the 'optical illusion' as well: like Briony he thinks that he is observing two people in the library when, in fact, he is only seeing avatars of Briony's literary conscience – creatures engendered by the chiaroscuro of memory.

One might notice that while the two figures have materialized in front of Briony, her sister's face remains inscrutable:

> Robbie moved in such a way that her view of her sister was completely obscured. Then Cecilia was struggling free, and he was letting her go. Briony stopped and said her sister's name. When she pushed past Briony there was no sign in Cecilia of gratitude or relief. Her face was expressionless, almost composed, and she looked right ahead to the door she was about to leave by. (123)

Cecilia's unreadable face may naturally be interpreted as McEwan's attempt to have the reader experience Briony's incomprehension towards the scene she witnesses. In that sense, the impenetrability of the young woman's face allows McEwan to build up the suspense until the next chapter – describing the encounter through Robbie's point of view. Yet, in that inscrutable face, one might also read the proof of Cecilia's inescapable Otherness. As Levinas explains it, it is in the relationship to the face that the Other becomes "absolutely Other"[27]. However, "the 'resistance' of the Other does not do violence to me, does not act negatively; it has a positive structure: ethical"[28]. In the heart of the library – a space of intimacy – one can read the traces of the unknowability of the Other.

Briony's attempt at atoning for her fault through the confrontation with Otherness echoes through the novel. Critics tend to regard *Atonement* as made of three separate, independent sections and a coda, and to focus more intensely on the first one. Yet, the three sections of the novel are far less separate than what may seem. An intricate web of correspondences and anamorphoses duplicates the spatial and narrative patterns of the first part. Then, the chiaroscuro of light and darkness, the difficulty in "containing" the Other that was so crucial to the library scene reverberates through the novel in a series of echoes. Thus *Atonement* depicts the endless return of the same, a never-ending rewriting of the past centred on the day when Briony "committed her crime" (156), in which spatial and architectural metaphors question the possibility "for a novelist" (371) to ever achieve atonement.

The numerous echoes emphasize the hauntingly circular quality of Briony's life and thoughts, while the web of connections is gradually amplified in order to reach beyond Briony's first urge to metaphorically retrace her steps through the rewriting of events. The global structure of the novel stresses this sensation: the book starts and ends with the performance of Briony's *Trials of Arabella* at Tallis House, thus bringing the narrative and spatial journey full circle. Indeed, the first section of the novel depicts the budding novelist as constantly going in and out of the house, striding the garden and the lawns, thus repossessing space – a perpetual movement both betraying her childish urge to control things and her desperate adult attempt at making sense of things by literally 'going over' them again.

Still, the metaphorical echoes of time and place are not limited to the first section of the novel: as the older Briony, assuming the position of narrator, strives for atonement, several series of echoes between section one, and the two other sections offer a curious sense of anamorphosis: Briony follows the rapist across the park in the dark in Part One, thinking she is following Robbie, just like in Part Three, going on a visit to Cecilia and Robbie leads her to Paul Marshall and Lola's wedding. The sense of anamorphosis is further heightened by the fact that Briony – expecting "a Gothic cathedral" (322) not unlike Tallis House – finds a church "like a Greek temple" (323) – ironically recalling the place where Paul and Lola's union truly began. One may also mention Robbie's rescue mission of the twins in section one which leads him to his downfall, just like in Dunkirk, his attempts to take Nettle and Mace safely back home only drive him closer his own death.

The parallels between Part Two and Three are of a different kind, for they are not thematically related to the 'criminal day' of section one but rather signal a return to the human. Yet, through all three parts, like in the library scene the process of reconfiguration and endless echoing seems to stumble against the irreducible unknowability of the Other, materialised by their blurred outlines, as Briony – caught "fogs of literary imagination" (370) struggles to literally and metaphorically 'define' it. Paul Crostwaithe, in his article on *Atonement*, has noticed how the Conradian technique of "delayed decoding" appears to be particularly relevant to the analysis of the novel (60). The parallel may be further developed, insofar as there is, at the centre of *Atonement*, what Forster called "a vapour rather than a jewel"[29] – not Jim's but Briony's guilt. Using a literary technique quite reminiscent of Conrad's, the difficulty in "entering the mind of the other" is expressed by the frequent visual blurring of the characters. The impossibility for Briony to truly enter Robbie's mind in order to atone for what she has done to him is enhanced by the elusive quality of his physical outline at key moments. When she sees him near the house, at the moment when he gives her the letter, Robbie is merely a "white shape which seemed at first to be part of the pale stone of the parapet. Staring at it dissolved its outlines, but within a few paces it had taken on a vaguely human form" (93). Still, as a writer, the very impossibility of ever capturing the essence of the Other is what makes the attempt so captivating: "that episode in the sunlight was not quite so as interesting as the dusk" (115). According to critic Bernhard Waldenfels, that discovery "does not mean that there is something behind the masks and clothes the other wears, it rather means that the other's otherness eludes every qualification we may apply"[30].

Moreover, this elusiveness is confirmed rather than dispelled, by moments of blinding clarity in part two and three as the faces of the wounded come into horrific focus. As Briony becomes a nurse like her sister, the possibility of an escape from the self-inflicted prison of her guilt is evoked, for compassion for another's suffering may be the true "entering the minds of others". Thus, Briony faces the gruesome death of a young soldier, just as a half-fascinated and half-horrified Robbie had to witness the tragic death of a Flemish mother and her child (236-7) and this parallel may offer a humane escape from the moral aporia of her guilt. When Briony takes care of a wounded French private, she discovers the strange power of his defenceless face:

> It was hard to think of him as a soldier. He had a fine, delicate face, with dark eyebrows and dark green eyes, and a soft full mouth. His face was white and had an unusual sheen, and the eyes were unhealthily radiant. His head was heavily bandaged. (305)

The description of the private's face is focused on its surface rather than the identity of the young man behind the face. Still the feeling of beauty lasts only a while and Briony soon discovers that the young boy has been horribly disfigured and is missing half his face. However, one might read in that encounter with the Other one of the final echoes of the book. By nursing a French soldier just out of Dunkirk, Briony symbolically tries to redress her wrongs. While it is not Robbie she takes care of, the fact that she accepts to simply be with the French soldier as he dies, shows to a certain extent that she now accepts the chaos inherent to life without trying to control it. Accepting Otherness also has a political dimension: for Levinas, seeing the Other's face and recognizing its fundamental unknowability is what prevents one from violence. Given *Atonement*'s powerful war subtext, the focus on Otherness is also a comment on World War Two, Nazi Germany and its radical attempt to obliterate Otherness through the Shoah.

It might be said that Briony's atonement consists in abandoning her "controlling demon", accepting Otherness as fascinatingly uncontrollable and ungraspable. *Atonement* – her house of fiction – may be interpreted precisely that way: its lack of resolution – especially in the much-discussed ending – eludes the reader's need for control, but offers him a enthralling textual maze in which to get lost, again and again. McEwan thus uses the artistic tradition in order to enhance the need to go back to history and to recognize its shortcomings in order to avoid an unjustified nostalgia. By focusing on the crucial importance of Otherness in the war context, the novel spurns the 'consolations of History' in order to make a political point about the necessity of a critical reading of the past.

Notes

1 Henry James: *Portrait of a Lady*, Harmondsworth, 2003, p. 7.
2 Silverblatt, Michael: *Interview with Ian McEwan* in "Bookworm", July, 11, 2002, KCR <http://www.kcrw.com/etc/programs/bw/bw020711ian_mcewan>.
3 Mark Girouard: *Life in the English Country House: A Social and Architectural History*, New Haven, 1979, p. 272.
4 Ian McEwan : *Atonement*, London, Vintage, 2002, p. 19. 'Further references to this edition will be included in the text.'
5 Girouard 1979, p. 27.
6 "'Invented tradition' is taken to mean a set of practices, normally governed by overtly or tacitly accepted rules and of a ritual or symbolic nature, which seek to inculcate certain values and norms of behaviour by repetition, which automatically implies continuity with the past. In fact, where possible, they normally attempt to establish continuity with a suitable historic past." Hobsbawm, Eric & Ranger, Terrence: *The Invention of Tradition*, Cambridge, 1983, p.1. Similarly, the building of Tallis House – a neo-Gothic house – is aimed at creating an apparent continuity with the past, making the Tallis a long-established family instead of newly-rich.
7 E.M. Forster: *Howards End*, Harmondsworth, 1989, p. 206.
8 Evelyn Waugh: *Brideshead Revisited*, Harmondsworth, 2003, p. 318.
9 Frederick Jameson: *Postmodernism or, the Cultural Logic of Late Capitalism*, Durham, 2005, p. 17.
10 *Ibid* 18.
11 *Ibid* 4.
12 Jean Baudrillard: *Simulacra and Simulation*, Ann Arbor, 1995, p. 4.
13 Susana Onega, & Christian Gutleben, Christian: *Refracting the Canon in Contemporary British Literature and Film*, p. 7

14 Linda Hutcheon : *Poetics of Postmodernism: History, Theory, Fiction*. London, Routledge, 1988 p. 26.
15 Philippe Hamon: *Du descriptif*. Paris, 1993, p. 106.
16 E.M. Forster: *Aspects of the Novel*, 1990, pp. 73-81.
17 Roland Barthes: *Camera Lucida*, New York, 1981, p. 76.
18 Ibid. 76.
19 Dominic Head: *Ian McEwan*, Manchester, 2007, p. 168.
20 In a letter to his brother, dated 22 December, 1817.
21 Emmanuel Levinas : *Ethique et Infini*, Paris, 1982, p. 73. (my translation)
22 Gaston Bachelard: *The Poetics of Space*, Boston: MA, 1994 p. 35.
23 Ibid 137.
24 Ibid 137.
25 Ingersoll, Earl G.: "Intertextuality in L. P. Hartley's The Go-Between and Ian McEwan's Atonement", *Forum for Modern Language Studies* 40.3 (July 2004), 250.
26 Philippe Hamon: *Du descriptif*, Paris, 1993, p. 175.
27 Emmanuel Levinas : *Totality and infinity: an essay on exteriority*, Springer, 1979, p. 40.
28 Ibid 197.
29 E.M. Forster : "Joseph Conrad: A Note" in Abinger Harvest, London, 1953, p. 138.
30 Bernhard Waldenfels: "Levinas and the Face of the Other" in *The Cambridge Companion to Levinas*, Cambridge, Cambridge U.P., 2002, p. 71.

Bibliography

Bachelard, Gaston: *The Poetics of Space,* Boston: MA, Beacon Press, 1994.
Barthes, Roland: *Camera Lucida*, New York, Hill and Wang, 1981.
--- *Mythologies*, London: Paladin, 1972.
Baudrillard, Jean: *Simulacra and Simulation*, Ann Arbor, University of Michigan Press, 1995.
Forster, E.M.: *Howards End,* Harmondsworth, Penguin Books, 1989. [1910]
---: "Joseph Conrad: A Note" in *Abinger Harvest*, London: Edward Arnold, 1953, pp. 136-141.
---: *Aspects of the Novel*, Penguin Books, 1990.
Girouard, Mark: *Life in the English Country House: A Social and Architectural History*, New Haven, Yale UP, 1979.
Hamon, Philippe: *Du descriptif*. Paris, Hachette Université, 1993.
Head, Dominic: *Ian McEwan*, Manchester, Manchester University Press, 2007.
Hobsbawm, Eric & Ranger, Terrence: *The Invention of Tradition*, Cambridge, CUP, 1983.

Hutcheon, Linda: *Poetics of Postmodernism: History, Theory, Fiction*, London, Routledge, 1988.

Ingersoll, Earl G.: "Intertextuality in L. P. Hartley's *The Go-Between* and Ian McEwan's *Atonement*", *Forum for Modern Language Studies* 40.3 (July 2004): 241-258.

James, Henry: "The Art of Fiction". In *The Art of Criticism,* University of Chicago Press, 1988: 165-196.

---: *Portrait of a Lady*, Harmondsworth: Penguin Classics, 2003.

Jameson, Frederick: *Postmodernism or, the Cultural Logic of Late Capitalism*, Durham: Duke University Press, 2005. [1991]

Lawrence, D.H.: *Lady's Chatterley's Lover*, Penguin, 1997.

Levinas, Emmanuel: *Ethique et Infini*, Paris, Le Livre de Poche, 1982.

---: *Totality and infinity: an essay on exteriority*, Springer, 1979.

McEwan, Ian: *Atonement*, London, Vintage, 2002. [2001]

Onega Susana, & Gutleben, Christian: *Refracting the Canon in Contemporary British Literature and Film* (Postmodern Studies 35), Rodopi, 2004.

Waldenfels, Bernhard: "Levinas and the Face of the Other" in *The Cambridge Companion to Levinas*, Cambridge, Cambridge U.P., 2002, pp. 63-81.

Waugh, Evelyn. *Brideshead Revisited*, Harmondsworth, Penguin Books, 2003. [1945]

Caroline Lusin (University of Heidelberg)

'We Daydream Helplessly'.
The Poetics of (Day)Dreams in Ian McEwan's Novels

1. 'The Imagination Spins'. Ian McEwan and the Device of the Dream Play

In a *Guardian* article entitled "Only Love and Then Oblivion" (2001), Ian McEwan shared his thoughts on the impact of 9/11 with the public, focusing on the emotional narrative which the events of that day instigated:

> I suspect that in between times, when we are not consuming news, the majority of us are not meditating on recent foreign policy failures [...].
> Instead, we remember what we have seen, and we daydream helplessly. Lately, most of us have inhabited the space between the terrible actuality and these daydreams. Waking before dawn, going about our business during the day, we fantasize ourselves into the events. What if it was me?[1]

Beyond their specific point of reference, these comments can be read as a general meditation on the effect media coverage of such events has on our minds. In fact, they encapsulate a central aspect of Ian McEwan's poetics. In all of his novels, McEwan takes a profound interest in the way in which the experience of traumatic events impinges on people's lives.[2] *The Child in Time* (1987), for instance, concerns the abduction of a child, *Enduring Love* (1997) a fatal balloon accident, *Atonement* the rape of a girl,[3] and *Saturday* (2005) a plane accident that seems to be a terror attack. However, McEwan focuses not so much on the way such events change life externally, but on how they bear upon what Virginia Woolf called "the dark places of psychology".[4] Human imagination and the precarious boundaries between dream and reality play a crucial role in all of McEwan's novels from *The Cement Garden* (1978) through to *On Chesil Beach* (2007). In this respect, (day)dreams often form the core of the narrative, serving as a crucial means of depicting the psyche and concerns of characters, or narrators.

Actually, the principle of daydreaming which McEwan describes in "Only Love and Then Oblivion" – and two decades earlier in the introduction to his oratorio *Or Shall We Die?* (1983)[5] – has been a popular narrative method throughout literary history. Particularly Romantic authors like Alexander S. Pushkin and E.T.A. Hoffmann favoured the so-called dream play, which applies to all genres, and did so for a good reason: The dream play is geared at presenting a subjectivity which creates its own reality according to its individual desires and fears.[6] What appears to be reality within the narrated world actually takes place only in the dreamer's consciousness. The mechanisms and idiosyncrasies of an individual's imagination thus become the focus of a work of art.[7] As Strindberg puts it in his programmatic author's note to *A Dream Play* (1901):

> [T]he author has in this dream play sought to imitate the disjointed yet seemingly logical shape of a dream. Everything can happen, everything is possible and probable. [...] [T]he imagination spins, weaving new patterns on a flimsy basis of reality: a mixture of memories, experiences, free associations, absurdities and improvisations.
> The characters split, double, multiply, evaporate, condense, dissolve and merge. But one consciousness rules them all: the dreamer's [...].[8]

Although the transitions between dream and reality are in some cases clearly marked, they are more frequently almost or entirely imperceptible.[9]

While the dream play has thus been a common enough narrative device for centuries, Ian McEwan criticism has so far ignored the fact that it tends to play a prominent role in his works, too. The aim of this article is to show how McEwan has used the dream play throughout his career, focusing on *The Cement Garden*, *The Child in Time*, *Saturday* and, finally, *The Daydreamer* (1994), which can well be considered McEwan's poetological manifesto. Hence Peter Childs has suggested that "*The Daydreamer* may profitably be read in terms of themes that have preoccupied McEwan throughout his fiction since the short stories and consistently in his novels from

The Cement Garden to *Saturday*".[10] As the following analysis will show, this also holds true to the literary device of the dream play, which McEwan employs and functionalizes in different ways.

2. 'A Fascinating Violation'. The Cement Garden *(1978)*[11]

At first glance, *The Cement Garden*, "an introverted first-person narrative of burgeoning adolescent sexuality",[12] seems to be a rather straightforward, if weird, story. From the perspective of fourteen- and later fifteen-year-old Jack, it gives an account of four orphaned siblings who conceal their dead mother in a tub of cement in order to avoid being put into foster care. Left to themselves, the children – apart from Jack seventeen-year-old Julie, twelve-year-old Sue and six-year-old Tom – live beyond the customs and laws of society: While the corpse in the cellar and discarded food in the kitchen are rotting away, Tom alternately cross-dresses as a girl or regresses into a baby, Sue retreats into the world of her imagination, and Jack and Julie embark on an incestuous relationship. Although critics have observed that sleep is a central motif in *The Cement Garden*,[13] its real significance has never been thoroughly looked into.

Sleep and dreams play a crucial role in Jack's story from the beginning. He makes a habit of daydreaming[14] and sleeping through the days: "I woke late in the morning, masturbated and dozed off again. [...] Some afternoons I fell asleep in the armchair even though I had only been awake a couple of hours." (85) Especially during the holidays, the lack of an everyday routine allows Jack to drift and lose contact to the outside world to such a degree that the boundaries between sleeping and waking dissolve (see for instance 128-129). Suspended between sleep and wakefulness, he whiles away his time, centred completely on himself and his (day)dreams. Towards the end of the story, Jack describes his strange dreamlike state to Julie, drawing attention to his experience of utter timelessness and seclusion: "'Except for the times I go down into the cellar I feel like I'm asleep. Whole weeks go by without me noticing, and if you asked me what happened three days ago I wouldn't be able to tell you.'" (134-135) His condition is such that it becomes difficult to distinguish what is imagined and what is real.

The final sentence of *The Cement Garden* suggests that Jack's story in fact exemplifies his inner life, and at the same time implies that the reader is implicated in a collective daydream with the boy. At the novella's end, Julie exclaims: "'There!' [...] 'wasn't that a lovely sleep.'" (138) Julie's words, which gain additional emphasis through their position at the very end of the story, have several meanings. First, they are simply directed at Tom, who has been roused from his sleep by the police. Second, they refer to the fact that the arrival of the police will put an end to the children's self-sufficient existence beyond parental and social authority.[15] Third and most importantly, set apart from the rest of the paragraph as they are, these words appear as a framing comment on the whole text: They underpin the story's dream-like character and question its status as lived reality within the narrated world.[16] As Lars Heiler has revealed in his perceptive analysis, readers are involved in this waking up, too, having been drawn into a 'collective daydream' in the sense Hanns Sachs proposes in his psychoanalytic study *Gemeinsame Tagträume* (1924; *Collective Daydreams*).[17] According to Sachs, literary texts have a social character, for they constitute collective daydreams in which the unconscious and repressed find their way into language. This psychoanalytic dimension of *The Cement Garden* finds expression on several levels.

Significantly, Jack's sexual initiation coincides with the death of his father, which provides a hint that the novella exemplifies Jack's unconscious. The very first sentence introduces the topic of oedipal rivalry, which the narrator develops into a set of correspondences between pairs of sexual images. Jack's introduction could hardly be more laconic: "I did not kill my father, but I sometimes felt I had helped him on his way." (9) Having become too frail to tend to the highly artificial garden in the pedantic way he used to, the father decides to cover the whole space in concrete. From the start, the imagery linked to this cement garden bears strong sexual connotations. Instructing the men delivering the cement where to store it, the father "pointed with the wet stem of his pipe at the coal hole" (10), which represents a thinly disguised image of penetration, as the pipe is identified with his penis.[18] During the work, the father suffers a heart attack while Jack experiences his first ejaculation. However, this blatantly obvious sexual imagery only introduces a more comprehensive sexual metaphor. Describing a by no means innocent game of doctor and patient, Jack identifies Sue's vulva as a "little flower made of flesh" (12), and later he depicts his drying first semen in terms of a thin layer of concrete: "As I watched, it dried to a barely visible shiny crust which cracked when I flexed my wrist." (18) Due to this analogy between flowers and the female on the one hand and concrete and semen on the other, the father's abortive attempt to pave over the garden – he dies before he can complete the task – turns out to be a metaphor for failing male dominance and oppression.[19] Hence, Jack sees his progenitor's endeavour to cover the garden with concrete as a "fascinating violation" (17), which reinforces the motif of violent male domination.

It is one of the central conceits of the story that Jack himself fails in a similar task, which is as much part of his unconscious as his oedipal longing. Soon after the father, the mother dies, too, and the children bury her corpse in a tub filled with concrete, thus repeating the initial "fascinating violation" their father enacted.[20] Unluckily, the concrete cracks, the stench of the decomposing body permeates the house, and Julie's friend betrays them to the police. As Kiernan Ryan maintains, "[i]n bringing Mother's corpse down from the upstairs bedroom and burying it in the basement, the children physically enact the metaphorical interment of the lost mother in the unconscious".[21] Like a Gothic novel,[22] *The Cement Garden* relies on the analogy between space and psychological processes, which is laid bare in the identification of the house with a person, suggesting that the events occur just in the narrator's mind: "Seen from across the road it looked like the face of someone concentrating, trying to remember." (23) In fact, the mother's interment takes place on so many levels of the narrative that the seemingly realistic action of the children dissolves in metaphoric correspondences. It is enacted in a science fiction novel Sue gives Jack for his birthday[23] and in a nightmare that repeatedly plagues him. In this nightmare, Jack is pursued by someone with a mysterious box he wants to avoid looking into by all means:

> The lid was lifted half an inch or so, too dark to see inside. I ran on in order to gain time, and this time I succeeded in opening my eyes. [...] I knew there was a small creature inside, kept captive against its will and stinking horribly. (27)

On waking up, Jack sees his mother sitting on his bed, who then embarrasses him by a lecture on the dangers of masturbation, which accounts for his need to banish her into his unconscious. The box Jack is so afraid of in his dream foreshadows the chest in which the children later hide the corpse; the creature's stench parallels the smell caused by the body's decomposition, which due to a crack in the cement pervades the house. Taken together, these motifs combine to form a disturbing portrait of adolescence.[24]

The Cement Garden, then, invites readers to witness the inner life of first-person narrator Jack through his story, which purports to be a realistic account of events, but can be read as a projection of Jack's unconscious wishes and fears. However, although the story is told from the first-person perspective, readers do not gain detailed emotional insight into Jack. The carefully wrought imagery and impersonal vocabulary in which he tells his story distance readers from Jack's emotions and make him appear strangely uninvolved.[25] Likewise, Jack's sometimes highly formalised style appears oddly incongruous with the fairly primitive language to be expected from a rather uneducated teenager,[26] which lends the story a strangely artificial character, even considering that the narrating I may differ from the experiencing I in both age and education. These devices are ultimately less geared at avoiding the reader's "emotional self-identification with the narrator"[27] for ethical reasons, but above all add to the narrative's dreamlike character. They create a discursive distance analogous to the experiential distance between the dreamer and his persona within the dream, which turns the dreamer into a detached witness of himself. Readers therefore share the detached perspective of the dreamer, and Jack's unconscious movements remain as inaccessible to them as to Jack himself.

3. 'The Elaborate Time Schemes of Daydreamers'. The Child in Time *(1987)*

As far as the phenomenon of daydreaming is concerned, McEwan's third novel *The Child in Time* gives an almost exemplary rendition of the mechanism he describes in "Only Love and Then Oblivion". The protagonist Stephen Lewis, a successful author of children's books whose name calls to mind Lewis Carroll (*Alice's Adventures in Wonderland*, 1865) and C.S. Lewis (*The Chronicles of Narnia*, 1949-1954), has a marked propensity to slip into extensive daydreams. Traumatized by the disappearance of his three-year-old daughter Kate in a supermarket, Stephen has largely lost his grip on the present. This is primarily because in his urge to understand how his daughter could vanish right under his nose, and in order to come to terms with her disappearance, he feels compelled to retrace this fateful episode again and again: "Later, in the sorry months and years, Stephen was to make efforts to re-enter this moment, to burrow his way back through the folds of events".[28] For him this is less a matter of trying to remember actively, than of slipping more or less involuntarily into his memories:

> Stephen ran memories and daydreams, what was and what might have been. Or were they running him? [...] A roomful of people did not lessen his introspection [...] so much as intensify it and give it structure. [...] At home [...] he lacked the concentration for sustained thought. He daydreamed in fragments, without control, almost without consciousness. (5-6)

Correspondingly, *The Child in Time* consists to a large extent of the protagonist's daydreams. In fact, his being immersed in daydreams or roused from them is a veritable leitmotiv of the narrative (see 79, 146). Yet, these daydreams concern not only the events surrounding Kate's disappearance, but Stephen's whole past, including his childhood. Participating in a committee to confer on children's education in reading and writing, for instance, Stephen does not listen to the chairman, but is transported to his schooldays: "When Parmenter outlined [...] the morning's work ahead Stephen heard his teacher's soothing Welsh lilt croon the glories of Charlemagne's court". (7) Accordingly, the narrative moves smoothly from the present, when Stephen is sitting in the committee, to his schooldays and from then on via free association to the day he lost his daughter:

> Through the window he saw not an enclosed car-park [...] but, as from two floors up, a rose garden, playing fields, [...] then rough, uncultivated land [...]. This was a lost time and a lost landscape – he had returned once to discover the trees [...] felled, [...] and the estuary spanned by a motorway bridge. And since loss was his subject, it was an easy move to a frozen, sunny day outside a supermarket in South London. (ibid.)

Since a considerable part of the story is thus told in flashbacks into Stephen's past occasioned by his daydreams, these turn out to be the very motor of the narrative.

In this context, McEwan is primarily interested in the issue of time and in how the experience of trauma affects our relation to reality and time. As a predominantly covert, heterodiegetic narrator carefully controlling the distribution of information tells the story,[29] the fact that the narrative is largely structured along the lines of Stephen's daydreams, following his thoughts, easily escapes notice. Even though the daydreams may be read as simple analepses into his past, the committee's sessions actually provide the backdrop for a considerable part of the story. Hence there is not just a single linear story which occasionally takes the reader back into the past, but two stories that proceed simultaneously. The narrator specifically stresses this concurrent existence of two parallel stories and timelines. Stephen's present activities in the commission are explicitly shown to parallel his search for Kate, which he recapitulates in another daydream:

> Stephen raised his hand for what he knew to be a useless alphabet. It hardly mattered for he was crossing a broad strip of cracked and pot-holed asphalt which separated two tower blocks. [...] He knocked on doors and spoke to mothers who were first puzzled, then hostile. (19-20)

Concerning the novel's time structure, this is essential, for the fact that Stephen's daydreams run parallel to his present existence highlights the concurrent presence of present and past, which seem to be going on concomitantly. No matter where Stephen is or what he does, he is literally seldom ever 'present', but relives his past in prolonged daydreams: "He was always partly somewhere else, never quite paying attention, never wholly serious." (114) The power of his daydreams is such that Stephen associates even the train (which is due to its connection with timetables traditionally a symbol for the compulsions of clock time) primarily with the opportunity to daydream undisturbed (see 51). In short, Stephen's traumatic loss of Kate profoundly influences his relation to the present, but this forms only the starting point for more fundamental reflections on the nature of time.

McEwan embeds Stephen's specific relation to time in a number of other, divergent temporal concepts. Most important among these is the contrast between Stephen's being out of touch with the present and the experience of time linked to childhood. As Stephen muses, taking his daughter as an example:

> Kate would not be aware of the car half a mile behind, or of the wood's perimeters and all that lay, beyond them, roads, opinions, Government. The wood, this spider rotating on its thread, [...] would be all, the moment would be everything. (113)

In other words, childhood represents the ability to live in the pure moment, or the knowledge of "how to fill the present and be filled by it to the point where identity faded to nothing". (114) However, the novel suggests that this state of 'pure time' cannot be attained permanently in adult life. This becomes obvious in Stephen's friend Charles, a successful publisher and politician, who trying to realize his obsession of being a boy again resigns and moves to a secluded country house: "He used to say he wanted to escape from time, from appointments, schedules, deadlines. Childhood to him was timelessness, he talked about it as though it were a mystical state." (222) Ironically, though, Charles achieves this only in his death by freezing at the foot of a tree, when he is truly 'frozen in the moment'. Stephen, on the other hand, embodies a conclusion drawn by the physicist Thelma, who stresses the complexity of time:

> [W]hatever time is, the common-sense, everyday version of it as linear, regular, absolute, marching from left to right, from the past through the present to the future, is either nonsense or a fraction of the truth. (127)

Thinking beyond the everyday version of time, Thelma envisions a new theory that "would refer to a higher order of reality", which she understands as "an undivided whole of which matter, space, time, even consciousness itself, would be complicatedly related embodiments". (129) In order to achieve this, one would – as Thelma puts it – have to concentrate on

> the really important conversations about time [...] – the mystic's experience of timelessness, the chaotic unfolding of time in dreams [...], the annihilated time of deep sleep, the elaborate

time schemes of novelists, poets, daydreamers, the infinite, unchanging time of childhood. (130)

In *The Child in Time*, McEwan uses the elaborate time scheme of Stephen's daydreams to initiate a similar conversation about time.

4. 'The White Noise of Solitary Thought'. Saturday *(2005)*

Just like in *The Child in Time*, the dream play in *Saturday* closely corresponds to what McEwan proposes in "Only Love and Then Oblivion", for the novel shows the impact current political reality has on the inner life of its protagonist. On the surface, *Saturday* reads like a gripping story, and it ostensibly depicts a day in the life of the protagonist, the ageing, but successful neurosurgeon Henry Perowne. In spite of its reflexive focus on Perowne's thoughts, the novel more or less follows the successful recipe of sex, crime and rock-'n-roll – in this case, blues. At the same time, though, *Saturday* contains various hints suggesting that it can be read as a (day-)dream of its central character, and it is in this reading that the novel's key concerns come to the fore most clearly.

Already the beginning of *Saturday* implies that the novel in fact represents a dream of Perowne, which is due both to the intertextual allusions it incorporates and above all to the peculiar state of mind it describes. Perowne wakes up in the small hours of the night and finds himself in a "curious mood",[30] calling to mind Kafka's *The Metamorphosis* (1915), which finds explicit mention in the novel.[31] At any rate, McEwan leaves no doubt that Perowne is experiencing something out of the ordinary:

> It's not clear to him when exactly he became conscious, nor does it seem relevant. [...] [T]he movement is easy, and pleasurable in his limbs, and his back and legs feel unusually strong. [...] It's as if, standing there in the darkness, he's materialised out of nothing, fully formed, unencumbered. [...] [H]e's alert and empty-headed and inexplicably elated. (3)

Apparently, Perowne is in a most unusual, dreamlike state. For the novel's plot this is crucial, because Perowne's extraordinary frame of mind, his "sustained, distorting euphoria" (5), suggests that he might just be experiencing a dream.

In the subsequent airplane scene, McEwan provides the reader with the incentive for Perowne's dream play. Having moved to the window, Perowne sees a light traversing the sky. First he mistakes it for a meteor, but then he realises that it is an airplane with one of its engines in flames. Although this later turns out to be a harmless accident involving a cargo plane, Perowne at the time immediately interprets the sight as a terrorist attack, brought about by "[a] man of sound faith with a bomb in the heel of his shoe." (17) Placed at such a prominent stage in the novel, the significance of the airplane scene for *Saturday* can hardly be overvalued. Some of the novel's most prominent themes can be traced back to that scene, above all the contrast between dream and reality as well as the opposition between helplessness and control. First of all, the airplane scene serves to pinpoint the problem of how we 'read' – or rather: tend to misread – reality, which McEwan also tackles in *Atonement* and *On Chesil Beach*. Second, the fact that Perowne *does* misread the airplane accident in this way shows how deep an impact the events of 9/11 – or rather: their overwhelming coverage in the media – have had on him. The result of the continuous presence of 9/11 is a feeling of insecurity and threat. Critics who read *Saturday* as a novel about happiness strangely ignore the fact that for Perowne, this disturbing feeling has at the end overruled everything else:

> All he feels now is fear. He's weak and ignorant, scared of the way consequences of an action leap away from your control and breed new events, new consequences, until you're led to a place you never dreamed of and would never choose – a knife at the throat. (277)

This feeling pervades the whole novel and proves to be the key to Perowne's dream play. The events of Perowne's Saturday should not be taken at face value, as reality within the narrated world, but as projections of his imagination, which are triggered by his half-conscious experience of the airplane accident as a terrorist attack.[32]

If one considers *Saturday* as a dream play, the links between the respective threats posed by terrorist attacks and the equally unpredictable thug Baxter pertain no longer – as critics have maintained so far – just to an allegorical level. Instead, Baxter (who breaks into Perowne's house threatening to rape Perowne's daughter) represents a direct imaginary embodiment of Perowne's disturbing fear that terrorism might impinge on his domestic life. Perowne's ultimate feeling of a deeply unsettling lack of control and being threatened is aroused first by the airplane incident and the meditations on terrorism it entails, and later on, much more concretely and immediately, by Perowne's encounters with Baxter. Baxter, in whose person terror literally invades Perowne's home, embodies Perowne's feeling of threat. This becomes apparent already in the description of Perowne's first encounter with Baxter, when Perowne is on his way to a squash game with his colleague Jay Strauss, that even within the narrated world, Baxter is not a real person, but really a figment of Perowne's perturbed imagination. Just before the neurosurgeon's Mercedes collides with Baxter's red BMW, Perowne sees this car out of the corner of his eye:

> [W]hen a flash of red streaks in across his [Perowne's] left peripheral vision, like a shape on his retina in a bout of insomnia, it already has the quality of an idea, a new idea, unexpected and dangerous, but entirely his, and not of the world beyond himself. (81)

This passage prefigures the dramatic scene to ensue as an imaginary encounter. Baxter, who is announced by the flash of red, is nothing but an "unexpected and dangerous" idea and has no existence beyond Perowne's imagination.[33] McEwan sets the scene for this imaginary dimension even beforehand, revealing the device of the dream play quite explicitly. On the occasion of Perowne's musings about his impending squash game, we learn that

> [h]is wellbeing appears to need spectral entities to oppose it, figures of his own invention whom he can defeat. He's sometimes like this before a game. [...] [T]he second-by-second wash of his thoughts is only partially his to control – the drift, the white noise of solitary thought is driven by his emotional state. (78)

From the point of view of the dream play, the squash game is a direct imaginary expression of Perowne's emotional state.

Reconsidered from this perspective, the entire story can profitably be understood as "the white noise of solitary thought" driven by Perowne's "emotional state". All the characters in the novel can be regarded as figures of Perowne's own invention. This accounts for the fact that, as critics have complained,[34] some of the characters are annoyingly flat, the plot seems overly constructed and improbable, and the story sometimes verges perilously on kitsch. Taken as Perowne's dream, the novel chiefly shows his unconscious trying to overcome his fears and to balance them with consoling fantasies. Some of the characters express Perowne's dark side or fears, like Baxter, Strauss or his mother Lily, and some function as beautiful, consoling fictions, like his children Theo and Daisy as well as his wife Rosalind. Baxter embodies Perowne's fear of irrationality, violence and loss of control, of terror infringing on his own life. Similarly, Lily, who suffers from dementia and has lost contact with the world, impersonates his fear of losing control through age, illness and death.[35] Rosalind, Theo and Daisy, on the other hand, embody Perowne's desire for a more or less undisturbed and harmonious domesticity in which everything is under control. They are, as if from a fairy tale, "the handsome healthy son with the strong guitarist's hands come to rescue him, the beautiful poet for a daughter, unattainable even in her nakedness, [...] the gifted, loving wife" (227-228). The squash game against Strauss, finally, mirrors Perowne's urge to control situations and to overcome his defects.[36] From this perspective, there is nothing gaudy about *Saturday*, for it is Perowne's consciousness that 'rules' the novel, which is indeed, as Strindberg has felicitously put it, "a mixture of memories, experiences, free associations, absurdities and improvisations".[37]

5. 'We've Dreamed Him Up'. The Daydreamer *(1994)*

It seems to be quite a leap from novels like *The Cement Garden* and *Saturday* to a children's book like *The Daydreamer*. And yet, *The Daydreamer* is a superb case in point for what Charles Drake tells the budding author Stephen in *The Child in Time*: "that the distinction between adult and children's fiction was [...] a fiction itself." (29) *The Daydreamer* is a collection of stories focusing on ten-year-old Peter Fortune, who has a sometimes precarious propensity to slip into daydreams and become completely oblivious to his surroundings. The stories thus consist mainly of the boy's daydreams, whose motto stems from Ovid's *Metamorphoses*: "My purpose is to tell of bodies which have been transformed into shapes of a different kind."[38] Some kind of metamorphosis takes place in each story,[39] concerning either things or people, and the most impressive have Peter himself undergo a transformation: He swaps bodies with the family cat, becomes trapped in his cousin's body or wakes to find himself turned into a giant, a grown-up.

Although the content of Peter's daydreams emerges directly from his current reality, it epitomizes central topics and mechanisms of McEwan's novels. This becomes particularly obvious in two of the stories, "The Cat" and "The Baby". While Peter is stroking the old family cat William, it prods him towards opening a kind of zipper in its fur, and Peter steps into the cat's body and vice versa. The lively descriptions that follow convey a keen impression of how he experiences being a cat, relishing the sensual pleasures involved: "What a delight, to walk on four soft paws. [...] His tread was light, and his fur was like the most comfortable of old woollen sweaters." (33) Conversely, when Peter is back in his own body, he has to adjust to it again: "This body did not really fit him. [...] It was like wearing boots four sizes too large." (38) Being William, he gets to know a different way of life and learns to value things he used to dislike, appreciating them through someone else's perspective: "The day passed just as he had hoped. Dozing, lapping a saucer of milk, dozing again, munching through some tinned cat food that really was not as bad as it smelled". (36) On a comparatively light and humorous scale, McEwan thus addresses a topic that pervades his early stories and his novels: "The Cat" originates in the inherently moral question of what it means to be someone else. In his daydream, Peter virtually enters the body and consciousness of the cat, experiencing something entirely 'other' to himself, and the reader shares this experience.

In "The Baby", McEwan develops the poetological implications of 'dreaming' oneself into others – the close connection between the experience of alterity and morality he also suggests in "Only Love and Then Oblivion" – even further. As Peter Childs has argued, imagination is, according to McEwan, "linked to morality because imagining oneself as another is at the core of compassion".[40] In "The Baby", this profoundly moral effect inherent in the experience of alterity comes clearly to the fore. When Peter's aunt arrives with her baby son Kenneth to stay for a while, Kenneth now becomes the centre of attention. Although far from admitting it, Peter takes an instant dislike to Kenneth out of mere jealousy. In his daydream, however, Peter imagines being magically transformed into Kenneth by a malicious spell of Kate's. As in "The Cat", Peter now experiences everything from the other's perspective. While his actions are thus severely limited, a whole new world opens up to him as regards his sensuous perceptions. The beautiful patterns cast on the wall by sunlit trees leave him spellbound (see 78), and he becomes transfixed by the taste of a boiled egg:

> The taste and smell, the color and texture and squelching sound overwhelmed his senses and scattered his thoughts. Egginess exploded in his mouth, a white and yellow fountain of sensation shot upward through his brain. [...] Until the egg was finished, Peter could think of nothing else. (ibid.)

Upon seeing something interesting, baby Peter feels possessed by an irresistible urge to explore things in any possible way. Due to the baby's compellingly intense, synaesthetic experience of the world, this urge is particularly powerful, as in the case of a simple brick:

> Yellow, yellow, yellow, it sang out. It vibrated, it glowed, it hummed. He had to have it. He lunged forward, and his hand closed around it, but he could not really *feel* it, not enough anyway. He raised it to his mouth, and with his sensitive lips and gums and tooth he explored the woody, painty, yellowy, cubey taste of it, until he understood it all. (82)

While Peter was before disgusted by Kenneth's habit of taking everything into his mouth, he now understands him well. This new understanding is based on his experience of Kenneth's perception of the world and his relationship to other people, particularly to Peter himself. In the daydream, the perspectives of Kenneth and himself are reversed; being the baby, Peter experiences his own reaction to Kenneth from Kenneth's point of view. Consequently, Peter-baby comes to feel the full antipathy from Kenneth-boy and recognizes its injustice: "He was staring at Peter with such loathing and disgust that it made dark ripples in the air." (80) Due to these instructive experiences, Peter's attitude towards Kenneth changes from dislike to comprehension and love: At the end of the story, Peter takes him for a stroll to the park. Hence, "The Baby" exemplifies the morally reforming effect of empathy McEwan sets forth in "Only Love and Then Oblivion": Having thought himself into Kenneth's mind, Peter is able to appreciate the baby's 'otherness', to reconcile himself to his difference and to adopt a mollified attitude towards him.

To put it more generally, by means of the dream play "The Cat" and "The Baby" reiterate an essential aspect of McEwan's novels: Characteristically, the reader is in most of McEwan's works through first-person narration or internal focalisation exposed to the inner life of characters deviating from the 'normal' – that is, from the set of attitudes, inclinations and opinions of the implied reader. In *The Daydreamer*, though, this feature has a pronounced self-reflexive quality, because Peter's experience of alterity functions as a scenic representation of what takes place in the process of reading. Just as Peter imaginatively enters William's and Kenneth's bodies in his daydream, readers in turn 'enter' his consciousness. From this perspective, the daydream can be understood as an allegory for the imaginative effort involved in reading.

At the same time, though, *The Daydreamer* also implies that the imagination creates its own reality. This is most apparent in "The Bully", which has an exceptional position in the collection as it is – apart from the introduction – the only story that does not surge into Peter's imagination. It takes its title from the school bully Barry, of whom everyone is terrified: "The very name Barry Tamerlane was enough to make you feel an icy hand reaching into your stomach." (49) One day, though, when he is invited to Barry's birthday party, Peter finds out that Barry is just a very normal, friendly boy, and wonders what on earth makes him change into a monster at school:

> 'It's obvious,' he thought. 'We do. We've dreamed him up as the school bully. He's no stronger than any of us. We've dreamed up his power and strength. We've made him into what he is. When he goes home, no one believes in him as a bully and he just becomes himself.' (55-56)

As soon as Peter has realized this, he and his school mates are no longer afraid of Barry, and Barry in the event loses his power. Last but not least, *The Daydreamer* thus highlights the creative potential and worldmaking power of imagination, which, as the narrator confirms, is going to make adult Peter a successful author (see 14).[41]

6. 'Inhabiting Other Minds'. Ian McEwan's Poetics of the (Day)Dream

Ian McEwan has in numerous interviews expressed his poetological conviction that the quintessence of novels is to give insight into others:

> For me the moral core of the novel is inhabiting other minds. That seems to be what novels do very well and also what morality is about: understanding that people are real to themselves as you are to yourself.[42]

Correspondingly, readers of McEwan's novels experience the state of mind of others, which is something McEwan considers an inherently ethical experience. According to him, the value of fantasizing oneself into others – be it real persons or literary characters – lies in being induced to recognize, adopt and accept other perspectives, which involves a considerable imaginative effort.[43] The question at the centre of "Only Love and Then Oblivion" – "What if it was me?" –, then, ultimately refers not only to real life events, but also to the way novels work. In this context, the dream play fulfils an important function, for it allows McEwan to go beyond the classic novel of consciousness and to visualise the protagonists' inner life in a more scenic, lively form. It provides him with a very flexible means of telling the emotional narrative constitutive for his characters, which is determined by imaginary projections of their wishes, anxieties and fears.

The subjects, motifs and thematic concerns McEwan links to the dream play, though, vary considerably. In *The Cement Garden* he illuminates the unconscious of a teenage boy, in *The Child in Time* and *Saturday* a psyche unsettled by the loss of a child and the events of 9/11 respectively, and in *The Daydreamer* the fantasies of an unusually imaginative child. In all cases, McEwan typically goes beyond the particular and uses (day)dreams as a starting point for addressing universal concerns. In *The Child in Time*, Stephen's daydreams are part of wide-ranging meditations on the nature of time. Similarly, Perowne's dream play in *Saturday* is motivated by topical anxieties occasioned by 9/11, but deals at least as much with overarching, timeless anxieties inherent in the human condition: the fear of ageing, illness and death. And, perhaps most surprisingly, *The Daydreamer* ultimately is about the creative potential of human imagination and the ethical benefits of literature. However, the dream play is by no means limited to these novels: In *Atonement*, too, the tendency of the protagonist and narrator Briony to create imagined worlds and dream up a reality fitting her own preoccupations is crucial.[44] Apart from appreciating the poetological value of daydreaming, then, Ian McEwan, who considers "literature and novels in particular as investigations of human nature",[45] addresses this phenomenon as a fundamental aspect of human existence.

Notes

1   McEwan (2001).
2   See Childs (2006: 6).
3   For Briony the really shocking event may be the love scene between Celia and Robbie, which sparks off her fantasy of him being a nymphomaniac.
4   Woolf (1966: 108).
5   In this introduction, McEwan (1983: 9) pinned down the effects of an imagined nuclear catastrophe: "Like others, I experienced the jolt of panic that wakes you before dawn, the daydreams of the mad rush of people and cars out of the city before it is destroyed, of losing a child in the confusion".
6   See Gerigk (1998; 2002).
7   See ibid.
8   Strindberg (2005: 3).
9   Examples of the former are James Thurber's "The Secret Life of Walter Mitty" (1939), which alternates between descriptions of Walter's cheerless everyday reality and self-aggrandizing daydreams, and Ambrose Bierce's "An Occurrence at Owl Creek Bridge" (1890), in which the protagonist imagines his escape before being hanged; an instance of the latter is David Lynch's psycho-thriller *Lost Highway* (1997), where dream and reality merge in a surreal psychodynamic scenario.
10 Childs (2006: 150).
11 I would like to thank David Malcolm for his suggestion to take *The Cement Garden* into consideration, too.
12 Childs (2006: 2).
13 See Wicht (1988) and Heiler (2004: 61).
14 See McEwan (1978: 37; 124; 128). Further references to this edition will be included in the text.
15 See also Heiler (2004: 73).

16 *The Daydreamer* contains an allusion to *The Cement Ga*rden that retrospectively confirms this interpretation. In *The Daydreamer's* final story, where Peter dreams to wake up as an adult, his mother confirms that he was just dreaming, using words strikingly similar to Julie's: "His mother waved at him. 'That was a good sleep. You needed that.'" (189).
17 See Heiler (2004: 73).
18 This image later occurs again with slight variations (see 5).
19 See Heiler (2004: 57-60).
20 See Ryan (1994: 22).
21 Ibid. 20.
22 See also Malcolm (2002: 52).
23 In this novel, Commander Hunt has to get rid of a monster corpse drifting through space (see 36). This reference underlines *The Cement Garden's* dreamlike character, which mirrors Jack's task to get rid of the mother's corpse. The fact that he identifies with the commander (see 87) besides associates him with another daydreamer, the protagonist of Thurber's "The Secret Life of Walter Mitty", who tries to escape his tyrannical wife and compensate his petty existence with dreaming himself into fearless characters, among them a flying boat commander. The parallel plots of Jack's science fiction novel and his story further encourage a reading of *The Cement Garden* as Jack's own "secret life".
24 In this context, it is crucial to bear in mind that *The Cement Garden* is the daydream not of its real, as Freud would have had it, but of its fictive author and narrator Jack. Other than 'psychodynamic' readings of this novella suggest (see Byrnes 2002), it is Jack's, not McEwan's psyche that comes to the fore here.
25 See Malcolm (2002: 47).
26 Ibid.
27 Ibid. 50.
28 McEwan (2001 [1987]: 9). Further references will be included in the text.
29 For exceptions to the narrator's covert attitude see Malcolm (2002: 92f.).
30 McEwan (2006 [2005]: 13). Further references will be included in the text.
31 It marks the beginning of Perowne's literary education (see 133).
32 The airplane scene actually calls the reader's attention to its ontological status as a dream. Envisioning the horror of the passengers, Perowne discards his initial idea of waking his wife: "Why wake her into this nightmare? In fact, the spectacle has the familiarity of a recurrent dream" (15).
33 In an interview, McEwan hinted at the abstract nature of Baxter himself: "What both Perowne and the reader bring to [this day] is the memory of 9/11. When it comes, the terrible thing, it will always surprise you. And so it does in this case – it's Baxter. When you're sending troops to war, it's very hard to control outcome. And when you have [a car accident], which is a personal version, a shrunken-down, tiny version of a war, you can't possibly design the result" (McEwan in Schilling).
34 See for instance Banville (2005).

35 McEwan alludes to the centrality of ageing and death already in the title, Sunday standing for death. In an interview, he thus stated concerning the things he shares with Perowne that "[we share] the slow decline of physical prowess, a real sense that Sunday is coming" (McEwan in Schilling).
36 See for instance this passage: "It's at moments like these in a game that the essentials of his character are exposed: narrow, ineffectual, stupid – and morally so. The game becomes an extended metaphor of character defect. Every error he makes is so profoundly, so irritatingly typical of himself, [...] like [...] some deformation in a private place" (106).
37 Strindberg (2005: 3). For a more detailed, in-depth analysis of *Saturday* as Perowne's dream play see Lusin (2008).
38 McEwan (1994: 5). Further references will be included in the text.
39 See Childs (2005: 127-128). Besides, the intertextual reference to Ovid suggests a linear development underlying the succession of stories. The *Metamorphoses* are composed of apparently independent stories, but follow a linear scheme, tracing the evolution of the world from its creation into the Augustan imperial order. Analogously, *The Daydreamer* on the one hand leads up to Peter's adolescence, ending as it does with a story about how Peter one days wakes up as a 'grown-up', which leaves him reconciled to his adult future (see 189-190) On the other hand, the stories herald Peter's future career as a writer, which is foreshadowed in the first story (see 18).
40 Childs (2006: 5).
41 See also Oeser (2004: 159).
42 See Appleyard (2007).
43 From this perspective, his superficially most outrageous texts paradoxically are also his most ethical. Similarly, Peter Childs (2006: 5) claims that "[...] McEwan has been taken to be an amoral writer, when in fact his interest in the marginal and the perverse has always aimed precisely at defining ethical limits." See also the article by Anja Müller-Wood in this volume.
44 Atonement directly relates to *The Daydreamer* in so far as "[i]n Briony, McEwan presents the child and the writer together, in that Briony's story is fictionalised by Briony herself, but also in the sense that the child and the novelist are both 'daydreamers' in the novel's terms" (Childs 2005: 131).
45 McEwan in Pim (2009).

Bibliography

Appleyard, Bryan: "The Ghost in My Family", *The Sunday Times*, 25 March 2007. http://entertainment.timesonline.co.uk/tol/arts_and_entertainment/books/article1563161.ece (last accessed on 22 July 2009).

Banville, John: "A Day in the Life. *Saturday* by Ian McEwan", *The New York Review of Books* 53:9, 26 May 2005. http:// www.nybooks.com/articles/article-preview?article_id=17993 (last accessed on 24 March 2007).

Byrnes, Christina: *The Work of Ian McEwan. A Psychodynamic Approach*, Nottingham, 2002.

Childs, Peter: "'Fascinating Violation'. Ian McEwan's Children". – In Nick Bentley (Ed.): *British Fiction of the 1990s*, London and New York, 2005, pp. 123-134.

--- (Ed.): *The Fiction of Ian McEwan*, Houndsmills, Basingstoke, Hampshire, 2006.

Gerigk, Horst-Jürgen: "Puschkin und die Welt unserer Träume". – In Ute Lange-Bachmann (Ed.): *Alexander Puschkin*, Baden-Baden, 1998, pp. 63-81.

---: *Lesen und Interpretieren*, Göttingen, 2002.

Heiler, Lars: *Regression und Kulturkritik im britischen Gegenwartsroman*, Tübingen, 2004.

Lusin, Caroline: "Metamorphosen des Selbst. Ian McEwans *Saturday* (2005) und die Poetik des Traumspiels", *Sprachkunst* 39:1, 2008, 77-96.

Malcolm, David: *Understanding Ian McEwan*, Columbia, 2002.

McEwan, Ian: *The Cement Garden*, London, 1978.

---: "Introduction". – In I.M.: Or Shall We Die?, London, 1983, pp. 7-20.

---: *The Child in Time*, London, 2001 [1987].

---: *The Daydreamer*, London, 1994.

---: "Only love and then oblivion. Love was all they had to set against their murderers", *The Guardian*. 15 September 2001. http://www.guardian.co.uk/world/2001/sep/15/september11.politicsphilosophyandsociety2 (last accessed on 18 August 2009).

---: *Saturday*, London, 2006 [2005].

Oeser, Hans-Christian: "Nachwort". – In Ian McEwan: *The Daydreamer*, Ed. H.O., Stuttgart, 2004, pp. 147-159.

Pim, Keiron: "McEwan's Novel Take on Climate Change", *EDP24*, 3 August 2009. http://www.edp24.co.uk/content/edp24/news/story.aspx?brand=EDPOnline&category=News&tBrand=EDPOnline&tCategory=xDefault&itemid=NOED03%20Aug%202009%2011%3A36%3A00%3A787 (last accessed on 20 August 2009).

Ryan, Kiernan: *Ian McEwan*, Plymouth, 1994.

Schilling, Mary Kaye: "Saturday Night Fever", *Entertainment Weekly* 813, 1 April 2005. http://www.ew.com/ew/article/ 0,,1041443,00.html (last accessed on 24 July 2009).

Strindberg, August: *A Dream Play*. In a New Version by Caryl Churchill, London, 2005.

Wells, Lynn: "The Ethical Otherworld. Ian McEwan's Fiction". – In Philip Tew & Rod Mengham (Eds.): *British Fiction Today*, London, 2006, pp. 117-127.

Wicht, Wolfgang: "Von *David Copperfield* zu Ian McEwans *Zementgarten*. Veränderungen im Diskurs der Ich-Erzähler", *Zeitschrift für Anglistik und Amerikanistik* 36:7, 1988, 1146-1156.

Woolf, Virginia: "Modern Fiction". – In V.W.: *Collected Essays*. Vol. 2. Ed. Leonard Woolf, London, 1966, 103-110.

Erik Martiny

"A Darker Longing": Shades of Nihilism in Contemporary Terrorist Fiction

This chapter aims to provide a brief overview of the fictional context surrounding Ian McEwan's novel *Saturday* (2006): it examines a number of responses to twenty-first century terrorism in the fiction of English and American writers such as Don Delillo, John Updike, Martin Amis and J. G. Ballard in order to explore the various ways in which the figure of the terrorist has been represented and define to what ethical and aesthetic ends the concept of nihilism has been formulated in recent times. It also attempts to position current fiction with respect to previous expressions of nihilism.

As we will see, there are many forms of nihilism and many different expressions of it that range from merely atheistic nihilism to Cosmicist nihilism to destructive nihilism (often imaged by the explosion and total atomisation of a character); as Perowne, the protagonist of Ian McEwan's *Saturday* points out, there are also acts which seem nihilistic but are in fact its exact opposite.

In his sequel novel, *The End of the Road* (1964), John Barth described his philosophical approach to existence in terms of "cheerful nihilism": ultimately a form of Keatsian "negative capability" based not only on the ability to accept doubt and mystery but also on a heroic transformation of the horrifying certainties of life into a source of revelry and humour. This upbeat, regenerative approach to nihilism can be traced back to Samuel Beckett's absurdism, and further back to Nietzsche's Dionysian or ecstatic nihilism in *The Gay Science* (1882) and the sometimes ludicrous optimists of Chekhov's *The Cherry Orchard* (1904). John Barth's happy formulation has since been used by critics such as Richard Hauck and Malcolm Bradbury to characterize postmodernist fiction since the 1960s. In the following survey, I will be considering in what measure post-9/11 fiction tends to put an end to this cheerful mode in the history of literary nihilism, signalling a return to the darker appraisals of Existentialist nihilists.

The title of Don Delillo's recent novel *Falling Man* (2007) provides multi-textual echoes of such novels as Saul Bellow's *Dangling Man* (1944), Albert Camus's *The Fall* (1956) and William Golding's *Free Fall* (1959), texts centred on Existentialist pessimism. Delillo's novel features a number of falling men. His central character, Keith Neudecker, who becomes a kind of fallen man, is in one of the twin towers when the suicide bombers attack. He also witnesses a man, or perhaps just the symbol of a man, falling in the very last sentence of the novel: "Then he saw a shirt come down out of the sky. He walked and saw it fall, arms waving like nothing in this life" (246). Apart from the verbal play intended in the word "nothing", the emphasis on emptiness is overdetermined here by the man's synecdochic reduction to a mere item of clothing. The image recalls the hollow men in *Heart of Darkness* (1902): Conrad is in fact a central figure for the study of terrorist fiction particularly because his novel *The Secret Agent* (1907) is considered as one of the three touchstones of the genre, alongside Dostoyevsky's *The Demons* (1872) and Henry James's *The Princess Casamassima* (1886).

While there are no direct allusions to Conrad in *Falling Man*, the disintegrative explosion of Stevie (a hyperbolic fragmentary image Conrad added to the real story of the bomber of the Greenwich Observatory) is a nihilistic image that echoes through the narratives of recent novels and films that centre on suicide bombings. When the protagonist of Delillo's novel is brought to hospital, he is covered in blood that is not his, an image frequently used in political fiction to suggest the protagonist's psychological breakdown, his guilt or a general descent into barbarity. The surgeon who cleans Neudecker's wounds informs him that he is looking for traces of what he calls "organic shrapnel", pellets of flesh that are often found in suicide bombings:

> The bomber is blown to bits, literally bits and pieces, and fragments of flesh and bone come flying outward with such force and velocity that they get wedged, they get trapped in the body of anyone who's in striking range. (16)

In Ridley Scott's recent film *Body of Lies* (2008), the lead character has to extract pieces of bomber's bone from his own body. Similarly, the terrorists in David Cronenberg's film *Existenz* (1999) fire a kind of dream-inspired gun that uses teeth for bullets. Conrad's metaphor for social disintegration is given added force in these recent images that literally describe the terrorist exploding into a kind of nothingness that gets under your skin, if not into your soul. Later in *Falling Man*, the protagonist's wife obsessively watches the television showings of the attack which is described in terms that evoke shrapnel: "The second plane coming out of that ice blue sky, this was the footage that entered the body, that seemed to run beneath her skin" (134).

Delillo's novel contains many images of self-loss and inner collapse. One encased narrative that holds the main character up, keeping his trauma at bay, runs counter to this fragmentary imagery. The legend that shores up his card-playing group recounts the story of "a cemetery in Germany, in Cologne, where four good friends, were buried in the configuration in which they'd been seated, invariably, at the card table, with two of the gravestones facing the other two, each player in his time-honoured place" (98-9). In the protagonist's mind, this story acts as a powerful antidote to the destruction of the two monumental buildings that seemed permanent fixtures of American identity. The novel oscillates between attributing major significance to the minute and relegating mankind to cosmic insignificance. When we last see Keith Neudecker sinking into total card-playing oblivion, the sounds of the game are compared to the sounds emitted by insects: "clay chips with smooth edges, rubbing, sliding, clicking, days and nights of distant hiss, like insect friction" (225). This entomological image evokes H. P. Lovecraft's Cosmicist nihilism, a philosophical doctrine according to which man is a limited and meaningless insect destined to disappear one day.

The novel has been criticised for the two paltry images it offers, a performance artist who suspends himself to imitate those who fell from the towers and a "self-absorbed man" who plays "stupid card games" (Kakutani), but that is just the point: the images are paltry because the attacks have made those it traumatised feel insignificant. Indeed one of the disturbing aspects of the novel is the unpleasant sensation that its characters are thinner than paper men and women. The author's minimal use of characterization techniques make them seem so disembodied that they have little more than a spectral presence: Delillo's postmodernist approach to characterisation appositely captures the trauma caused by the attacks. The same can be said of the protagonist of Philip Roth's novel *Everyman* (2007). While the aim of Roth's novel is to make the nameless protagonist seem universal, it could be argued that his somewhat anonymous, rather flat characterisation could be analysed as one of the 9/11 effects on literature.[1] The attacks also have a tragi-comic repercussion on Roth's protagonist who is so emptied of his manhood and so paranoid that he takes refuge by the sea after the attacks, leaving his wife and daughter alone in New York (66).

Falling Man presents the hijackers in acutely nihilistic terms. Seen from the perspective of another Islamist called Hammad, Mohamed Atta is described in terms that are very close to those that define nihilism. Islamic fundamentalism in the fiction I study here is generally portrayed as a kind of idealist's nihilism, in the philosophical sense of the term (idealism being a doctrine that relegates the value and substance of this world to a mere illusion). When Hammad asks him about the future victims, Atta's solipsistic nihilism defines other people in these terms: "there are no others. The others exist only to the degree that they fill the role we have designed for them" (176).

John Updike's second-last novel *Terrorist* (2006) takes a more extended look at Islamic fundamentalism from the point of view of a fictional future attack. The young terrorist Updike focuses on is named Ahmad Mulloy. In view of the existentially absurd frame of mind adopted by the protagonist, it seems probable that by giving his character an Irish mother, Updike also intended a nod towards the Beckettian absurdity embodied by the eponymous character of his novel *Molloy* (1951). The critic Robert Clark makes a similar comparison with regard to the names chosen for the domestic terrorist Baxter's twin-like henchmen, Nark and Nigel, in Ian McEwan's *Saturday*, a novel published the same year as Updike's *Terrorist*.

Like Henry Perowne in Ian McEwan's *Saturday*, Updike's more or less normative character, Jack Levy, begins the day troubled by insomnia at four in the morning: "his dreams are sinister, soaked through with the misery of the world" (19). Like Perowne, he just barely avoids disaster, here by ably reasoning with an Islamicized teenager who has decided to blow himself up in a strategic urban area. Through Levy (the protagonist's foil character) the novel juxtaposes two kinds of nihilism. Levy lacks Perowne's drive, his general buoyancy and affluence: his corpulent wife is little more than a heavyweight burden to him, he feels increasingly out of touch with the students he is supposed to counsel, he lacks lustre and his overall vision is generally rather sour and futureless. Although by contrast, Ahmad has everything going for him, America provokes a sense of existential disgust in him that pushes him to want to cleanse it through violent action. When the novel closes, the two main characters find themselves in a truck loaded with heavy explosives: while Levy initially seeks to dissuade the adolescent, it is ironically his own recently increased sense of nihilism which ultimately saves the day. In the final twist of the novel, Levy gives up, also wishing to die and this seems to unexpectedly cause the teenager to relent – Levy's death-wish reminds Ahmad that the Prophet Mohammad speaks of God as a Creator: "God does not want to destroy: it was He who made the world" (306). It is as if through Ahmad's consciousness, Updike seeks to undo Islamic nihilism from the inside, and although this philosophical twist descends upon the plot in the manner of a *deus ex machina*, its abruptness is ultimately convincing enough in psychological terms, as is the terrorist's ephemeral change of heart during the climax scene of McEwan's *Saturday*.

Terrorist also closes with another Cosmicist image of man as a mindlessly-mechanized insect:

> scuttling, hurrying, intent in the milky morning sun upon some plan or scheme or hope they are hugging to themselves, their reason for living another day, each one of them impaled live upon the pin of consciousness, fixed upon self-advancement and self-preservation. That, and only that. *These devils*, Ahmad thinks, *have taken away my God* (310).

This echoes the novel's opening words ("Devils, Ahmad thinks. *These devils seek to take away my God*" 3) suggesting that the plot charts the breaking, or perhaps merely the coming to maturity, of the central character's extremist faith. Taking a synoptic glance at Dostoyevsky's *The Demons* makes Updike's rendering of the thought processes of his character seem strikingly empathetic.

A number of reviewers have argued quite rightly that Ahmad is somewhat stereotypical and wooden. In his *New York Times* review of *Terrorist*, Michiko Kakutani very condescendingly describes "the would-be terrorist in this novel" as

> a completely unbelievable individual: more robot than human being and such a cliché that the reader cannot help suspecting that Mr. Updike found the idea of such a person so incomprehensible that he at some point abandoned any earnest attempt to depict his inner life and settled for giving us a static, one-dimensional stereotype.

Yet this method of characterisation is patently a deliberate attempt on the writer's part to suggest how alien the awkward adolescent terrorist feels, despite the fact that he was born and raised on American soil. If the young terrorist is representatively stereotypical, Updike does avoid the pitfall of demonising him, something Dostoyevsky did not refrain from at all. While Updike does give us a relatively conventional portrait of the terrorist (who suffers from a teenager's physical and sexual inhibition, an absent father figure and a sense of not belonging because of his half-Islamic roots), this is simply because terrorists, like many other human beings, also tend to be afflicted with rather conventional forms of maladjustment and emotional instability. Turning the other part of Kakutani's analysis on its head, I would add that some reviewers seem to be expecting a representation of the psychology of terrorist characters to be something like an encounter of the third kind, a far cry from the representation of an ordinary existentially and politically embattled, or indoctrinated, human being. Another noticeable feature of reviews dealing with post-9/11 terrorist fiction is their tendency to be almost invariably disparaging, even condescending, especially in the American press, as literary journalists (a shade naively) await the Definitive Terrorist Novel, a sort of 9/11 version of *Moby Dick*, a novel to end all novels, as it were.

While Ahmad's criticism of the American consumerist ideal is extreme, Updike quite obviously shares his nonmaterialist thirst for higher values, hence the writer's use of free indirect discourse, a style in which it is often hard to distinguish the author from his character. Through his misguided, but sympathetic protagonist, Updike reiterates Existentialist nihilism's critique of the modern world as inauthentic. Updike's terrorist gives us an often rather clear-sightedly defamiliarised version of the America we know – he is Albert Camus's Outsider conjoined to an Islamicized Catcher in the Rye.

Martin Amis's short story, "'The Last Days of Muhammad Atta'" in *The Second Plane* (2008), takes a direct look at the ringleader of the 9/11 attacks in a way that differs substantially from the ruthless portrait that we are given in Delillo's *Falling Man*. Amis's characterisation of Atta is very much a matter of deliberate hit and miss, however. Far from being the deeply fervent ideologist reports have made him out to be, the author makes Atta apolitical and non-religious: "He had allied himself with the militants because jihad was, by many magnitudes, the most charismatic idea of his generation. To unite ferocity and rectitude in a single word: nothing could compete with that" (101).

Of all the novelists studied here, Amis is without a doubt the one who comes closest to manifesting a degree of continuity with the general spirit of cheerful nihilism: while the story can hardly be said to be upbeat, it bears the stamp of Beckettian humour, most especially with its emphasis on bodily malfunction (Atta is prone to constipation for weeks before the attack and then has to submit to an onslaught of diarrhoea on the plane). The story is playful in that it elaborates a kind of writer's revenge by deliberately misrepresenting the terrorist on an ideological and religious level. The final twist of the story is also in keeping with this jokey vengeance as Atta is forced to relive his last day endlessly in a kind of paper hell designed by his writerly gaolkeeper.

Like Updike with Ahmad, Amis transforms Atta into a nihilist who cannot suffer the impurities of this world. His view of the world is a misanthropist's version of the doctrine propounded by the Greek philosopher Hegesis: since the hardships of existence far outweigh its pleasures, the only logical solution is suicide bombing. Amis also makes Atta almost inconceivably misanthropic. He is the ultimate misanthrope, exceeding any other man-hating literary character. Amis takes Sartre's existential nausea to its extreme in this story. The all-embracing loathing of existence that Amis attributes to his paper-bound captive is at least partly based on impressions of the real-life person. According to reports, Atta was said to walk into rooms without acknowledging the presence of those who were in them. He was described by his flatmates in Hamburg as inhabiting complete, almost aggressive insularity.

Set in London, like Ian McEwan's *Saturday*, J. G. Ballard's third-last novel *Millenium People* (2003) takes a similarly oblique look at 9/11. This novel explores the potential terrorist lurking in the heart of every man. The nihilistic strand it explores is akin to anomie, the disintegration of moral values in the individual and society due to boredom with the habitual. The narrator's wife observes that "We're like children left for too long in a playroom. After a while we have to start breaking up the toys, even the ones we like. There's nothing we believe in" (115). Inspired by the 9/11 attacks and fuelled by a kind of *début-de-siècle Ennui*, London's bourgeoisie decides to instigate a revolt against its self-constructed world as a way of abolishing its decadence by pushing it as far as it will go. Although the novel's scenario is improbable, it works well as a fable illustrating the desire for revitalisation through violence. While the purposeless, random violence perpetrated in the novel appears to express what one character calls "pure nihilism" (194), the intradiegetic narrator argues that it is

> [t]he exact opposite [...] It isn't a search for nothingness. It's a search for meaning. Blow up the Stock Exchange and you're rejecting global capitalism. Bomb the Ministry of Defence and you're protesting against war. You don't even need to hand out the leaflets (194).

By imitating the random functioning of the universe, the deranged instigators of the revolution also hope to beat the universe at its own game. Their irrationalist, motiveless acts are ultimately portrayed as a behavioural defence mechanism.

While the tone of *Millenium People* can hardly be said to be cheerful, the overall plot tends to bring out the *puer aeternus* in every man. Although Ballard has said in an interview that his greatest fear is terrorist attacks ("Questions and Answers" *Millenium People* 6), he has also claimed that

> there's a room for the terrorist novel and I've always thought of myself [...] as throwing a literary bomb into a rather smug [...] cafeteria. I think most people have a conventionalized view of the world and I'm interested in stripping away those conventions because the underlying psychological truth is there to be [...] exposed ("BBC Profile").

In this sense, McEwan's fiction can also be said to have something in common with Ballard's scriptorial terrorism.

In his "Faith and Doubt at Ground Zero" interview, McEwan presents the world deadlocked between Existentialist nihilism and the religious and political zeal that leads to annihilation: "I don't know, quite honestly, whether the world suffers from people not believing enough in things, or believing too much in things". The private drama enacted in *Saturday* depicts the plight of a family confronted with a nihilist who has lost all moral sense because of the disease that afflicts him. Baxter, who has been diagnosed by the novel's protagonist as suffering from Huntington's Disease, comes to represent the figure of the nihilistic terrorist on a domestic level. His loss of moral values is only partially caused by his incurable disease; he is also socially unfortunate: "He's an intelligent man, and gives the impression that, illness apart, he's missed his chances, made some big mistakes and ended up in the wrong company. Probably dropped out of school long ago and regrets it" (98). In the end, it is ironically his not quite complete nihilism which causes his downfall. A neurosurgeon, Perowne is also psychologically adroit: he is able to turn the tables by wedging a false element of hope for a cure into Baxter's mind on two occasions, first in order to save himself and then in the final scene to save the whole family: "Perowne is familiar with this impulse in patients, this pursuit of the slenderest leads" (97). In the final scene, Perowne leads Baxter away from his nihilism, literally up the stairs of hope to his office where, like Daisy who pretends to read her own poem, he aims to offer Baxter papers full of medical terms that he is about to pass off as evidence of a cure that does not in reality exist. McEwan's gift for mirroring effects is supreme: another fine instance of doubling is provided by the squash match Perowne has with a colleague of his after the first encounter with Baxter. The match cogently works as both a re-enactment of Perowne's first confrontation with Baxter and a suspenseful warning of a possibly negative resolution to the novel as Perowne ultimately thinks he has won the match only to be defeated in an unexpected extension of the game.

As in Updike's novel *Terrorist* in which the day is saved by the career counsellor's apparent bout of nihilistic indifference, it is the beleaguered family's use of Matthew Arnold's politically and existentially nihilistic poem "Dover Beach" (1867) that makes their assailant's acute sense of nihilism abate,[1] ironically just long enough for him to be defeated entirely as he careers down the stairs, becoming yet another Falling Man, a mere structuring element of the novel since his fall echoes the falling airplane that the protagonist, Henry Perowne, sees in the opening pages of the novel. In a way that recalls Amis's grimly playful punishment of Atta, McEwan imagines another form of writer's revenge against the figure of the terrorist.

With the last twist of his plot, McEwan provides a rather optimistic view of the power of literature. Although the resolution to the conflict is a bit improbable (perhaps especially the way Perowne's daughter Daisy is able to summon such powers of memory in the midst of an extremely anxiety-inducing situation), McEwan's greatness lies in his ability to make the unlikely feel utterly convincing. Asked to read from a collection of her own poems by the terrorist figure Baxter, Daisy (who is understandably shaken up and has been forced to strip naked) not only has the presence of mind to recite Matthew Arnold's "Dover Beach" instead of reading her own poem, she also suddenly has an extremely self-possessed actress's ability to do this and simultaneously pretend she is reading her own poem. And yet, we willingly suspend our disbelief in this scene as McEwan stretches suspense and our sense of the possible to its elastic limit when Baxter, almost silent with emotion, commands a second reading. Perowne acts as the reader's alter ego in the scene as his incredulity allays our own:

> Though his right hand hasn't moved from Rosalind's neck, his grip on the knife looks slacker, and his posture, the peculiar yielding angle of his spine, suggests a possible ebbing of intent. Could it happen, is it within the bounds of the real, that a mere poem of Daisy's could precipitate a mood swing? (221).

McEwan's use of Baxter's compulsive verbal repetitiveness also very convincingly portrays the mind of the enthralled, mentally impaired terrorist, capable of allowing the potentially pantomime-like change of heart to occur:

> Henry worries that a prompt from Nigel, a reminder of the purpose of the visit, could effect another mood swing, a reversion. But Baxter has broken the silence and is saying excitedly, 'You wrote that. You *wrote* that.'

It's a statement, not a question. Daisy stares at him, waiting.
He says again, 'You wrote that.' And then, hurriedly, 'It's beautiful. You know that, don't you. It's beautiful. And you wrote it.'
She says nothing.
'It makes me think about where I grew up.' (222)

Among contemporary novelists, McEwan is virtually alone in depicting a scene in which the pen is mightier than the penknife, to rephrase Edward Bulwer-Lytton's famous phrase. As the critic Margaret Scanlan observes, the only novels that have had any real effect on terrorists are those that have been misread or taken to extremes: she mentions the Unabomber's idealization of Conrad's character known as the Professor in *The Secret Agent* and Timothy McVeigh's use of William Pierce's anti-Semitic novel *The Turner Diaries* to bomb the Murrah Federal Building in Oklahoma City. Scanlan might have added Mark Chapman's misuse of *The Catcher in the Rye* to sanction his murder of John Lennon, a novel Theodore Kaczynski, the Unabomber, also admired, even going as far as to include it in one of his parcel bombs that fortunately did not detonate, sending literary shrapnel through the air.

The backdrop to Baxter's loss of values is provided by Perowne's reflections on Islamic fundamentalism which is conveyed in a more subtle and perhaps less Western-centred way than it is in Delillo or Amis who both emphasize the apparent aimlessness of Islamic terrorism. Although at first he is bemused by what he sees as a form of nihilistic terrorism that demands nothing in exchange ("Only hatred is registered, the purity of nihilism" 33), he later qualifies that statement: "But that's not quite right. Radical Islamists aren't really nihilists – they want the perfect society on Earth, which is Islam" (34). It is therefore unfair to say, as does Michael L. Ross, that Perowne's (and McEwan's) gaze is entirely "monoptic" (82).

McEwan found the ideal objective correlative for the Cold War and the partitioning of Berlin in *The Innocent* (1990) by imaging the cutting in two of a character called Otto: added to this perfectly organic image of severance, McEwan's recourse to palindromic onomastics in the choice of Otto's name appositely symbolises the broken wholeness of the city. Conrad's disintegration of Stevie (who is accidentally blown to pieces when he is forced by his morally defunct stepfather to carry a bomb because the latter feels trapped into organising an attack on the Greenwich Observatory) in *The Secret Agent* also acts as an apt image of moral disintegration. The same can be said of Don Delillo's performance artist, known as the falling man: the obscure, dimly-portrayed character is in fact more of a dangling man (which brings us back to the title of Saul Bellow's novel) who suspends himself from various buildings after the 9/11 attacks. The fact that so little is known about this character coupled to the fact that he is suspended in the air and thus as paralysed as the city itself after the endless falling of the towers functions well as an objective correlative, particularly also as a doubling image for the main character's sense of inertia after he has escaped from one of the Twin Towers. Whether or not Baxter functions as a solid symbol of the post-9/11 world is perhaps a bit more debatable. While he very concretely and dramatically embodies Perowne's post-9/11 paranoia and hatred of intrusion from the public domain, the fact that he has no real link to Islamicism or the 'war on terror' tends to make McEwan's dialogic discussion on whether or not to attack Iraq collapse into a thrilling, but politically uninteresting, defence of Perowne's home and the simple destruction of the 'devil' in the house, to reformulate Coventry Patmore's Victorian expression for perfectly domesticated and angelically disempowered femininity.

Although Perowne's general approach to life is very serious-minded and generally beset by the disturbing intrusions of the outside world which he calls "this infection from the public domain" (108), a number of his thoughts do come close to the wry spirit of cheerful nihilism. There is an instance of this towards the beginning of the novel when he performs his ablutions: after having moved his bowels, he remembers an article he read that claimed that at least one particle of his waste would one day evaporate and come down as rain on his head (57). The ludicrous thought makes him hum Vera Lynn's wartime song "We'll Meet Again": although it is not stated explicitly, his scatological recontextualization of the song is at least unconsciously, if not consciously, influenced by Stanley Kubrick's disjunctive use of it at the end of *Dr. Strangelove* when film footage of nuclear mushroom clouds is included to accompany the soothing sentimentality of the song. Generally speaking, however, Perowne's consideration of the state of the world is rather grave, revealing as in Ballard's novels, the sinister underside of nihilistic violence. While Ballard dramatises our sadistic need to destroy, McEwan views our obsession with terrorist attacks in more masochistic terms: using the participatory device of free indirect discourse, the narrator calls it "a darker longing in the collective mind, a sickening for self-punishment and a blasphemous curiosity" (176).

While recent fictional accounts of terrorist violence are not devoid of occasional flashes of dark humour, sustained examples of cheerful nihilism seem to be in recession even within the confines of generally more exuberant American fiction. Although Will Self's most recent novel *The Butt* (2008) actually won the Wodehouse prize for comic fiction, its account of the nightmarishly absurd consequences of the war on terrorism make Kafka's world feel almost reassuring by comparison. Will Self's nihilism in this novel is about as cheerful as a tombstone, and probably made poor P. G. Wodehouse turn in his grave. Admirable as Self's writing is, it was something of a relief to learn that no one laughed at his reading of an extract during the attribution of the prize.

All things considered, it is in the end probably misleading to attribute this trend towards dark nihilism entirely to the effects of 9/11. Serious novels that explore contemporary terrorism written before this ominous date are often also sombre and hopeless. The optimism implied in Doris Lessing's *The Good Terrorist* (1985), for instance, doesn't go much further than the title: in the final analysis, it is probably just as ironic and oxymoronic as Ford Madox Ford's *The Good Soldier* (1915).

Bibliography

Auster, Paul: *Man in the Dark*. London: Faber and Faber, 2008.
Amis, Martin: *The Second Plane*. London: Cape, 2008.
Ballard, J. G. "BBC Profile". BBC 4 <http://www.youtube.com>
---. *Millenium People*. London: Harper, 2003.
Barth, John: *The End of the Road*. New York: Avon, 1964.
Biaggi, Vladimir: *Le Nihilisme*. Paris: Flammarion, 1998.
Bradbury, Malcolm: *The Modern American Novel*. Oxford: Oxford University Press, 1992.
Clark, Robert: "Saturday", *The Literary Encyclopedia*. 12 April 2005. <http://www.litencyc.com>
Cronenberg, David: *Existenz*. Alliance Atlantis, 1999.

Delillo, Don: *Falling Man*. New York: Shribner, 2007.
Hauck, Richard Boyd: *A Cheerful Nihilism: Confidence and "The Absurd" in American Humorous Fiction*. Bloomington: Indiana University Press,1971.
Kakutani, Michiko: "A Man, a Woman and a Day of Terror", 9 May 2007. *The New York Times*. <http://www.nytimes.com>
---: "John Updike's 'Terrorist' Imagines a Homegrown Threat to Homeland Security". 6 June 2006. *The New York Times*. <http://www.nytimes.com>
Lessing, Doris: *The Good Terrorist*. London: Cape, 1985.
McEwan, Ian: "Faith and Doubt at Ground Zero". Frontline/PBS, April 2002.
---: *Saturday*. London: Vintage, 2006.
Nietzsche, Friedrich: *The Gay Science*. London: Dover, 2006.
Ross, Michael L.: "On a Darkling Planet: Ian McEwan's *Saturday* and the Condition of England", *Twentieth-Century Literature*. 54.1(2008): 75-96.
Roth, Philip: *Everyman*. London: Vintage, 2007.
---: *The Plot Against America*. Croydon: Vintage, 2005.
Scanlan, Margaret: *Plotting Terror: Novelists and Terrorists in Contemporary Fiction*. Charlottesville: University Press of Virginia, 2001.
Scott, Ridley: *Body of Lies*. Warner Brothers. 2008.
Self, Will: *The Butt*. London: Bloomsbury, 2009.
Updike, John: *Terrorist*. New York, Ballantine, 2006.

Helga Schwalm (Berlin)

Figures of Authorship, Empathy, & The Ethics of Narrative (Mis-)Recognition in Ian McEwan's Later Fiction

In a frequently quoted Guardian article published in the immediate aftermath of 11 September 2001, Ian McEwan formulates his vision of a morality based on empathy:

> Waking before dawn, going about our business during the day, we fantasize ourselves into the events. What if it was me? This is the nature of empathy, to think oneself into the minds of others. These are the mechanics of compassion: you are under the bedclothes, unable to sleep, and you are crouching in the brushed-steel lavatory at the rear of the plane, whispering a final message to your loved one. There is only that one thing to say, and you say it. All else is pointless. You have very little time before *some holy fool, who believes in his place in eternity* [my emphasis, HS], kicks in the door, slaps your head and orders you back to your seat. [...] If the hijackers had been able to imagine themselves into the thoughts and feelings of the passengers, they would have been unable to proceed. It is hard to be cruel once you permit yourself to enter the mind of your victim. Imagining what it is like to be someone other than yourself is at the core of our humanity. It is the essence of compassion, and it is the beginning of morality.[1]

"Empathy",[2] "compassion", and "love" – these are the key words that McEwan holds up against the onslaught of a 'foolish' and 'inhumane' terrorism. He does so in a twofold way: Firstly, "our" response is one of empathy with the victims during their last minutes/ hours – "we" imagine ourselves in their place, and McEwan is confident that we would have all resorted to those "universal" words of love. Secondly, terrorism would be impossible in the face of empathy: "The hijackers used fanatical certainty," McEwan proposes, "misplaced religious faith, and dehumanising hatred to purge themselves of the human instinct for empathy. Among their crimes was a failure of the imagination."[3]

McEwan is treading on difficult ground here. He calls up empathy and imagination as fundamental, universal qualities ("the core of our humanity"), and by implication a community of value, but does not extend his imagination to the other side, choosing not to think about what could have possibly driven the terrorists to such terrible acts (they are nothing but "holy fools"). McEwan's vacillation between universalist notions on the one hand and occidental enlightenment assumptions on the other; between claims of reciprocity and one-sidedness of intersubjective relationships, seems to be symptomatic also of his literary productions before and after 9/11. Notoriously, McEwan did proceed to write a novel which stages in its opening scene a protagonist awaking in bed before dawn to see an aeroplane on fire in the London sky; terrorism, physical violation and empathy play a key role in *Saturday* (2005). As a mode of intersubjectivity and authorial control, empathy also operates at the strategic heart of his earlier novels *Atonement* (2001) and *Amsterdam* (1998). Located at the intersection of aesthetics and ethics, the nexus of empathy, intersubjective recognition, and its authorial/narrative staging[4] is the subject of this paper. My contention is that McEwan's novels *Amsterdam*, *Atonement*, and *Saturday* display and explore various dimensions of authorial and figural patterns of empathy and thus reveal its paradoxical nature as a fundamental quality of intersubjectivity and as a transgressive act of 'usurpation', of authorial appropriation, and of potential misrecognition.

Drawing on Axel Honneth's social philosophy and its key concept of recognition may illuminate the social and political significance of McEwan's extra- and intra-fictional preoccupation with empathy and love. Honneth assumes the priority of intersubjective relationships of recognition (and struggles for recognition as the core of social conflicts), spelling out three different modes and forms of recognition: 1) "emotional support"/"love, friendship"; 2) "cognitive respect", "rights"; 3) "social esteem", "solidarity". Correspondingly, there are different modes of misrecognition at the heart of social and interpersonal conflicts: 1) "abuse and rape"; 2) "denial of rights, exclusion"; 3) "denigration, insult".[5] Honneth argues that the three distinct, increasingly abstract modes of recognition make up three distinct stages in the development of individuals, each with "quite different social and political implications."[6]

Reconsidered in terms of Honneth's philosophy of recognition, the fundamental and at the same time limited nature of McEwan's perspective becomes visible. McEwan singles out one particular mode of intersubjective recognition – empathy and love – pertaining to primary, concrete relationships and involving complex reciprocal processes of love and mutual support. While empathy represents the reciprocal quality of projecting oneself into the mind of another person, love signifies an intersubjective emotional bond, recognizing both the needs of the other and their separate individuality.[7] In Honneth's model, this basic relationship of recognition is followed by two more abstract modes of recognition: "cognitive respect" and "social esteem", relating to the spheres of "rights" and "solidarity" respectively.[8] Significantly, McEwan does not engage with these more abstract spheres and correspondent modes of recognition. Yet in the context of Honneth's model, McEwan's authorial obsessions with the themes of sexual and psychological deviation, physical violence, and assaults on the one hand and explorations of forms of love on the other hand make sense indeed: Psychological pathology and violence represent "forms of disrespect" which Honneth defines as love's "negative equivalents".[9] They threaten the "physical integrity of individuals". While love implies both "an affective confidence in the continuity of shared concern" and a "recognition involving the cognitive acceptance of the other's independence",[10] disorders of love relationships can be grasped as "one-sidedness in the direction of one of the two poles of the balance of recognition."[11]

In *Amsterdam*, empathy as a projection of oneself into the minds of others operates on various levels of plot and narration. Quite obviously and deliberately staged, it does not ground any moral sense or self-awareness. Neither does it feature as part of the principle character's aesthetic imagination. In the key scene of the novel set in the Lake District, when the composer Clive witnesses the assault on a woman, he fails to overcome his egotistic concerns and decides not to help a female stranger. Romantic authorship/ composership, evoked through the Lake District topography, remains unconnected from any will or ability to support an other. Art needs to be unbothered by the world. Clive's self-centredness is indeed so strong that he is not prepared to engage with real others:

neither with the female stranger nor with the group of school children, whose presence tempts him to change his itinerary. Exclusion from the world is felt as a prerequisite of artistic creativity – unlike Wordsworth's crucial inclusions of companions and encounters with locals in his topographical poems, but sharing with Wordsworth the objection to mass (in this case: children's) tourism which, as the composer laments, reduces the Lake District "to a trampled beauty spot".[12] He also shares with Wordsworth the pathetic fallacies and the belief in the regenerative power, both aesthetically and morally speaking, of the Lake District.[13]

Ironically, Clive's Wordsworthian confidence to be on the verge of artistic regeneration, of finding the key element to his finale, proves an illusion. What he believes to be the perfect theme to conclude his symphony, the ultimate sign of genius, turns out to sound "quite absurd", like "a giant bagpipe in need of repair". "The absence of variation had wrecked his masterpiece."[14] Yet while Clive is ultimately forced to see/hear the flaws in his composition during the rehearsal, he does not achieve any insight into his cognitive and moral failings.

Clive's perception of others, including their response to him, is repeatedly revealed to be erroneous, particularly in the case of his statement at the police station when he fails to identify the suspect.[15] This tendency towards misperception even applies to the relationship with his best friend. While they agree at an early stage in the plot to give 'ultimate support' to each other, promising 'reciprocal euthanasia', the novel's ending exhibits both friends in a kind of parody of intersubjective reciprocity. Cold-heartedly anticipating and calculating the actions of the other, they both fail to recognize their opposite's equally nasty schemes. Thus *Amsterdam* concludes with a scenario of perfect mutual, reciprocal misrecognition. It is a misrecognition generated by the structures of an intrigue gone wrong: If the dramatic device of intrigue 'normally' stages deliberately asymmetrical, semi-intransparent structures of communication, the narrative arrangement of the ending, in contrast, doubles the intrigue to blast its design into a perfect symmetry of failed operations, which ironically serve the purpose of murder after all. While on the diegetic level the authorial plan of deliberate intersubjective asymmetry goes out of control, the extradiegetic narrator has composed a perfectly arranged scenario which coolly displays the emotional, cognitive, and moral shortcomings of his characters.[16] The effect is cold, merciless satire in the services of (fictional) authorial power reminiscent of the early Nabokov.[17]

Atonement gives the figures of authorship, empathy and intersubjective recognition a metafictional twist. Critics have agreed that the first three parts of the narrative initially appear to be the product of a heterodiegetic narrator employing Virginia Woolf's modernist technique of multiple focalization through free indirect discourse. Empathy thus features by way of the narrator's imagination of the minds of others qua free indirect discourse or psycho-narration" with (strong) "consonance".[18] In other words, narrative empathy projects the authorial self into the mind of a character, translating vicarious narrative into the mode of experientiality.[19] In this context, the presence of Jane Austen, both in terms of stylistic influence and explicit quotation,[20] reinforces the thematic link between subjective points of view, rendered by free indirect discourse, and social misunderstanding. The iterative narration of the fountain scene precisely exhibits the limitations and distortions of subjective perspectives, particularly the cognitive and emotional restrictions of adolescence and of class prejudice.[21] Richardson's *Clarissa,* another prominent pretext in *Atonement,*[22] again – apart from suggesting Romance and epistolary intrigue – evokes the precariousness of intersubjective relationships based on sympathy/empathy; at the same time it alludes to the difficulty of maintaining ultimate authorial control over one's text.[23]

In *Atonement*, the problem of authorship and empathy emerges in the final part when the logic of narration undergoes a sea change: the heroine Briony turns out to be the intradiegetic author-narrator of the preceding narrative, which is the revised and extended version of her earlier war-time prose attempt referred to in part III.[24] It is Briony herself who, as an old woman, explains the motivation behind her authorship – atonement for the wrong she has committed as a young girl. Among others, Claudia Schemberg has suggested in this context that what Briony as narrator attempts is a redemption through placing herself in the mind of another.[25] Indeed, to some extent this makes her novel a loving exercise in an empathetic 'semi-vicarious' narrative which seeks to overcome her own limited point of view according to her insight "that other people are as real as you. And only in a story could you enter these different minds and show how they had an equal value."[26]

Briony herself, however, concedes the impossibility of atonement through "impartial psychological realism".[27] As a novelist, she has placed herself in a God-like position, having the "absolute power of deciding outcomes",[28] and as such she has no one to appeal to but herself – this is her paradox of authorship. Yet her insight does not extend to the question of narrative mode. She does grant others a mind of their own,[29] but from a position of adopted authorial superiority that, in a way, repeats her will to authorial control, the "controlling demon"[30] of the young girl with literary aspirations. Her modernist choice is one that seeks to pretend the independent existence of individual minds by limiting the visibility of her authorial power. In a way she confirms what John Bender has shown with regard to the historical origins of free indirect discourse: as a narrative device of creating transparent minds, it entails structures of control through an invisible presence of authorial power.[31]

Bound to a homodiegetic third-person narrative, Briony's fictional transparent minds acquire the status of overt fabrication; however, in the pragmatic context of seeking impossible atonement, they are particularly suspicious in suggesting a hidden agenda behind the authorial concealment and a kind of usurpation of the other for Briony's own purposes.

Such a self-serving undercurrent comes to the surface in part II. For what is the purpose of the lengthy descriptions of Robbie's Dunkirk experience? Whereas the narrator's fictional ending, which brings the lovers together (and does not allow Briony forgiveness), may be an act of love and atonement, part II seems to fulfil a more complex and more ambivalent function. The war section includes less focalized narrative passages (with Robbie as "Turner") attempting to 'storify' a deeply fragmentized and chaotic experience, which in its details must have eluded the author's knowledge, well researched as her novel may be. In fact, specific events such as the failed rescue of the Flemish mother and child need to be taken as the product of her imagination, although to some extent based on letters and corrected or verified by an army veteran.[32] (Had she taken the details of the episodes from Robbie's letters, the corrections by her military advisor[33] would not have been necessary.) Apart from translating historical knowledge into an experiential narrative of war, from foregrounding "the horror of death and mutilation"[34] in these largely invented scenes, the fictional author possibly generates a certain relativity of her own guilt by juxtaposing it with ubiquitous guilt, individual and collective, and by projecting the consciousness of this onto her character, freeing herself from any suspicion of self-interest: "But what was guilt these days", Robbie reflects on his way to the beach. "It was cheap. Everyone was guilty, and no one was."[35] Leaving the issue of the empirical author's ethical soundness with respect to his war scenes aside,[36] Briony certainly makes use of her empathetic account not solely for the impartial purposes of psychological realism and recognition of the impossibility of making good, but also for merging her deed into larger events. Thus Briony's war writing, in effect, allows her "crime to be subsumed in – and overshadowed by – the larger movements of twentieth-century history"[37] – or by larger scales of guilt.

With *Saturday*, McEwan explores the limits and failures of empathy in relation to (authorial) control further,[38] and he also takes up again the negative equivalents of primary forms of recognition: rape and physical violation. Terrorism and the impending Iraq war make up the large-scale analogies to face-to-face forms of misrecognition. Notably though, the sight of an aeroplane on fire does not inspire compassion in the protagonist. Perowne, who is a family man constitutionally destined to love his wife only and forever, to love his children so much that he can even tolerate his son's Blues career (the middle-class assumptions behind this!), Henry Perowne on this potentially horrific occasion simply recollects his own thoughts and fears as a post 9/11 traveller: "the spectacle has the familiarity of a recurrent dream. Like most passengers, outwardly subdued by the monotony of air travel, he often lets his thoughts range across the possibilities while sitting," and "[p]lastic fork in hand, he often wonders how it might go".[39] This is a far cry from McEwan's post 9/11 *Guardian* universal man. Outside his home, Perowne tends to project himself into other persons not by imagination or compassion, but by neurological knowledge and observation. McEwan's protagonist can read the mind and anticipate the actions of his opponent Baxter, and he also 'literalizes' empathy in the sense that he intrudes into the minds of his patients through surgery. Just as he needs to stay aloof in the operating theatre, Perowne manages to maintain the upper hand in his first encounter with Baxter because of his professional authority. Class status, professional knowledge and command of his rational powers allow him to defeat his opponent. Perowne walks away believing himself to be in authorial control of his world. (The victory, of course, is not quite complete as he fails to anticipate the extent of Baxter's provocation.) Only later, when his family is seriously in danger, does he attempt "to see the room through his [Baxter's] eyes, as if that might help predict the degree of trouble ahead"[40] – one might call this 'empathy as survival strategy'.

Perowne assimilates everything and everyone into his view of the world, and the narrative does not transcend his angle. It is his scientific epistemological frame and his class and professional habitus of superiority and detachment that make McEwan's protagonist so unsusceptible to literature. Significantly, whereas he is capable of at least noticing his failure to have perceived Daisy's pregnancy symptoms, he is not capable of fully grasping his failures as a reader. The (present tense) free indirect discourse brilliantly exposes him to hear in his daughter's or rather Matthew Arnold's words the projections of his own mind only. The Iraq war thus invades Arnold's poem: "desert armies stand ready to fight".[41] On hearing the poem read a second time Perowne "discovers" there is "no mention of a desert",[42] but still does not comprehend what is going on. Finally, he fails to realize that this is not his daughter's poem – he is, after all, a true middle-class "Philistine", to use Arnold's word,[43] whereas it is Baxter who is capable of aesthetic response. Thus, in a "curious kind of parody of literature's civilizing mission, he [i.e. Baxter, H.S.] becomes a kind of Arnoldian best self, transformed by a literary conversion" as opposed to the determinism of his disease.[44] What Perowne and Baxter share, however, is the wrong identification of the author.

McEwan, then, brilliantly displays various scenes of misrecognitions and failures of empathy. Along with that he reminds us in his novel of the postmodern condition of mutually incompatible systems of knowledge, frameworks and discursive rules. However, by again pathologizing the encounter with the other (outside those obnoxiously happy family relations), McEwan reduces the phenomenon of intersubjective misrecognition, the problem of legitimacy of violence etc. to a somewhat simple scenario of primary relationships. He excludes the larger, more abstract issues initially evoked by the 9/11 allusions. And while he does reveal the empathetic shortcomings of his focalizer-protagonist, he has largely cut out the complex issues of the author's position in the processes of empathy which *Atonement* stages. Perowne's command of events has only been impaired temporalily, the outcome reasserting his professional English middle-class world. The threat to physical integrity is caused by a pathological opponent, and the hero's own misappropriations of others remain secondary; they are not subjected to alternative viewpoints as the narrative constructs Perowne as sole focalizer. Fallible as Perowne may be as focalizer,[45] the implied author remains invisible (or inaudible) behind him. With its absence of metafictional and epistemological reflections and the narrative invisibility of its author, the text disengages author and protagonist from empathy as well as compassion, while leaving empathy as the authorial act of creating transparent minds in place.

Empathy as a fundamental quality of reciprocity is strikingly absent in *Saturday*; so are other, more abstract or general forms of recognition (or misrecognition, for that matter). Only fleetingly does Perowne catch a glimpse of Baxter's reproach of social exclusion as he is tumbling down the stairs:

> Henry thinks he sees in the wide brown eyes a sorrowful accusation of betrayal. He, Henry Perowne, possesses so much [...] and he has done nothing, given nothing to Baxter, who has so little that is not wrecked by his defective gene.[46]

The issue of cognitive respect and social esteem, or exclusion and insult, is reduced to a sad genetic phenomenon. Apart from this brief moment in the final scene, the larger social and political issues of rights and legitimacy, the question of how inclusive McEwan's community of value is, are at best faintly present by implication – after all, the London march serving as the novel's backdrop was about the (il)legitimacy of the impending Iraq war.

Returning to McEwan's *Guardian* response to the terrorists' attacks, it needs to be acknowledged that he formulated his credo of empathy, love, and compassion at a highly emotional point in time, and he never aspired to speak as a social philosopher or to formulate a comprehensive theoretical view in the first place. Yet his novels, especially *Saturday*, which is explicitly positioned in the post 9/11 world, appear curiously oblivious to the limits of their own normative framework, excluding other, more general forms of recognition and misrecognition, such as the denial of rights, exclusion, denigration, insult, although these generalized forms of recognition, which go beyond interaction with concrete others, are pertinent to the modern world and certainly even more so to the post 9/11 world. The novel remains curiously silent on the larger issues at stake, leaving the reader puzzled as to its political and ethical stance.

Notes

1   McEwan (2001).
2   The Oxford English Dictionary defines empathy as "the power of projecting one's personality into (and so fully comprehending) the object of contemplation".
    http://dictionary.oed.com/cgi/entry/50074152?single=1&query_type=word&queryword =empathy&first= 1&max_to_show=10 [1-3-09].
3   McEwan (2001).
4   Various critical voices have testified to the "'emphatic proximity and intensive interconnectedness'" of these aspects in McEwan's novels, see James (2003: 93).
5   Honneth (1995: 129), Figure 2.
6   Blunden (2009).
7   Honneth speaks of empathy only with reference to Winnicott. While empathy represents this reciprocal quality (signifying the fundamental quality of reciprocal role taking at the core of interactive relationships), love signifies an intersubjective emotional bond, recognizing both the needs of the other and their separate individuality.
8   Honneth (1995: 129).
9   Ibid., 93.
10 Ibid., 107.
11 Ibid., 106. In "pathological cases", Honneth explains, "the reciprocity of the intersubjectively suspended arc is destroyed by the fact that one of the subjects involved is no longer able to detach himself or herself either from the state of egocentric independence or from that of symbiotic dependence." Ibid. – McEwan's Enduring Love features such constellations especially.
12 McEwan (2005a: 83).
13 See especially Book One of Wordsworth's Prelude, 1805 version (1979).
14 McEwan (2005a: 160-161).
15 Ibid., 154.
16 Clive, in contrast to the narrator's structuring, believes their friendship to be imbalanced, see ibid., 65.

17 According to Lynn Wells, the architectural structure of *Amsterdam* invites the reader to reflect on the issue of ethical preferences (2006: 123). However, Wells ignores that the satirical staging refuses its characters the faculty of empathy.
18 Cohn (1978: 21-57). Dorrit Cohn's term allows for more authorial visibility than pure free indirect discourse.
19 As Monika Fludernik (1996) has argued, this is the hallmark of the novel proper, realized in modernist fiction.
20 The epigraph of *Atonement* is taken from Austen's *Northanger Abbey*.
21 McEwan (2002: 29-30 vs. 38-40, and 312-313).
22 Briony's sister Cecilia reads *Clarissa* (2002: 21), while the heroine of Briony's melodrama, Arabella, shares her name with the sister of Richardson's heroine.
23 For Richardson and sympathy see Schwalm (2007: 172-176).
24 See also Head (2007: 156-158).
25 Schemberg (2004: 85-86).
26 McEwan (2002: 40).
27 Ibid., 41.
28 Ibid., 371.
29 See also Schemberg (2004: 85).
30 McEwan (2002: 5).
31 Bender (1987: 211-213, 227-228). – Placing Jane Austen within the tradition of the eighteenth-century novel, so deeply engaged in juridical discourse, her narrative empathy would appear as a product of authorial power, a power seeking to invade and make transparent the consciousness of another.
32 McEwan (2002: 359). Head argues similarly (2007: 166).
33 McEwan (2002: 359).
34 Head (2007: 156).
35 McEwan (2002: 261). – Furthermore, Briony also achieves a kind of self-justification through repetition staging her misperceptions as inevitable, see Head (2007: 165).
36 On this issue see, e.g., Ibid., 166–167.
37 Ibid.,171.
38 Lynn Wells, for instance, has suggested that McEwan's later fictions include "staged scenes of ethical confrontation that call into question the individual's true ability to deal compassionately with the other", complicated by McEwan's "evolving aesthetic [...] towards greater textual self-consciousness and generic manipulation". Wells (2007: 117).
39 McEwan (2005b: 15).
40 Ibid., 207.
41 Ibid., 221.
42 Ibid., 222.
43 Arnold (1960: 101).
44 Amigoni (2008: 162).

45 I am indebted to Martin Middeke for this observation.
46 McEwan (2005b: 227-228).

Bibliography

Amigoni, David: "'The luxury of storytelling.' Science, Literature and Cultural Contest in Ian McEwan's Narrative Practice". – In Sharon Ruston (Ed.): *Essays and Studies 2008. Literature and Science*, Cambridge, 2008, pp. 161-168.
Arnold, Matthew: *Culture and Anarchy. An Essay in Political and Social Criticism*, London, 1960.
Bender, John: *Imagining the Penitentiary. Fiction and the Architecture of Mind in Eighteenth-Century England*, Chicago & London, 1987.
Blunden, Andy: "Honneth's "Struggle for Recognition"', http://home.mira.net /~andy/works/honneth.htm (accessed 23 February 2009), n.pag.
Cohn, Dorrit: *Transparent Minds. Narrative Modes for Presenting Consciousness in Fiction*, Princeton, 1978.
Fludernik, Monika: *Towards A 'Natural' Narratology*, London & New York, 1996.
Head, Dominic: *Ian McEwan*, Manchester, 2007.
Honneth, Axel: *The Struggle for Recognition. The Moral Grammar of Social Conflicts*, Cambridge, 1995.
James, David: "Masculinities in McEwan's fiction", *Textual Practice* 17:1, 2003, 81–100.
McEwan, Ian: *Amsterdam*, London, 2005a.
---: *Atonement*, London, 2002.
---: "Only love and then oblivion. Love was all they had to set against their murderers", *The Guardian*, 15 September 2001, http://www.guardian.co.uk /world/2001/sep/15/september11.politicsphilosophyandsociety2 (accessed 17 February 2009), n.pag.
---: *Saturday*, London, 2005b.
Lawson, Mark: Review, *The Guardian*, 22 January 2005, http://www. guardian.co.uk/books/2005/jan/22/bookerprize2005.bookerprize (accessed 18 February 2009), n.pag.
Schemberg, Claudia: *Achieving 'At-one-ment'. Storytelling and the Concept of the Self in Ian McEwan's The Child in Time, Black Dogs, Enduring Love, and Atonement*, Frankfurt, 2004.
Schwalm, Helga: *Das eigene und das fremde Leben. Biographische Identitätsentwürfe in der englischen Literatur des 18. Jahrhunderts* (text & theorie 7), Würzburg, 2007.

Wells, Lynn. "The Ethical Otherworld: Ian McEwan's Fiction". – In Philip Tew & Rod Mengham (Eds.): *British Fiction Today*, London, 2006, pp. 117-127.

Wordsworth, William: *The Prelude*, 1799, 1805, 1850. Ed. Jonathan Wordsworth, M. H. Abrams, & Stephen Gill, New York & London, 1979.

Barbara Puschmann-Nalenz (Ruhr-Universität Bochum)

Ethics in Ian McEwan's Twenty-First Century Novels. Individual and Society and the Problem of Free Will

1. Introduction

Some headlines above the reviews of McEwan's post-millenium novels reveal – beside the reviewers' diverse readings – an acknowledgement of the writer's obvious and lasting concern with ethical problems which individual characters face in a social environment shaped by history. A few examples prove this: about *Atonement*: "Unforgiven", "Schuld und Sühne", "Tea in the Garden of Good and Evil", "And when she was bad she was ..."[1]; about *Saturday*: "The Enemy on your Doorstep", "Have Mercy: The Subtle Study of Moral Sympathies", "The Age of Anxiety", "One Saturday after 9/11", and about *On Chesil Beach*: "No Sex, please, We're British!", "Love in England before the 60s started to swing", "A stark reminder of less liberated times".[2]

While these titles stress principles of right and wrong in *Atonement* and *Saturday*, they also hint at the significance of social and cultural history, most obviously in *Chesil Beach*. McEwan's own recent interpretation of his works will leave many readers surprised, since the expression of its ethical purpose echoes not only the humanistic tradition, but also the words of the Bible in an atheist's confession:

> For me the moral core of the novel is inhabiting other minds. That seems to be what novels do very well and also what morality is about: understanding that people are as real to themselves as you are to yourself, doing unto others as you would have done to yourself.[3]

McEwan can also be very sober and rational when he states in the aftermath of 9/11 that to use the notion of "Evil" may be tempting in the face of monstrous misdeeds, but "that it would be 'better to try and understand it in [...] political or psychological terms'".[4] For McEwan, empathy, or feeling for others, is an undisputed central value and as such ethically required; morality, as he defines it, consists of understanding another person, not imposing or self-imposing laws, imperatives or commandments. According to McEwan and late twentieth-century critics like Wayne C. Booth, Martha Nussbaum, Richard Rorty and Colin McGinn, fiction invites identification, moves the emotions and is therefore perfectly suited to fulfil his preconditions of ethical convictions.

Reflections about the importance of sympathy and compassion as the main purpose and responsibility of fiction, however, lead to an inevitable twofold moral dilemma. First, where will the demand to understand completely, "to inhabit" another mind, steer the reader? Does it mean extending solidarity, excusing or pitying, perhaps also suspending one's judgment or even giving up notions of Good and Evil? This is the question, for example, about which two survivors of 11 September 2001, who worriedly discuss this paradox in Don DeLillo's novel *Falling Man,* keep wondering: "First they kill you, then you try to understand them", which takes these protagonists to an even graver paradox, namely that terrorists only emerge as individuals with names, biographies and beliefs after they have killed.[5] What if fiction explores "cases where sensitivity itself can be put to unethical purposes, as in the novels of de Sade"?[6]

Second, how far may the author of the real-life novel go? Is it unethical or indecent to exploit and exhibit as if by a scalpel a character's innermost secrets? Wayne Booth brings up this question when he pointedly asks: *"What Are the Author's Responsibilities to Those Whose Lives Are Used as 'Material'?* Are there limits to the author's freedom to expose, in the service of art or self, the most delicate secrets of those whose lives provide material?"[7] Is the author being irreverent in dissecting someone's feelings? In his chapter on *Atonement* Dominic Head investigates the question of the writer's ethical responsibility in an innovative way. As a result he even tentatively states something "ethically unsound" and "morally dubious" about the novelist's work.[8]

McEwan's own comment on the role of fiction quoted above rejects an ethical instruction in the sense of communicating particular principles as well as the normative generalisation of a singular action as proof of its validity. The latter is required in Immanuel Kant's concept of the categorical imperative as the foundation of his moral philosophy.[9] McEwan's view of the novel emphasises above all the importance of the emotional sharing of an experience, and his fiction again raises through its characters the subject – more than two hundred years after Kant and the Age of Enlightenment – of autonomy versus heteronomy and of free will in moral choices versus contingency.

It will be the first and foremost objective of this article to explain how the reader's response in sharing a specific experience with the characters of the three novels in question is achieved; the second one is to point out once more the issues raised above in Harpham's and Booth's criticism, which are located on the extra-textual or metafictional level and concern the fiction writer's ethical position in regard to his occupation. Of McEwan's earlier work a critic said that it exemplifies the "negative capability" defined by the romantic poet John Keats.[10] My third and still hypothetical goal is to challenge this evaluation in respect to McEwan's latest novels. My attempt eventually leads to the question whether these fictions present a binding value-system and reliable truths, reliable because they are based on authority.

Even when we consider that writers' explanations of their own works have to be applied with caution, the reader can in the above quotations from interviews easily detect the confidence with which this author positions literature in the tradition of realist fiction. This affinity becomes evident in his novels because they have a structured and coherent composition with a time-concept that is clear if not linear, with a recognisable setting, with plot and event, a protagonist and discernible characters based on the notion of a personal identity, and, in sum, mimetic intent – features the readership gratefully accepts and that are eagerly welcomed by the reviewers of McEwan's work, because they lead us into a world resembling the well-known. Readers can distinguish a storyline and even sympathise with characters that open up their comprehensible minds and souls, in other words, they are able to imagine the universe of the novel as conforming to empirical reality. This, like "looking for the moral core of the novel", contrasts with the criteria of overtly postmodern fiction. Nevertheless, as numerous critics of *Atonement* maintain, significant elements of deconstructionist writing are also implemented in these novels.

While the relevance of ethics in fiction and literary criticism, which at first seemed to dwindle in the age of postmodernism after 1970, and later, around 1990, became topical once more in both fiction and theory[11], McEwan's latest novels display an undisputed interest in the diegetics of modernist storytelling. *Saturday,* which also repeats the time-structure of Part I in *Atonement,* is a conspicuous post-nine-eleven variation of Virginia Woolf's novel *Mrs. Dalloway* (1925), *On Chesil Beach* celebrates, like *Atonement* before it, multiperspectivity and stream-of-consciousness technique. The individual mind as narrative centre and an awareness of the self are not subverted.

The reviews also show that the two most recent novels, *Saturday* and *On Chesil Beach*, owe their great popular success not only to "The [thematic] conversion of Mr. Macabre", as the review of *Saturday* in *The Sunday Times* on 23 January 2005 calls the author's development, but equally to the waiving of experimental and therefore potentially alienating narration in the postmodern turn. *Atonement,* however, which precedes them and is often termed his finest novel[12], makes an in-depth use of the characteristics of historiographic metafiction.

Another reason why the author has gained tremendous acclamation and such a broad readership lies in his shift from the eccentric – some say, the abnormal – to protagonists and incidents presenting the unique in ordinary life. I consider his recent novels an urgent invitation to discover the same in others and relate to others, not the Other. The "once in a lifetime" singularity of an event, experienced by a normal individual as ordeal, excitement or elation, confronts the characters of a novel with unexpected and unprepared-for necessities to respond in some way, either to reach a decision or to disclaim the familiar, well-known security of the mind. The moment of decision-making serves here as a central motif of the novels and lends itself to the investigation of the ethical questions and possible answers inherent in each novel.

2. Atonement

The shifting or "variable internal focalisation" in *Atonement,* which discards a homogeneous narrative perspective, results for the reader in an intricate process of constructing the imaginary world, a process in which he is frequently granted the advantages of being better informed than the respective reflector figure, because the reader also gets to know the inside of the "other minds" in the story. It is worth remarking, however, that we are actually never led to inhabit the mind of the rapist who profits from war and ends up a publicly celebrated benefactor in *Atonement*;[13] even the demiurge-like Briony prefers to spend only a few moments of angry speculation on the person, whose crime(s) certainly testify to a failure of empathy (337).

In *Atonement*, the effects of shifting focalisation are impressive in the several representations of crucial moments in Part I: first the fountain-scene, depicted by the implied author (28-29), thirteen-year-old Briony (35-37) and finally by Robbie (74). Similarly the rendering of discrepant perception and the accompanying feelings about the scene in the library (Briony 116 and Robbie 126-131) not only has a similar impact and enables the reader to share the emotions of different individuals, but also gives him or her the foreboding of a tragic misunderstanding rooted in Briony's immature mind. This evaluation is made possible since the narrative voice is that of an implied author, apparently mature and near-omniscient. Briony Tallis' own programme for fiction, which bears a striking similarity with that of McEwan in the interview with Appleyard, is revealed early in the novel:

> [to] show separate minds, as alive as her own [...] to grasp the simple truth that other people are as real as you. And only in a story could you enter these different minds and show how they had an equal value. That was the only moral a story need have. (*Atonement* 38)

This appears as pure irony considering the girl's subsequent misinterpretation, which is, however, not totally alien to the performance of several other characters in the novel. The victim, Robbie, actually spends a considerable amount of thinking about the circumstances of Briony's slander which earned him a prison sentence. It proves, however, impossible for him to really enter the mind of another person. The fact that an imaginative girl of ten or thirteen has ideas very different from those of a young adult and moreover possesses an emotional unsteadiness characteristic of late childhood and puberty[14] is foregrounded in Part II through Robbie's erroneous interpretation of Briony's destructive action; for years he has been trying to see through motives for her accusation, and he has come to a conclusion: "Only one theory held up." (215) He ascribes it to disappointment arising from unrequited love, which as a ten-year-old she had confessed to him: "In her mind he had betrayed her love by favouring her sister [...], in the library [...] the whole fantasy crashed." (219-220) Robbie tries to "inhabit another mind", but he cannot do it – only the fiction writer is capable of that.[15] In "fact", Briony, as we know, is neither motivated by jealousy nor bitterness or revenge, but has long forgotten her confession, and instead childishly confuses love-making with violent attack and a confused expression of desire with deviant behaviour. In addition, she is obsessed with order, but what reigns is confusion – an insight which ironically she seemed to have gained earlier that day in her reflection about literary genres: "It wasn't only wickedness and scheming that made people unhappy, it was confusion and misunderstanding;" (38) – how true!

Actually none of the main characters are exempt from misunderstanding, as the later dialogue in Balham and Briony's disclosure of the rapist's identity also show, about which Cecilia and Robbie maintain misapprehensions even five years after the event (196, 317, 319, 326-327). It remains an interesting detail that Cecilia as well as Robbie is convinced that Danny Hardman must be the culprit, because paradoxically class prejudice is here at work in them as well – as seen by the fictional author, Briony. No one is able to utter a suspicion against Paul Marshall.[16] He is "immune" even before becoming an MP.

The device of mirroring the same scene in different perspectives to create that "moral core of the novel" mentioned above raises the reader's psychological interest in the complexity of characters and heightens his/her ability for empathy. The reader's repeated surprise at the status of this self-conscious narrative – what is "fact", what fiction in this novel? who tells the story? – can have an opposite, destabilising effect on the notion of 'reality'.[17] As critics have stated, a second reading of this novel starts with a quite different consciousness, after the recipient has been obliged to revise several times his/her realisation of the identity of the narrator – is he an omniscient third person? – and of the implied author, who is finally, after justified suspicions, unveiled as "B.T.". The reader not only recognises that what he/she read was a novel in a novel, that what eventually became Part I of the final draft was first written in January 1940 (*Atonement* 349) – that means before the evacuation of the British Expeditionary Force at Dunkirk took place – and largely corresponds to the short story Briony finds is rejected by *Horizon* in Part III. The reader also realises that the whole purpose of the novel is a very peculiar one.

While the metafictional elements of *Atonement*, which make it outstanding and link the realistic novel to modernist and additionally to postmodernist stances, have frequently attracted the attention of critics, we intend to focus in the following on the emphasis laid on the representations of decision-making in the novel. At its beginning Robbie has already made up his mind to read medicine after his first class degree in literature, "whatever Dr. Leavis said" (86) obviously concerning the central significance of the arts and humanities. Robbie regards choosing medicine as a liberating act of autonomy. Moreover, he intends to continue his studies in a metropolitan city, which to him appears as a stronghold of "freedom" (85).

Ironically, this elated consciousness of a deliberate new start, personal as well as professional, is immediately followed by Robbie's mistake in handing over the wrong letter, his "obscene draft" (89), to Briony. Without having made a decision, but out of mere accident, he becomes fortune's fool, when he realises his error and Briony is already gone.

Whereas bewilderment caused this error, the road he takes in search of the twins that evening proves a fatal decision, and the narrator stresses his heightened awareness: "he had already decided: if it could not be with Cecilia, if he could not have her to himself, then he too, like Briony, would go out searching alone." (135) The momentousness of this decision will accompany him throughout the years to come; the fact that he acts and often fantasises "like Briony" turns out as another instance of dramatic irony, but also a sign of their relatedness.

She also resolves to walk by herself, taking decisions of an even wider scope: "Her childhood had ended, she decided now as she came away from the swimming pool" (150). In doing so she clearly overestimates her own judgment, since this is not a matter of an abstract decision or a deliberate act like that of breaking off the rehearsal of her play. Generally she – like Robbie – overrates her capacity of decision-making and the significance of her autonomy, as her insistence on a resolute manner predicts when she walks away from the house: "After waiting a while she decided to turn back." (*Ibid.*) The idea that she is mistress of her own, autonomous master of her ways and later on of her vision and its interpretations, guides her actions. She discards all other options and takes the path which leads to her "crime", as the implied author's temporal prolepsis repeatedly calls it (146, 152).

This "crime" of false accusation, however, shows no signs of conscious decision-making, even though free will is conjured up by Briony herself. The process which leads from her first rhetorical question when addressing Lola, "It was Robbie, wasn't it?" (156) to her repetitious "I saw him" – where believing is seeing – is preconditioned by her earlier impressions of Robbie during that day. Nevertheless, she regards her false testimony as an act of will: *"I can. And I will"* (158), parodying a heroic act of saving an innocent victim. It is her self-image of being her sister's protector and the advocate of justice – and not her environment – which pressures her to give evidence; she is a prisoner of her own idealised self and her fantastic scenarios. "She trapped herself, she marched into the labyrinth of her own construction, and was too young, to awestruck, too keen to please [...]" (160).

Relentlessly, the narrator calls her action a crime and speaks of guilt, thereby leaving no doubt about the moral evaluation, though the explanation of Briony's making up her mind would render her a victim of her own state and condition, thereby exculpating her at least partly. This paradox, which Robbie and Cecilia discuss in Part III, results from ethical stances of the author(s) and at least for this novel answers our question raised above, whether understanding means suspension of judgment, in the negative. Briony's "decision", the one with the most grievous consequences, is psychologically fuzzy, ironically in spite of the protagonist's declared willpower and belief in the myth of her new marvellous, free-willed self. It is revealed as a child's new-born self-importance and assumed clarity of things.

Part I, the story of one day in June, covers the period of major decisions; what follows shows the contingency of life in crises where decisions of the individual are not asked for or even tolerated. But before the war starts that crushes all independence or resolution, Cecilia, who had felt "bored and confined by the Tallis household" (75), who believed that "there was no choice" in her family home (96), decides for Robbie and against her own family when everybody believes in his guilt: "[T]here had to be a choice – you or them." (197) While the narrator emphasised Briony's insisting stress on making decisions, her sister's life-changing determination is hardly commented on and later represented in her letter as "[r]ealistically" (*Ibid.*) made. Though earlier on Cecilia felt that smoking on the stairway during her father's absence was a "revolt" (44) and cost her some effort, her great rebellion, which also defeats all of Briony's fantasies about Robbie, appears almost natural.

Briony's later decisions all attempt at atoning for her crime: being trained as a nurse instead of going to college, writing her story of that day in 1935 which is not accepted, and finally in 1940 attending Lola's wedding in a church on Clapham Common, where the minister pronounces the words of the wedding ceremony that seem to reflect – for those who know the secret – the bridegroom's crime committed and concealed five years previously.[18] Briony's own crime in giving a false testimony and that of the wedding couple in conspiring against verity cannot be atoned for by proclaiming the truth here and now, as Church and law would demand.

Once again, after leaving the church and the newly-weds, Briony's sense of selfhood is challenged, as happened so often before, and there are a few similarities with her fuzzy decision-making in 1935: "A decision had been made – without her, it seemed." (311) An "unreal feeling" accompanies her steps towards Balham to visit her sister. This direction is marked in the text as "the road not taken"; it remains fantasy inside fiction, with one part of her self, which the implied author calls "the imagined or ghostly persona" (*Ibid.*), walking into the direction of Balham, the other self going back to the hospital. The indeterminacy evoked by this image dismisses the notion of a unified self once more, and simultaneously the reader receives a signal that the fantasised meeting of all three characters, with the lovers united after all and a perspective of atonement agreed upon with Briony, who is "at one" once more with the two individuals closest to her, might be wishful thinking. Her "unreal feeling" (*Ibid.*) becomes the reader's uneasy feeling about the "reality" and veracity of this part of the story.

The atonement Briony chooses and reflects on in the epilogue of her work is based on her final and conscious decision to write. It actualises a literary topos far older than Shakespeare's *Sonnets* – the eternizing conceit or immortalisation through literature that is to the writer much more effective against oblivion than other means.[19]

However, we must not overlook that even in the author's – Briony's – own view she is not only taking "a stand against oblivion", but against "oblivion *and despair*" (351, my emphasis), against "bleakest realism" [...] "that they never met again, never fulfilled their love" (350). Her wish, which has materialised in her novel, that everything should turn out different from the "facts" of imprisonment and death in the war, her longing that love would have defeated all obstacles and made all crime and guilt – personal and historical – undone accentuates again the problems of the author's ethical self-interpretation: is she above all bound to truthfulness, or is it her responsibility to give hope? For Briony, the writer, the answer is apparently clear at the end of Part III, even though it is quite subjective: her atonement consists in that happy end in the imagination of her "ghostly persona", who provides a fortunate closure to the tragedy.[20] What she kept in mind and what sustained her will to go on, "it was her sister with Robbie. Their love. Neither Briony nor the war had destroyed it." (330)

In agreement with Müller-Wood's unambiguous judgment (154), I consider not only Briony's heroic and sacrificial life as a war-time nurse "dwarfed by her inexcusable guilt" (*Ibid.*), but also think that neither it nor her final draft's conciliatory closure can undo the 'reality' of the consequences of her false testimony. "*Atonement* is essentially a novel about the narrator's protracted non-atonement" (*Ibid.* 148), if the reader gains distance from the writer's persona.

The text imposes criticism of the thirteen-year-old as well as the 77-year-old Briony on the reader, especially regarding honesty and courage; the disapproval of the girl is explicit, that of the old woman losing her mental capacity is left to the recipient's discretion. On the diegetic level the narrative produces the "inescapable question 'How should one *live*?'"[21] and claims that "living an ethical life is central" (Seaboyer 31). It stigmatises Marshall's as well as Emily's and, of course, Briony's conduct as unethical, nor is Lola totally spared. Briony herself, the author, on the concluding metafictional page of her work, denies atonement to the novelist because of yet another paradox: the writer's god-like position. Where free will and autonomous decisions are withheld from the human characters, the author is omnipotent. In the immanence of the work she is god and no transcendent authority can forgive her, even if the author is an atheist and does not believe in the existence of god (*Atonement* 351).

Beyond the back cover of the book, however, we return to the initially asked questions about "the ethics of representation" or "How (and what) ought one to *write*?" (Seaboyer 31, my emphasis). In doing so we face a challenge, which both McEwan's novels and his personal statements trigger off. Not only the "Ethics *in* Fiction", but also the "Ethics *of* Fiction" are burning issues. If we take the answer from the author Briony, it is as "a final act of kindness" (351) ethical to offer hope to the novel reader, to take a final stand against despair, to eternalise the lovers and thereby on the one hand to fulfil the reader's expectation of poetic justice and on the other his supposed "metaphysical yearning for a meaningful universe in which all fates are resolved"[22] – a purpose that would certainly be rejected with vehemence by any existentialist. Does the reader believe in this contract with the implied author, whose personal goal was to atone for her own guilt? Concerning the Ethics of Fiction, McEwan in *Atonement* hands his reader, at least temporarily, over to the ambivalence of writing and imagination, which one critic rightly calls "Briony's gift and her curse" (Childs 135); another exclaims "woe betide those who confuse the two [spheres of the real and the fictional]."[23]

Briony's double role as main character in the fictional story and as its implied author, for whose identity the reader finds a number of clues in Parts I to III of the narrative, receives a final twist of uncertainty in the epilogue. This confirms the assumption that she is the author and brings a circle to completion with the performance of Briony's youthful play about the melodramatic *Trials of Arabella*.

I think it is justified here to repeat the question radically phrased by Wayne Booth: "Can art be bad for you?" (Booth ix). For Briony the girl art's influence was ambivalent, her mind being shaped by "stories" or fairytales and ready to engage in ever new scenarios which intervene with her perception of reality and tempt her to form an over-confident self-image that "[t]here was nothing she could not describe" (146, 155) and "she was able to build and shape her narrative in her own words" (169). This is the writer's strength and temptation. The 77-year-old writer would have to answer "yes and no" to Booth's question.

The coda from 1999 ends with Briony's evaluation of the novelist's Olympian position outlined above. Scepticism and criticism aroused by it in the reader, however, reach beyond the self-critique of the protagonist and continue to probe the writer's authority.[24]

As a result of the reading we can state that a responsible and morally intact life – and that would mean one of empathy with others – can without ambivalence or hesitation be called a central issue of this novel, but we can equally argue that the recipient may also nourish a certain doubt about a writer's obligation to kind forgivingness. We are kept in "uncertainties, Mysteries, doubts" still, as shown by the two different endings, the "good" and the "bad" one – the "bad", the one of "bleakest realism" being "the road not taken", only hinted at by the author. Is it possible to evade the claims raised with regard to the novelist in Part III and the coda and yet take a stand against despair? I think that a novel can avoid despair as well as an opportunistic giving way to readers' hopes, and the author as the "governing intelligence" shows how this can be done: by making it a subject of the novel and reflecting it from diverse sides, instead of simply satisfying the reader's longing for the victory of the good, as popular literature would want to do.

Questioning the moral function of writing and reading emerges as one result initiated by the author standing behind *Atonement,* a second is the iconoclasm of the myths of social class and national history, a topic which exceeds the limits of this article.

3. Saturday

A distinguishing mark of *Saturday* often goes unnoticed, a circumstance as surprising as the nature of this characteristic: the book is written in the present tense.[25] If we follow the statement of Käte Hamburger (qtd. from Genette 245) that the use of the past tense in the novel ('episches Praeteritum') is nothing other than the expression of the narrative's fictionality and by no means diminishes the temporal directness of the narrated story,[26] we may ask ourselves if the immediacy or the mimetic impact is increased by the use of the historic present here.

Even though *Atonement* seems to be the one novel by Ian McEwan that deals most intensively with ethical problems his subsequent fictions put similar questions of autonomy, free will and moral values in a different context. Modernist narrative techniques, the recurrent thematic use of literature, family issues and friction between the demands of society and individual self-fulfilment are all familiar to the readers of his previous novel. The historic moment captured in the personal experience of a "community of anxiety"[27] after 9/11 and the terrorist attacks in Madrid and before the bombings in London provides the setting. The epistemological indeterminacy as well as the metafictional element introduced in *Atonement* is missing in *Saturday*; two poets and a musician instead represent one of "the two cultures" (C.P. Snow), with the protagonist Henry Perowne standing for the second, that of the sciences.

"Inhabiting" Henry Perowne's mind leads to a view of free will and autonomous decision that is not primarily restricted by social, cultural and historical conditions, but by physical nature.[28] The question of ethical values and the freedom to live them becomes even more pointed through the narrowed vista of someone familiar with neurological conditions; this is underlined by the monoperspective from which the narrative is told.

The repeatedly bipolar structure of themes and characters leads to an explicit argument about the "ethics" of the impending war on Iraq, carried out in dialogues between Perowne and his two children, especially with Daisy who arrives later in the novel. It is, however, the implicit ethical problems of Perowne I want to focus on. These result from the protagonist's medical profession, the "requisite norm [...], governed by the Hippocratic oath, which obliges reverence of life" (Head 2007: 187).

Though determined by genes and various uncontrollable accidents during his life Henry Perowne firmly believes that man in his normal state of health is able to make decisions. So that when at the end of Part 4, with the attackers just defeated, during the telephone call which he receives from Jay Strauss at the hospital, Henry makes up his mind and "thinks he knows what it is he wants to do" (232) we can be sure about his resolve, but not at all about its content. Will the "requisite norm" work here, and in what way? Is there really that temptation to take revenge on Baxter, which Rosalind briefly hints at before he leaves at the beginning of Part 5? What does "revenge" mean? To leave the operation to an inexperienced junior surgeon – or worse? To save his life and thereby commit Baxter to the torture of his illness, as the final page concisely and cynically summarises the outcome, calling it "Revenge enough" (278)? Or to what other solution will reverence for life oblige this doctor? The reader here is clearly kept ignorant, in uncertainty and speculates, perhaps worriedly, about the outcome and the hero's emotional stability.[29] Later it turns out that Perowne decides something which is for the reader quite unexpected here: to prevent Baxter's being taken to court and being held responsible for the mugging, even to the point of perversion of justice (*Ibid.*).

This conclusion seems almost superhuman and certainly heroic in its altruistic humanism. To Perowne, the healthy competent man, "[d]ecisions are all" (22) from the beginning through to the end of the day where it is time to "decide precisely what should be done" (263), while he sees in Baxter "biological determinism in its purest form" (93). Perowne has to struggle with the question *how* to apply the ethics of the medical profession rather than *whether* to do it. This protagonist, however, also has a very personal motive for forgiving Baxter so radically: to atone for his feelings of superiority, which made him "act unprofessionally, using his medical knowledge" (111) to humiliate Baxter earlier in the day and secure his own escape.[30]

Throughout the novel Perowne is concerned about the 'ethics of fate' – though he believes in "pure chance and physical law" rather than fate (128).

> It troubles him to consider [...] the accidents of character and circumstance that cause one young woman in Paris to be packing her weekend bag with the bound proof of her first volume of poems [...], and another young woman of the same age to be led away by a wheedling boy to a moment's chemical bliss that will bind her as tightly to her misery [...] (65).

When facing the young people in the square he gets the impression "that he owes them an apology" (146). It troubles him to think of his own genetically determined future when he visits his mother, watching her " [m]ental death" (165). And most of all he feels guilty when Baxter looks at him while falling down the stairs with the expression of

> a sorrowful accusation of betrayal. He, Henry Perowne, possesses so much – the work, money, status, the home, above all, the

> family [...] and he has done nothing, given nothing to Baxter who has so little that is not wrecked by his defective gene [...]. (227-228)

Partly Perowne feels that there is a debt he has to pay, to atone for the inequality of chances in life. Yet he is not a saint, perhaps not even an over-idealised hero. His is a lifetime decision made as a result of his interest in and enthusiasm for the medical profession; to be good at it becomes an obligation, nonetheless a very rewarding one, and what most strongly carries him through the fatigue, spontaneous anger and regret which might tempt him to violate the ethics of the Hippocratic oath, is the everyday routine (230) which makes him act almost automatically.[31]

His discussions, especially with Daisy, about terror and war ended in a deadlock, the pros and cons of the Iraq war seeming mere sophisms which might disturb domestic peace. Whereas Henry's position seems rather weak in this dispute – it appeared weak in the act of violence in the street – he is strong at the moment when "the opportunity of mercy close to home" (Childs 140) presents itself in the operating theatre. It is an opportunity where his professional competence excises all doubt from his own mind.

His steadfastness in this moral choice proves part of his identity and contrasts with the stalemate of his response to terrorism and dictatorship.[32]

When a critic claims that *Saturday* represents an attempt at outlining a "third culture" (Head 2007, 200), it seems justified to add that an intermediary 'third way' leads out of the conflict with the 'enemy' in this novel.[33]

4. On Chesil Beach

McEwan's latest novel so far acutely raises once more the extratextual question of the writer's responsibility expressed by Wayne C. Booth: is it unethical to use the lives, minds, innermost secrets of live human beings as material for a novel?

The book also emphasises the author's involvement with the development of society, as reflected in individual lives. While *Saturday* was striking because of its closeness to the reader's historical experience, this novella moves back to the early sixties of the twentieth century – almost one generation before Henry Perowne. Regarding time and place McEwan moves from World War II in *Atonement* zig-zag to London in the aftermath of 9/11 and back to England in the Cold War a few months before the Cuban Missile Crisis and half a decade before the peak of the countercultural movement.

Well known for his involvement with borderline psychological conditions the author breaks a taboo here as well and makes the detailed exploration of a crucial situation in the life of individuals a principle of his narration. The disastrous because irreparably damaging wedding night of the young couple Florence and Edward in the summer of 1962 poses moral questions inherent in the fictional text, while the above-mentioned writer's dilemma has tempted one or two critics to address the novella as voyeuristic or a parody of pornographic writing.

While Head (2009) believes that it is beyond the capacities of the art form novella to represent society and history, because the genre is determined to make an event its central issue, I regard the short form allowing for a highly concentrated channelling of a cultural situation portrayed "in a nutshell".

McEwan's interviews added to my conviction that the intention "to inhabit other minds" is being seriously pursued here too in spite of the comic effect of an anti-climax and the extremes represented in the protagonists' social backgrounds and upbringings. The implied author achieves what the main characters fail to accomplish: to show insight, understanding and patience and to communicate innermost feelings. Depicting the sexual dilemma of two young people who are not only sexually inexperienced before the cultural watershed of the later sixties presents an opportunity for a revaluation of an ultra-conservative society and the few tentative 'exotic' attempts to break through the rigid and paralysing effects of an authoritarian and often retrospective culture.

According to the serious purpose evident in the narrative the immanent ethical and moral problems are focused on in a very pointed way, and they go beyond the mere sexual failure of a couple's wedding night. The breaking of a taboo actually does not so much consist in the explicit description of failed sexual intercourse but in the outspoken verbalisation of feelings which are 'forbidden' because they are unorthodox or "inadequate": absurdity, disappointment, disgust. Ethical and moral principles apply here very well –

or was it accepted to regard the preparations for the "consummation" of a marriage as clumsy or ridiculous, for a young bride to think that a forty-minute ceremony in church could not make much of a difference in an otherwise strange and scaring moment for which she is badly prepared? After all, the phrase from the Book of Common Prayer "with my body I thee worship" seems fairly abstract, in its own way as insufficient as the manual used by Florence which gives technical instructions about intercourse. What no person and no institution are obviously able or willing to communicate at this point is the sense of "guiltless elevation of sensual pleasure" (161), to admit passion or sexual satisfaction as an aspect of human life and the circumstances under which they can be achieved, to talk openly about sexual difficulties – a topic which on moral grounds is still taboo to parents, manuals, church and teachers alike. The implied author leaves no doubt that it has to be considered rather unethical and wrong to silently insist on this "innocence" – a concept which is problematised more than once in McEwan's fiction (cf. Groes 123).

Of the two young people Florence is more severely afflicted by their ignorance (7), and she mistakes Edward's behaviour as a sign of multiple experience. That she will not stay totally unresponsive becomes obvious to the reader (86-88), mediated by the knowing third-person narrator:

> For the first time, her love for Edward was associated with a definable physical sensation [...]. Now here at last were the beginnings of desire, precise and alien, but clearly her own; (87)

while Edward remains ignorant of Florence's hidden nature, like herself: "[S]he had no interest in him. She was unsensual, utterly without desire." (135) This is Edward's misapprehension. I disagree with the reading of Dominic Head (2009: 120-121), who ascribes the girl's insecurity and subsequent repulsion for sex to child abuse by her father – I believe her reticence can be understood without assuming that. Conflicting emotions characterise her development. Several hints point to a different psychological constellation: she replaces a son in her father's eyes, to whom he would like to give all the opportunities and potential (54), regardless of her disposition. Being sensitive, she sees both her parents as unattractive and distant, her younger sister as a nuisance, and, of course, feels guilty about each instance of disharmony (50-51). It is difficult for her to regard herself as part of a group or community outside her professional occupation with music. The emotional separateness and isolation which she experiences is even soothed by her discovery of sexual maturity: "It was undeniable she was not a separate subspecies of the human race. In triumph, she belonged among the generality." (88) Her difficulties in socialising are greater than Edward's, who also has this "sense of a concealed self" (75).

It is evident that the embarrassment or discomfort which apart from the protagonists also an occasional reader feels exposes the gap, which is also a moral insufficiency of the imagination – the gap between individuals, the lack of communication, the difficulty in dealing with intimate questions. An additional ethical dilemma, which is the author's, is stated in the following:

> Beyond this, there is something arch about the novel, governed by a sexually knowing narrator manipulating his innocent creations. Indeed, the gap between their understanding and experience, and the knowledge of the narrator – and also the author, as the governing intelligence – is discomfiting. (Head 2009: 122)

To this, the following extract from an interview McEwan gave in December 2007, may be regarded as an apt reply:

> I want narrative authority. [...] I want the authorial presence taking full responsibility for everything. Although the narrator of *On Chesil Beach* is not a character you could describe, or has any past or future, it is a presence which assumes the aesthetic task of describing the inside of two people's minds. Then the reader can make a judgement.[34]

The sexually knowing reader might feel equally superior, amused or outraged, according to disposition, yet the narrative offers another chance: to gain an insight into a culturally very different era, into minds shaped by social constraints and inhibitions inspired by class, social politics, religion, and sexual repression (96). The "dividing line" between "before" and "after" the liberalisation of the sixties is, according to a critic, metaphorically represented by the shoreline separating land from sea – the beach thereby becoming a "symbolic setting" (Head 2009: 118). The crucial event of the narrative is set on the brink of the great change which happened a little later, and it is important to observe that much more than a sexual liberation took place. The novella marks 1962 as a date where a shift of generations was approaching and a fundamental change caused by the independence of British colonies much argued about, where the class system had equally begun to crumble, and educational opportunities and wealth were spreading.

The focalisation of the narrative, which alternates between Edward and Florence, refrains from ridiculing them as young persons, even though there are feelings of ludicrousness and comical effects more than once. The narrator treats them with equal sympathy and understanding, yet does not spare them criticism of their demeanour either, when the outcome is disastrous, since both their lives have definitely been impaired. It strikes the reader that towards the end Florence 'leaves the site' quite literally, but also diegetically (157); the concluding flash-forward represents exclusively Edward's perspective. Both the immediate sequel of the failed night and the outlook into the future of the characters leave the girl's point-of-view completely to our speculation, with one exceptional moment: the narrator tells us that she stealthily glances at Edward's presumed seat in the Wigmore Hall where her quartet gives its triumphant debut six years later. She obviously remains unmarried.

Using this structural imbalance as closure the author explores only the regret and futility in the young man's later life, whose achievements do not attain the public acknowledgement of Florence's. His life, though not bad, shows no further ambition in professional or personal matters, unlike the expectations which he had nourished during his year with Florence. His interests remain circumscribed and provincial, his historical activities amount to playing "a part in the restoration of the ancient watercress beds in Ewelme" (164). When he is over sixty years old he is able to admit that he has never again loved a person as much as the girl with the violin, and that much that went wrong after they separated would possibly have taken a better turn if he had found the right word to say, "that the sound of his voice would have been a deliverance, and she would have turned back. " (166) He could have helped to stop her self-accusation and her sense of insufficiency, but he did nothing, feeling self-righteously offended, left with the burden of shame and failure, yet, as a consequence," [i]n his misfortune, he felt almost noble" (158).

The focus on Edward at the end mitigates the fact that here the ending is bad and unhappy, considering the mutual insult and harm caused by the scene on the beach where they argue about their failed lovemaking. Readers sometimes have polarised opinions about who is more to blame for the "mess", he or she. While Florence immediately expresses a sense of regret and guilt, Edward comes to see his fault only much later, as an elderly man.

"Guilt", as in the two previous novels, remains a key term with varied meanings in different situations: carelessness, lovelessness, failure and reproachfulness (e.g. 51, 70, 139, 161,); "free", as with the protagonists of *Atonement,* is another one, like "liberty" repeatedly used at crucial points (e.g. 6, 18, 47, 91, 96, 130, 142, 154-155, 160). Much of the cultural criticism of this work revolves around the tension between the individual's longing for freedom and social constraints.

One decision Edward had taken before he met Florence was to abstain from violence (95). Up to the street fight with a stranger in order to defend his fellow student he had thought it all right to engage in occasional brawls, even felt the desired "freedom" in a fist fight (91). Later he found out that it was not socially approved of to engage in it as a college student. Surprisingly, or not surprisingly at all, he feels overcome by the temptation to be violent again in the moment after sexual failure, not sure if he can control himself. The connection between sex and violence re-emerges in several of McEwan's fictions, but physical violence is also connected to class, to the lower classes, most obviously with Baxter in *Saturday*, where the protagonist uses violence only in self-defence after all verbal means have been exhausted. To Edward Mayhew with his isolated, disorderly upbringing and his keen interest in fanatical medieval religious cults violence seemed to be a part of life, until he became familiar with the standards of the educated classes. Violence there is judged unethical; Mrs Ponting sternly rejects all sympathies for eastern European political systems mainly on the grounds of tyrannous force exerted by them (52-53). Edward eventually manages to suppress his impulse to use violence against Florence on the beach (156). It is, nevertheless, an extreme situation in which control over the momentum of an urge cannot be taken for granted, while Florence is no longer in control of her verbal aggression.

The finish is partial insofar as it focuses on Edward only and reflects melancholy and resignation: "This is how the entire course of a life can be changed – by doing nothing." (166) His silence also constitutes a kind of guilt, but it points most of all to damage done to himself, as he recognizes. Decision-making appeared as a process and a sign of maturity on the threshold of young adulthood; to revoke the decision to get married is left to their respective parents (160). Individual responsibility proves again determined by society, historical situation and accidental circumstances.

When John Fowles was writing *The French Lieutenant's Woman* he remarked that this was not a novel which the Victorian novelists forgot to write, but one which they failed to write.[35] Accordingly, one could apply this not only to *Atonement*, but equally to the early nineteen-sixties and *Chesil Beach*, which turns out to be far more than a "fine anti-romance".[36] The distance in time brings about the effect of cultural criticism as well as of psychological probing.

5. Conclusion

To conclude, the question of the author's responsibility towards the implied reader has to be reconsidered.

From the often-quoted interview that Ian McEwan gave to the *Guardian* after the terrorist attack on the World Trade Center on 11 September 2001:

> As I said at the time, what those holy fools clearly lacked, or clearly were able to deny themselves, was the ability to enter into the minds of the people they were being so cruel to. Amongst their crimes, is, was, a failure of the imagination, of the moral imagination. (Interview with Helen Whitney in April 2002)

We know that at least to this novelist fictionalizing is only morally permitted if it serves the social and psychological good. Insofar it gives a definite answer to the question of *author*ity and values.[37]

Furthermore, as Wayne Booth (127) maintains, the writer's goal to aim at artistic success, to "think of the pursuit of excellence as itself a matter of duty" is complementary to the reader's demand on him to do so, and that in the process of dialectic reasoning the corresponding claim must be that the author should be demanding towards his reader. "That question always leads to ethical (or if one prefers, ideological or political) appraisals, as in Sartre it leads to judgments about how well the fiction serves the reader's freedom."[38] What literary theory states here is paralleled by McEwan's comment in the interview quoted above sixty years later, that the reader can make his own judgment after the writer has fulfilled the aesthetic task of describing the inside of people's minds.

Notes

1. This heading refers to the English nursery rhyme which opens "There was a little girl" and ends "when she was bad/ She was HORRID."
2. www.ianmcewan.com/bib/criticism.html and bib/books.html (accessed 11 June 2009). Where not otherwise indicated, all quotations from published reviews follow this website. Interviews and reviews are also extensively covered by Peter Childs (Ed.): *The Fiction of Ian McEwan. A reader's guide to essential criticism.* Basingstoke: Palgrave Macmillan, 2006, and Bernie C. Byrnes: *Ian McEwan's 'Atonement' & 'Saturday'.* Nottingham: Paupers' Press, 2006.
3. "The Ghost in my family". Interview of Ian McEwan with Bryan Appleyard in *The Sunday Times* 25 March 2007.
4. Helen Whitney: "Faith and Doubt at Ground Zero" (interview accessed 20 August 2009). *Frontline* April 2002 (omission in the text).
5. Don DeLillo: *Falling Man.* London: Picador, 2007, 113.
6. Geoffrey G. Harpham: "Ethics and literary criticism". In: Christa Knellwolf & Christopher Norris (Eds): *The Cambridge History of Literary Criticism* vol. 9. Cambridge: CUP 2001, pp. 371-385, 379.
7. Wayne C. Booth: *The Company We Keep: An Ethics of Fiction.* Berkeley: University of California Press, 1988, 130 (emphasis in the text). The title of Booth's study is a slightly altered quotation from Shakespeare's *King Henry IV*, Part 1.
8. Dominic Head: *Ian McEwan.* Manchester: Manchester UP, 2007, 166.
9. Immanuel Kant's text says: "Act only according to that maxim whereby you can at the same time will that it should become a universal law." (dtv-Lexikon vol. 9, entry Imperativ. München: Deutscher Taschenbuch Verlag, 1967. Engl.: *Groundings for the Metaphysics of Morals*, trans. J. W. Ellington [1785] (1993), 3rd ed., 30) http://en.wikipedia.org/wiki/Categorical imperative, accessed 28 September 2009).
10. Kiernan Ryan. *Ian McEwan.* Plymouth: Northcote House, 1994, 65. – The term "negative capability" refers to the poet's special capacity of "being in uncertainties, Mysteries, doubts", unlike the philosopher without offering a solution (John Keats: Letter to George and Thomas Keats. In *The Letters of*

John Keats 1814-1821 (Ed. H.E. Rollins), 2 vols, Cambridge: CUP, 1958, vol. 1, 193).

11 For this debate cf. Vernon Gras: "The Recent Ethical Turn in Literary Studies." *Mitteilungen des Verbandes Deutscher Anglisten* 4.2 (1993), 30-41; also Heinz Antor: "The Ethics of Criticism in the Age After Value". In: Rüdiger Ahrens & Laurenz Volkmann (Eds): *Why Literature Matters. Theories and Functions of Literature*. Heidelberg: Winter, 1996, pp. 65-85.

12 Representative examples are Head (2007: 156 and n. 1) and Frank Kermode (qtd. from Childs 132).

13 *Atonement*. New York: Anchor, 2003 (2001).

14 Brian Finney: "Briony's Stand Against Oblivion: The Making of Fiction in Ian McEwan's *Atonement*". *Journal of Modern Literature* 27:3, 2004, 68-82, ascribes Briony's 'errors' completely to the influence of fiction on her impressionable mind (69, 80), while I consider the novelist's psychological investigation of her youth and class to be equally important.

15 Judith Seaboyer asks, following Booth, if this seductive capacity of the writer regarding Part II of the novel presents in fact "a violation, a colonisation" and is therefore ambivalent ("Ian McEwan: Contemporary Realism and the Novel of Ideas". In James Acheson/Sarah C.E. Ross (Eds): *The Contemporary British Novel Since 1980*. New York: Palgrave Macmillan, 2005, pp. 23-34, 32); concerning the death agony scene in Part III Dominic Head (2007: 172) reaches the same conclusion that "inhabiting" is 'invading' the minds of others, but here he clearly defends the prerogative of writing, however discomforting it is.

16 Anja Müller-Wood summarizes: "The different viewpoints [...] also suggest that misinterpretation is ubiquitous and unavoidable and hence cannot be blamed on Briony alone." ("Enabling Resistance: Teaching *Atonement* in Germany". In: Steven Barfield et al.: *Teaching Contemporary British Fiction. Anglistik und Englischunterricht* 69, 2007, 143-158, 152).

17 A thorough analysis of self-referentiality on the different narrative levels in the novel is given by Merle Tönnies in her article "A New Self-Conscious Turn at the Turn of the Century? Postmodernist Metafiction in Recent Works by 'Established' British Writers". In: Christoph Ribbat (Ed.): *Twenty-First Century Fiction: Readings, Essays, Conversations. Anglistik und Englischunterricht* 66, 2005, 57-82, here 67-74; cf. Finney 68-82, who moreover criticises reviewers who banish all metafictional traits in the novel to the coda. Alistair Cormack opposes a classification of the novel as postmodernist with the characteristic relativism and self-consciousness and marks it as belonging to the tradition of English empiricism ("Postmodernism and the Ethics of Fiction in *Atonement*". In: Sebastian Groes (Ed.): *Ian McEwan. Contemporary Critical Perspectives*. London: Continuum, 2009, 70-82, 82).

18 The quotation on p. 305 from *Atonement* is taken from the 1552 and 1662 versions of the Canon Law in *The Book of Common Prayer*, which was not altered before 1979/80.

19 Briony's guilt and wish for penitence render her work a special case which adds to the act of saving the lovers and their hopes from oblivion the personal motive; she acts in the service of art and self (cf. Booth).
20 The late seventeenth- and eighteenth-century versions of Shakespeare's *King Lear* and *Romeo and Juliet* which were performed with a happy ending could be added here. For further literary associations and intertextual references cf. Finney's discussion of numerous reviews (70-74).
21 Claudia Schemberg: *Achieving 'At-one-ment'. Storytelling and the Concept of the Self in Ian McEwan's 'The Child in Time', 'Black Dogs', 'Enduring Love', and 'Atonement'.* Frankfurt/M.: Peter Lang, 2004, 31 (my emphasis).
22 Schemberg 90. This critic considers the 'obligation for hope' not only linked to the human search for a good life, but equally to the concept of the unity of the self, and believes the successful struggle for the latter indispensable in human life; Finney speaks of "the compensations and limitations which [the fictional world] can offer its readers and writers" (69).
23 Cormack 82. I agree with him about the absence of a lasting ontological uncertainty like that produced by simulacra; the novel does not celebrate fiction as the only reality.
24 Cf. Head (2007, 156), who is more restrictive here. But he also admits that one effect is to question the morality of the author-figure in regard to truth (*Ibid.* 160). Echoing Keats, Dominic Head calls this fruit of the narrative a "cultivated uncertainty" (*Ibid.*).
25 Head (2007, 192-193) also observes this and interprets it as a tension-raising device which repeats the experience of reading a book – the reader always lies level with the reflector figure (cf. n. 29, which contradicts this thesis).
26 E.g."Morgen war der Tag, an dem sich alles entscheiden sollte." Or: "this music, in his lifelong view, was far superior to the fey three-minute music-hall ditties from Liverpool that were to captivate the world in a few years' time." (Ian McEwan: *On Chesil Beach.* London: Cape, 2007, 38. Further references to this edition will be included in the text.)
27 Ian McEwan. *Saturday.* London: Cape, 2005, 176. Further references to this edition will be included in the text.
28 Bauder-Begerow/Lusin point to the connection of these themes (250-251).
29 This incident contradicts Head's statement that by the unconventional use of the present tense "nothing is being withheld" (Head: 2007, 193).
30 Cf. Head (2007, 194). I consider the proposition that Henry wants to atone "for his own genetic privilege" (*Ibid.* 195) in successfully operating on Baxter too unalloyed as a motive; it is a hybrid impulse which causes him to do it.
31 McEwan's comment on the reception of his character reads: "Some critics were shocked by the description of a man who wasn't having a divorce, who loved his wife after 20 years, who got on well with his teenage children. To some intellectuals this was an abomination. It shocked people more than any of my child-raping short stories ever did." ("Journeys with-

out Maps: An Interview with Ian McEwan, by Jon Cook, Sebastian Groes and Victor Sage". In: Groes (Ed.), pp. 123-134, 130).
Obviously "the attempt to describe happiness in a troubled world" (*Ibid.*) also signifies the breaking of a taboo. Or "Happiness is a hard nut to crack" as the reviewer of the *Calcutta Telegraph* writes on 18 March 2005. Mild criticism of the plot is expressed by Sarah Compton's review in *The Telegraph* on 16 February 2005: "I was both worried and moved by a conclusion in which the power of literature to transform and heal assumes a melodramatic role."

32 The implied author indulges in dramatic irony when he has Perowne say to the Prime Minister at the opening of Tate Modern "'You're making a mistake'" (144), as he confuses him with an artist; what kind of fault Blair will commit a little later is still unrevealed to the general public as it is to the hesitantly pro-war citizen Perowne.

33 A recurring bi-polar structural pattern in McEwan's novels (e.g. rationality vs. mysticism in *Black Dogs*) perhaps renders a "reconciliation" of oppositions also a matter of ethics for the writer, and in McEwan's later narratives the impact of scientific thinking widespread in neuro-biology and socio-psychology takes on a conciliatory function; Baxter, for example, is not simply an evil, but above all a sick person.

34 Groes, pp. 123-134, 133 (omission in the text).

35 Review of *Atonement* by Geoff Dyer in *The Guardian*, 22 September 2001.

36 Review by John Cruickshank in *Chicago Sunday Times*, 3 June 2007.

37 For this argumentation I am indebted to Roland Weidle's presentation published in this volume.

38 Booth's translated quotations refer to Jean-Paul Sartre's essay *Qu'est-ce que la littérature?* published for the first time in 1947.

Bibliography

Acheson, James & Ross, Sarah C.E.: *The Contemporary British Novel Since 1980.* New York: Palgrave Macmillan, 2005.

Adamson, Jane/Freadman, Richard/Parker, David (eds.): *Renegotiating Ethics in Literature, Philosophy, and Theory.* Cambridge: CUP, 1998.

Antor, Heinz: "The Ethics of Criticism in the Age After Value". In: Ahrens, Rüdiger & Volkmann, Laurenz (edd.), *Why Literature Matters. Theories and Functions of Literature.* Heidelberg: Winter, 1996, 65-85.

Bauder-Begerow, Irina & Lusin, Caroline: "Der englische Roman zu Beginn des 21. Jahrhunderts: Ian McEwan." In: Nünning, Vera (ed.). *Der zeitgenössische englische Roman*. Trier: WVT, 2007, 243-258.

Booth, Wayne C.: *The Company We Keep. An Ethics of Fiction.* Berkeley: University of California Press, 1988.

Byrnes, Bernie C.: *Ian McEwan's 'Atonement' & 'Saturday'*. Nottingham: Paupers' Press, 2006.
Childs, Peter (ed.): *The Fiction of Ian McEwan. A reader's guide to essential criticism*. Basingstoke: Palgrave Macmillan, 2006.
Finney, Brian: "Briony's Stand against Oblivion: The Making of Fiction in Ian McEwan's *Atonement*." *Journal of Modern Literature* 27:3 (2004), 68-82. Abstract in: http://muse.jhu.edu/journals/, accessed 4 July 2009.
Genette, Gérard: *Die Erzählung*. München: Fink, 1998.
Groes, Sebastian (ed.): *Ian McEwan. Contemporary Critical Perspectives*. London: Continuum, 2009.
Harpham, Geoffrey Galt: "Ethics and literary criticism". In: Knellwolf, Christa & Norris, Christopher (edd.). *The Cambridge History of Literary Criticism*, vol. 9. Cambridge: CUP, 2001, 371-385.
Head, Dominic: *Ian McEwan*. Manchester: Manchester UP, 2007 (Contemporary British Novelists).
James, Harold: "Narrative Engagement with *Atonement* and *The Blind Assassin*." *Philosophy and Literature* 29:1 (2005), 130-145.
Malcolm, David. *Understanding Ian McEwan*. Columbia: U. of N. Carolina Pr., 2002.
McEwan, Ian: *Atonement*. New York: Anchor, 2003 (2001).
---: *On Chesil Beach*. London: Cape, 2007.
---: *Saturday*. London: Cape, 2005.
McGinn, Colin: *Ethics, Evil and Fiction*. New York: OUP, 1997.
Müller-Wood, Anja: "Enabling Resistance: Teaching *Atonement* in Germany." *Teaching Contemporary British Fiction* (ed. Merle Tönnies). *Anglistik und Englischunterricht* 69 (2007), 143-158.
Reynolds, Margaret & Noakes, Jonathan (edd.): *Ian McEwan – the essential guide to contemporary Literature*. London: Vintage, 2002 (Vintage Living Texts).
Ryan, Kiernan: *Ian McEwan*. Plymouth: Northcote House, 1994 (Writers and their Work).
Schemberg, Claudia: *Achieving 'At-one-ment'. Storytelling and the Concept of the Self in Ian McEwan's 'The Child in Time', 'Black Dogs', 'Enduring Love', and 'Atonement'*. Frankfurt/M.: Peter Lang, 2004.
Slade, Jack: *Ian McEwan*. New York: Macmillan, 1996 (Twayne's English Authors Series).
Tönnies, Merle: "A New Self-Conscious Turn at the Turn of the Century? Postmodernist Metafiction in Recent Works by 'Established' British Writers". *Twenty-First Century Fiction* (ed. Christoph Ribbat). *Anglistik und Englischunterricht* 66 (2005), 57-82.
Julie Ellam's study *Ian McEwan's 'Atonement'* (London 2009) was not yet available.

Contributors' Addresses

Dr. Elsa Cavalié, CAS, Université de Toulouse 2 – Le Mirail, 5, allées Antonio Machado, 31 058 Toulouse Cedex 9, France

Prof. Dr. Peter Childs, University of Gloucestershire, Fullwood Villa, The Park, Cheltenham, GL50 2RH, England.

Dr Lynn Guyver, Centre for Applied Linguistics, University of Warwick, Coventry CV4 7AL.

Dr. Lars Heiler, Universität Kassel, Institut für Anglistik und Amerikanistik, Georg-Forster-Straße 3, D-38127 Kassel.

Dr. Caroline Lusin, Ruprecht-Karls-Universität, Anglistisches Seminar, Kettengasse 12, D-69117 Heidelberg.

Dr. Erik Martiny, International School of Aix-en-Provence (University of Cambridge), 200, rue Georges Duby, 13080 Luynes, France.

PD Dr. Pascal Nicklas, Universität Leipzig, Beethovenstraße 15, Philologische Fakultät, Institut für Klassische Philologie und Komparatistik, 04109 Leipzig.

Prof. Dr. Anja Müller-Wood, Johannes Gutenberg-Universität Mainz, Department of English and Linguistics, Anglophone Cultures, D-55099 Mainz.

Dr. Barbara Puschmann-Nalenz, Ruhr-Universität-Bochum, Englisches Seminar, Universitätsstr. 150, D-44801 Bochum.

Prof. Dr. Helga Schwalm, Humboldt-Universität zu Berlin, Institut für Anglistik/Amerikanistik, Unter den Linden 6, 10099 Berlin.

Prof. Dr. Roland Weidle, Ruhr-Universität-Bochum, Englisches Seminar, Universitätsstraße 150, D-44801 Bochum.